For Tiffany

Acknowledgments

The Unbroken Series is about friendship and the bonds that can't be broken. I'm truly blessed to be surrounded by a group of incredible women that support me through all my crazy ideas and adventures. Thank you for going above and beyond to help make this endeavor a successful one. Our past has helped me develop these characters and the situations they find themselves in. No one character is entirely you. However, all characters have a piece or two. My tribe: Linda, Cherie, Tammy, Holly, Nancy, Marie, Shiela, Lisa, Gabrielle, Carol, and Sandy, this dream wouldn't be a reality without you.

My husband, Ali, for supporting me every time I've wanted to reinvent myself. Whatever I've needed, you've helped provide. You kept my writing in the conversation, knowing ultimately, that's where I'd end up. You've gently nudged me since the days of our first email communications over twenty years ago. You told me you were impressed by how I put sentences together…I've never forgotten.

Tiffany, my daughter, one of my most proud accomplishments, you've been one of my first readers and critics as I dove into this realm. Thank you for your honesty, support, and love, as I've traveled these unchartered waters. I'm so grateful for the relationship we have.

My cover designer Anjanee, WOW…you are so talented. I know I drove you crazy—I'm such a perfectionist, thank you for your patience and taking my vision to the next level. You once again created an eye-popping, unique, and stunning cover for *Deja Vu*. I can't wait to see what we come up with for the final book, *Cést la Vie*.

I was fortunate when I found my editor, Kimberly Hunt. You're paying someone to critique your work, to point out the mistakes. Drink a few glasses of wine and prepare yourself, this isn't going to be easy. Kimberly has such a great way of not only finding the areas that need correcting but also pointing out the positive parts that moved her, whether it was laughter, heartache, or sometimes, revolting her. That positivity helped ease the pain. Thank you for helping me be a better writer.

Finally, I'd like to thank YOU, dear reader, for choosing *Deja Vu* out of the vast literary sea before you. I hope you enjoy reading the Unbroken Series as much as I have had writing it. It's so exciting to find these twists and turns along the way. It's been so much fun! I genuinely wish I could write faster—I have so much more to say.

Introduction

If you've read *Facade*, Book I in the Unbroken Series, then I know how anxious you are to read *Deja Vu*.

- Did Debra lose the baby?
- Was Ashanti hurt in the park?
- If not her, who?
- What caused the blood Dominque coughed up?
- Will Amber and Patrick ever make it work?
- Where has Brandy been all this time?

Facade left you with so many unanswered questions. The answers to these and so many more are revealed in the next 350+ pages.

The majority of *Deja Vu* was written under quarantine from COVID-19. The stress of the pandemic at first made getting into my characters' world difficult. Soon, I found the escape to be a much-needed diversion as I watched the numbers, suffering worldwide, grow each day. Boy, was I glad I was not writing a book about a contagion.

My characters have taken some unexpected turns in this continuation. For one of our beloved characters, it turns quite dark when she's sexually assaulted. I mention this with respect for anyone reading who may have experienced this as well. Many times I didn't know what would happen until the words appeared on my screen. I gasped, laughed, and cried quite a few times. I still do each time I reread it. I wish people would stop hoarding tissues; I really need them.

One of the character's health issues was very difficult for me. My beta readers commented I needed to add more emotion…it was tough. I would have to relive the anguish and terror I felt in 1998 when I was fighting for my life.

At one point, I was eager to get on stage and share my story, giving hope. Since my grandchildren came into the world, I crumble every time I try to share. My eyes are tearing up as I'm writing this—tissue please. How do you tell your fifteen-year-old daughter you have cancer? (I was thirty-five and a single mother.) I prayed every day—I wanted to live. I wanted to see her graduate high school, be the mother-of-the-bride one day…watch my future grandchildren be born.

I'm so grateful my prayers were answered. Not only have I witnessed all of the above, after a second diagnosis ten years later (new primary—not a metastasis), I've dared to set new goals. Publishing my first book was one of them, and now with *Deja Vu*, I'm sharing my second one with you. Last tissue, stop hoarding people—please!

I had so much fun writing this one, especially as I was coming to the end. *Deja Vu* leaves you with a few unanswered questions, just like *Facade*. I knew where this one would end, but when I finished, I had to keep going—I needed to know! All will be answered in the exciting conclusion to the Unbroken Series, Book III, *Cést la Vie,* due out later this year.

When you have finished *Deja Vu*, please write a review. That is one of the kindest things you can do for an author. Be honest, but please be kind. We bare our soul when we share our work. We do try to please everyone, knowing it's impossible. We want to know what you think, but remember, with great power comes great responsibility—be kind—we need more of that.

Melody Saleh

DEJA VU

A Novel

Chapter One

A frantic Amber comes barging through the Emergency Room entrance looking all around for familiar faces. This new year, only a few days old has already lost the *Happy* part. There are so many people here. It never surprises her, how in sunny South Florida, so many injure themselves by do-it-yourself projects, roller-blading, or worse, this year's craze—scooters. Driving down the iconic Las Olas Boulevard, they're every-where. A few patients even have burn injuries from their fire-places. It did get down to sixty-five degrees last night.

Just as Tina spots Amber through the glass of the wait-ing room, another version of her comes up behind her looking pissed off and very agitated. Shock registers on Tina's face as she sees…two Ambers!

Amber, forgetting she had to bring Brandy with her, reads the shock as something terrible has happened to one of her friends. She rushes to Tina with tears already streaming down her face. Tina stands as Amber rushes to hug her, "Is it Debra? The baby? Who? Please tell me—WHO?"

Tina is dumbfounded and unable to speak. As Amber pulls away, she sees Tina's wide eyes looking past her at the doorway.

Amber turns and is brought back to reality as Brandy leans up against the doorway, with one foot propped in the door jam, examining her fingernails.

"Oh, I'll explain," Amber says as she turns back to Tina. "Please, first tell me what you know about Debra and Dominque."

A tall man in green scrubs comes into the waiting room and walks over to a couple sitting in the corner. Her crying halts as he approaches.

In a hushed tone, the doctor says, "Your son is stable, for now. He's still in very serious condition. Mitch lost a lot of blood; the next twenty-four hours is going to be rough. If that young girl had not stayed and helped, we would be having a very different conversation right now. She saved your son's life."

Mrs. Morris's face turns beet red—her eyes like daggers. "That girl is the reason he's in here in the first place. She didn't save him—she tried to kill him! She needs to be locked up in a cage where she belongs!"

Mr. Morris tries to quiet his wife. "It's okay honey; he's gonna be okay." Then, addressing the doctor, he says, "That's great news, thank you, doctor. When can we see our son?"

"He's still in recovery. A nurse will come out for you once we get him settled in ICU."

"Is that witch still here in the hospital?" Mrs. Morris spits out. "If she is, I swear I'll kill her. Her kind needs to go home and never come back!"

The dark-skinned doctor, who had turned to leave, turns back around, with his eyes bulging and fists clenched. "Because she's black, Mrs. Morris?"

"Well, yes, that, and she's Muslim. They're nothing but terrorists—they all need to leave!"

Tina's eyes get big as saucers as she realizes they're talking about Ashanti, her partner's daughter. The anger begins in the pit of her stomach, and she swears she's going to explode. Stacey senses this and grabs her mother's hand. "Breathe, Mom, just breathe. She's narrow-minded and was fed all of the talking points. She screams anger and hatred...please don't lower yourself to her level."

Tina's eyes water as she hugs her daughter. Her heart swells as she reflects at how blessed she is to have such a levelheaded, intelligent, kind-hearted girl. *Wow, I did something right.* She's lost in her thoughts as her eyes gaze up, then she closes them, enjoying the affection. It takes a second to register, and then her eyes flash open as her head snaps up. She's seeing double. She pulls away from Stacey, with her mouth agape, and points to Brandy while looking at Amber for an explanation. "What?" she says, unable to take her eyes away from Brandy.

Amber sits down next to her. "I did tell you I have a sister...I might have left out the fact that she's my identical twin."

At that, Brandy sashays over and sits in a chair across from Tina. "Yeah, the bitch is back," she says.

Amber gives Brandy a dark look and grabs Tina's hand, getting her attention. "Brandy has been—shall we say—not able to visit for a while. Imagine my surprise when she showed up on my doorstep the other day," Amber says as she looks Brandy's way, stressing the last few words.

Brandy responds with venomous eyes, "Not able to visit because I was in the slammer! Had you come to see me, my dear sister, you would have known I was being released." She turns in her seat to address Tina. "You see, my sister here is a bit embarrassed by her exact copy, trying to push me off to some distant relative, so she wouldn't have to deal with me. Guess today is your lucky day." Brandy stands and heads toward the vending machines.

Tina's mouth is open. She's at a loss for words.

Amber comes over, trying to explain and smooth over the shocking news of her evil replica showing up, unannounced. How do you tell your friends, the sister you've been hiding all these years, is your identical twin, but can't be any more opposite?

As Amber gets closer, she notices Stacey looking down at her hands with tears rolling off her cheeks. "Oh, honey, are you okay?" she asks, sitting in the chair next to her, putting her arm around her shoulders.

Tina is brought out of her stupor as she sees the same tears, making her turn toward her daughter and rest her hand on her leg.

"We haven't heard about Ashanti either. I hope she's okay." Stacey says in a tiny voice, never looking up.

Amber looks at Tina for an explanation. "What's wrong with Ashanti? I thought Debra was here?"

With tears also threatening to fall, Tina explains, "Ashanti, Debra, and Dom are all here. You know about Debra, Tad brought Dom in because she coughed up blood; I'm still waiting to hear from him. Ashanti has been bullied at school all year—today, it escalated. Ashanti defended herself, but the young man is badly hurt as you heard the doctor just say. Ashanti's shoulder was dislocated in the attack, but it's the boy who might not make it. That couple over there..."—Tina points to Mr. and Mrs. Morris— "that very racist couple are his parents. Ashanti saved his life, but all they care about is her going to jail. Or better yet, back to Africa!"

Amber had no idea her three closest friends are all here fighting for themselves or their loved ones. She's always been the glue that holds their tribe together, but now, she feels so helpless...there's nothing she can do. One who's always been able to fix things, she lacks the tools and knowhow to help any of them. At a time when she needs to lean on someone, the man she loves—the one man she allowed herself to love—can't even return her call.

As if on cue, Patrick comes running through the emergency room doors. Seeing Amber, he wants nothing more than to turn around and run. She is the last person he wants to see right now. His concern for Debra forces him to continue inside. He's relieved to see Tina, so he doesn't have to speak to Amber.

"Tina, please tell me, Debra and the baby, are they okay?" he asks, never looking Amber's way.

Amber is immediately hurt and confused, but she addresses him anyway. "Patrick, I'm so glad you got my messages. Thank you so much for being here." She slides over to him, hoping to feel comfort and strength in his arms.

He pulls away as if she's contagious with a deadly disease and says, "I'm here for Debra; this has nothing to do with you."

As he steps away from her, something catches his eye, coming down the hallway. *She looks exactly like Amber,* he says to himself—completely stunned. As she gets closer, he realizes…she's Amber's double.

At first, Amber is stunned, her mouth hangs open, her eyes huge. Finally, after a moment to calm down, she asks, "What did I do? I honestly have no idea why you are treating me like this. If you wanted to end our relationship, why not be a man and do it with honesty and integrity. You've taken the chicken's way out."

Brandy slides up to Patrick and says in a sultry voice, "If you like her looks, but you want something a little hotter, a little more dangerous—more adventurous, I'd say you're exactly my type."

"What?" is all Patrick can say.

Stewart comes in behind him. "I finally found a parking space. Sorry it took so long."

Patrick looks at him with an angry snarl. "What is this?" The only words he can muster as he points to the twins. "It wasn't Amber I saw you with, was it? Why would you let me go on thinking she was cheating on me—with you?"

Patrick takes two steps forward as Stewart takes two steps back.

"Wait, wait, wait…" Stewart quickly explains, "She begged me not to tell you. She wanted to tell you about Brandy herself—her own way."

Amber begins to connect the dots. "Wait a minute… that's what this is all about? You thought I was with Stewart?" Amber can't help but laugh, which stings Stewart a little. "And you,"—pointing her index finger, over and over, hard into Stewart's chest— "you let Patrick think it was me? Couldn't you call me and explain? Oh, it all makes perfect sense now."

She turns with fists clenches toward Patrick. "The worst part is you didn't trust me enough to ask at least. You know, our whole relationship has been like this. Both of us so quick to think the worst. Maybe this is the universe's way of telling us we're not meant to be." Amber removes the Claddagh ring Patrick gave her at Christmas—a promise ring, and hands it to him.

Amber turns on her heel, walking down the hall to the restroom. She wants to be confident and strong as she walks away, not show him she is utterly crumbling inside, hurt for the last and final time by Patrick Simpson.

"Amber, wait please, you're absolutely right, I should not have jumped to conclusions, but come on. I knew you had a sister, but an identical twin sister? What are the chances of that?" Patrick asks.

With Amber's back turned to him, her anger starts to wane, wondering if she's overreacting. Without turning around, "I get that, but you could have at least thought it was a possibility," she says, realizing just how ridiculous she sounds as the words are spoken. She can't help but break out in spontaneous laughter. Maybe it's from the stress, anxiety, fear—the hysterics just pour out.

"I'm so glad you find this all so humorous," Patrick says, as he moves up behind her, turning her around. "Can we please start over? I think the universe does want us together; it's just throwing us these curveballs."

Amber looks into Patrick's eyes, and her heart does a flip. She thought he was the one. Knowing she could be setting herself up for more hurt, her heart begs her to give him one last chance. *We'll go slow this time*, the voice inside her head.

She extends her hand, "Hi, I'm Amber. You might not remember me, but I interviewed you for "The Ethical Attorney" article last year in *The South Florida Magazine*."

Patrick shakes her hand. "Yes, I do remember you. I'm so glad to see you again. Maybe we can have coffee sometime."

"Okay. Double-espresso, right?" Amber asks.

They turn and begin to walk to the hospital cafeteria. Patrick says, "I know we're starting over, but can I still get the lap dance from Candy? Maybe this time, I'll be allowed to touch more?"

Amber stops abruptly, looking confused. "What do you mean? Who's Candy?"

Patrick's face drains of all color. They've never discussed his birthday stripper before. Stuttering, trying to find the right words. "My um, birthday stripper…um, you in a platinum wig…um, us on the conference table, in my office?"

Amber turns around, glaring at Brandy. Her fists balled up; she takes giant steps toward her until they are practically nose to nose. "You—you seduced Patrick? How did you know? Just how long have you been out of prison? Have you been stalking me?"

Brandy, still cool as a cucumber, says, "You deserved it. I called you so many times, and you never answered—you never called me back. Do you know how much that hurt? I needed you, and you just couldn't be bothered. I needed money and a place to stay so I took a job, any job I could find. I thought I'd give a hand at stripping when I saw the marquis for Ladies, Ladies, Ladies. I went in to ask about a job and overheard someone needed a stripper sent to some hunky man's office for his birthday celebration. The real stripper was canceled, and I, or should I say, Candy, took her place. He had a very sexy—hot birthday. Funny how the universe works sometimes, isn't it?"

Angry and hurt, she addresses Patrick. "She looks just like me—you mean to tell me, you didn't even question her?"

"She looked familiar. I didn't know it was you—her at the time." Patrick blurts out and motions with his hands toward Brandy. "She had a wig on, and her eyes were blue."

Brandy sashays over to Patrick, "Duh…I didn't want to lose my job before I even started. I didn't want anyone to recognize me in case they frequented the titty bars."

Pushing her body up against Patrick, her mouth just inches from his, she says in a sexy voice, "And all that kissing, grinding, and touching we did—I guess it's not allowed. You got way more than you should have. I hope it was just as hot for you." She stresses the word 'hot,' blowing a puff of air out as it's said.

Amber, so mad, pulls her fist back, wanting to punch her sister in the mouth, but Patrick grabs her arm on the backswing. "You really don't want to do that," he says.

"Oh, yes, I do—you have no idea the shit she's put me through. The guilt she's piled on. She drove a wedge so deep between my father and I. Our dad passed away thinking I didn't love him, thinking I didn't want him in my life. She played us both. I'll never get the chance to say goodbye to him now. I'll never be able to tell him how much I loved him and what a wonderful father he was, especially after our mom passed away. He was told I didn't return any phone calls. Calls I never received; ones SHE made sure I never got."

She realizes Brandy is toxic, and she's better off without her. "I'll never forgive you for that. I thought I might be able to —and I tried—I really did, but your jealousy, and your ego, always got in the way. I'm done trying. I don't care if I never see you again as long as I live. My friends are more family to me then you've ever been. You've used me for the last time. Get out, and don't you ever, and I mean EVER, come back again...you're dead to me!" Amber turns and walks away, not daring to let her sister see the tears.

Brandy responds as if in a horrible, dramatic acting scene. "No, wait...how could I have known you were hot for lover boy. Oh, and the birthday gift I sent you,"—turning toward Patrick— "keep it as a token of my admiration." Laughing, she pushes herself from the wall and struts out the hospital emergency room doors.

Chapter Two

Brian can't think straight. Ever since Amber called him about Debra, his heart hasn't stopped pounding. His head is in a fog—he can't get to her fast enough.

He had to cancel his appointments—that took time.

Brian finds a spot outside the Emergency Room entrance, the last one. He was rushing out of the car when he sees Amber coming out, laughing. *That's strange, why would Amber be laughing at a time like this?*

"Amber, is Debra okay? Little George, is he okay?" Brian practically yells as he runs over to her.

Brandy just can't help herself—she put the E-V-I-L in evil. "Oh, so sorry, but it doesn't look good...for either of them. I'm afraid you're too late."

Seeing the color drain completely from Brian's face, she bursts out laughing.

Brian can't move; his legs won't work. He slowly turns around to watch Amber's double walk away.

Brian looks up toward the hospital and sees Amber through the glass doors. She sees the back of Brandy walking away from him and the color drain from his face.

She runs to him. "Brian, I don't know what she said to you, we don't know anything yet."

It's that very second, he realizes he can't live without Debra. The fear, the anguish he felt those few seconds when he thought he had lost her—he has to make her his. He's hopelessly in love with her.

Brian grabs Amber and hugs her tight. "Oh, thank God. I love her Amber. I can't live without her. Help me make her mine."

"Of course I will. You two were made for each other." Amber takes Brian's hand, walking him into the hospital. "We haven't heard anything yet about her or the baby. I was just about to ask one of the nurses. Come on, let's go together."

Brian leans up against the elevator wall looking off into space—wearing his heart on his sleeve.

"By the way, you going to explain who that was in the parking lot?" Brian asks.

"It's a long story…"

☯

His slippery wet body slides against her back—his erection, growing rapidly, nestles between her cheeks—as the hot steamy water cascades down their bodies. His hands are lathering across her pregnant stomach, inching ever so slowly upwards until one hand completely entraps her breast. Her nipple immediately stands at attention, begging for his skilled fingers to caress it. Tremors begin deep inside as her wish becomes his command. She grabs his hand and pushes it lower over her ever-expanding belly; her shyness preventing her from taking him all the way.

He obeys, slowly creating small circles down to her hips until he reaches the small patch of pubic hair she refuses to lose.

Debra tries hard not to writhe and undulate, but her body has a mind of its own. She arches her back as his hand continues lower, exploring deeper. She pushes herself closer—so close, it's as if she's trying to merge them into one. His cock, now fully erect, he pushes it between her legs. He doesn't enter her. He slowly begins to thrust his hips so she can feel the extreme length of his manhood—so hot—so slippery, sliding between her legs.

He pulls the hair away from her neck, planting tiny kisses up to behind sensitive earlobes. How he's maneuvering both of his hands, and his lips—his hips—is a crazy talent. It's more than her body can handle. She wants to enjoy this moment forever, but the heat inside is burning hotter with every second.

Debra can't take it anymore. She pushes his hand down between her legs, and without hesitation, he slides his finger inside. The feeling of all her nerve endings coming alive makes her catch her breath. She swallows, trying to calm the fire inside. She wants to enjoy this…she needs to slow down. However, he has plans of his own. Just as she feels she's gained some control, his hand pushes the head of his cock inside her. With one thrust—he's buried. His finger finds her button—the one to push—to throw her over the edge.

Her head thrashes, side to side, as the convulsions come one after the other. He doesn't stop until they subside.

Her knees go weak, but his strong arm catches her, bringing her back up. With one swift push, he's again inside. She feels as if she's going to split in two—and catch fire—both at the same time.

He thrusts slowly at first until she can catch his rhythm.

Her hands against the shower wall, legs spread far apart, they begin to move in unison.

"I've been thinking about this day for a very long time. As much I want nothing more than to explode inside you, I want to take my time, savor every moment...I hope you don't mind," he says, as he enjoys every second he pulls out—then pushes himself back in, as far as possible. Each time, he tries to reach in farther; her hips til back just enough for him to accomplish his fete.

He surrenders to his passion, increasing his tempo, faster—faster in sync with her moans echoing off the shower walls. Just as he's going to release, he rubs her engorged clit, determined to climax together.

Their bodies convulse together as they both shout out, calling to the higher power.

She turns around to kiss him, ...the man that has stolen her heart and makes her feel alive. The one who makes her feel like she's never felt before. The man she loves—Brian?

Debra wakes with a start! *Why was I dreaming about Brian? Did I say his name out loud? Was I moaning in my sleep?* The look on Roberto's face, the question mark she can see floating over his head. *Oh, my God! What do I do now? Did I make the right decision with Roberto? Is little George okay?*

Reality hits her in the face as she wakes enough to re-member she's in the hospital and why she's there. Her heart begins to pound as she thinks, *It's too soon; he has to stay put for just a little while longer,* while her hands go to her belly, rubbing, comforting Little George from the outside.

❦

The doctor comes rushing in, frantic. It's obvious he's swamped. He quickly introduces himself, then gets right to the point—no small talk. "Mrs. Harris, the bleeding is caused by partial placental abruption. In other words, the placenta has started to detach from your uterine wall. It's only partial at this point, and hopefully, it won't detach anymore. You still have a few weeks to go. If necessary, you can deliver now, but we'd like to keep your son there as long as possible to let his lungs fully mature."

She confused being hit with all these words at once, and yet relief, knowing the baby is okay.

Debra asks, "What can I do to help keep him safe for a few more weeks?"

"Not what you probably want to hear, but complete bed rest for the next few weeks. Every day we delay labor, the bet-ter off he'll be."

Roberto, in his thick Italian accent, jumps up from the side of the bed and shakes the doctor's hand. "No problem, I take care of her now. Can she make love?"

Debra is worried about her son's life, and Roberto wants to have sex? An immediate flush run through her body, *he heard me, he knew I was dreaming about Brian.*

The doctor's cold facade breaks, he chuckles and shakes his head. "I think we need to take sex off the table for right now. An intense orgasm might cause contractions big enough to cause the placenta to pull away more. Let's steer clear there."

While Debra feels a huge weight lift from her chest— relief the bleeding is subsiding, she fears if she has another wet dream, she may cause harm to Little George. *Another wet dream, that's the least of your problems, girl. You've said yes to the wrong man!* The little, sometimes way too harsh voice, reminds her.

Debra is afraid. If he heard her call out for Brian, he's going to confront her.

She watches as Roberto ushers the doctor out of the room and prepares herself for the fight that's about to happen. Hoping the ugly side she saw of him, a few weeks ago, was a fluke.

"We have to marry quickly. I need to be here for you all the time. I will ask your friend Amber to setup."

She's confused—shocked! She shakes off the whiplash from the turn of events.

Without giving Debra a chance to respond, he turns and leaves the room. Debra snaps out of her stupor and calls out to him, but his name bounces off the closed door.

What have I done? How do I fix this? Can I fix this?

Tears start streaming down her face as she realizes the mistake she's made. Never wanting to cause problems, she immediately begins to defend Roberto and convince herself, life with him won't be so bad. It's crazy, so soon after George's death, she's stuck in a love triangle with Roberto, who she met while she was in Milan last summer at Zya's fashion show, and her therapist, Brian...the one who makes her heart goes pitter-patter whenever she thinks about him.

Debra's husband George was killed on his fortieth birthday last June. Debra met Brian right after her husband's passing. He was her therapist recommended by Amber. After she featured him in an article, his practice has boomed. He was the best in his field. He owed her.

She gushed to him about meeting Roberto over the summer. She was so excited and animated when she talked about him. It never dawned on her, he—Brian, also cared for her.

Before long, Debra found herself with both men fighting over her. Not just for her love but also for her hand in marriage. The catch, they couldn't sleep with her. This put Brian at a disadvantage. By that time, Debra and Roberto had spent a weekend together—the weekend just before they became entangled.

She was numb dealing with losing her husband and being pregnant, it never really sank in what was happening, until now. She was living in a dream, or a Hollywood movie, where everyone lived happily ever after.

How could I let them do this? I'm not ready to marry anyone. I want this all to stop. This drama has to end! Oh, George, how I wish you were here right now. I need to keep our lives calm.

Amber's phone rings as she and Brian enter the hospital. "Roberto, thank you so much for calling me, is everything okay with Debra and little George?"

His accent is thicker and harder to understand now that he's agitated and stressed. "Debra, she is good, Little George good too. The doctor say bed rest. I ask Debra to marry me; she say yes. We want to marry quickly. You arrange for us, yes?"

Not the conversation she expected to have, she's thrown completely off guard. "Um, sure—I'm happy to help. What does Debra have in mind? Can I talk to her?"

"I have left on my way to courthouse to get marriage paper, and I need to go to Italian Embassy. We need priest—Catholic priest to come to hospital today."

The hairs on the back of Amber's neck stand up. He sure is being pushy. Debra would never want to be married in the hospital, and not by a Catholic priest either.

"Can we slow down a little Roberto? Don't you think this is all happening just a bit too fast?"

"No, not fast. If you cannot, I will ask someone else. This is how it is to be," he impatiently responds.

Desperately needing to speak with Debra, Amber decides the easiest thing to do now is just to agree and get him off the phone. "No, no, I'll take care of it. You go to the courthouse, and I'll call you back."

Hanging up the phone, Amber grabs Brian's hand, pulling him along to Debra's room.

She motions Brian to wait outside, and she taps on her door. Without waiting for an answer, she enters.

Seeing her tear-stained cheeks, Amber rushes over to the bed and hugs her. Debra can't hold back any longer—the sobs start, full force, with no end in sight.

After what seems like an eternity, Amber wipes Debra's cheeks with a tissue, then dries her own. "I was so scared for you and Little George. I'm glad to hear you just need bed rest to keep him cooking."

She is happy he's okay, but also distressed with her sudden emergency nuptials. "Yeah, I know, great news. I should be so happy."

"Roberto just called me…he says you want to get married, right away?" Amber asks.

"I'm so confused; I don't want to hurt anyone's feelings. Oh, I've really messed things up."

"Do you want to marry Roberto?"

"I thought I did, but now I don't think so. He's become so bossy—controlling. He's making all these decisions without even asking me. I didn't want to worry anyone, but I've seen an evil side to him before. I thought it was just a one-time thing, he was angry, and I understood why. But today, I saw that side again—it might be who he is."

She picks up Debra's hand to try and comfort her. "You don't worry about a thing, I've got you. You're allowed to change your mind, and don't you think twice about him getting angry. You need to think about yourself, Tracey, and Little George. You need to do what's right for your family."

Debra thinks about her little content unit. Her smart and funny six-year-old daughter, Tracey, and her soon to be perfect little man. Complete would include George, but she can't think about that right now, she has to be strong.

Amber continues, "Roberto called me and told me about your engagement and wedding plans. Let me guess, they're his plans... not yours?"

"I don't want to get married yet. I thought we'd have plenty of time after Little George gets here."

"Well, first things first, Mr. Romantic wants to get married—today! He instructed me to get a Catholic priest here to perform the ceremony. He's on his way to the courthouse for your license and then to the Embassy for his paperwork."

"What!" Debra shrieks as she bolts upright in bed. "No way—what is he thinking! This isn't what I want. What do I do? How do I stop him?"

Amber gently presses her back, so she's laying down again. "Let me handle it, okay?"

"Okay. Why did I allow all of this to happen in the first place? What was I thinking letting two men compete over me for my hand in marriage? George isn't even gone for a year yet, what kind of person does that?"

Amber reaches down, pulling her into a hug, smoothing her hair to calm her. "You were hurt...you were lost. You lost George just as you finally got pregnant. I think the right question might be, how did we let you? You just seemed so happy; he was romantic and so patient—and smooth. There were no red flags. Well, not until now. As for Brian, he was your therapist. And honey, we all see why women fall in love with him. He's pretty awesome."

"I've been kind of crazy, huh?"

"We all have. First, I need to stop a wedding."

She remembers just as she's about to leave, thinking this is exactly what she needs right now. "Deb, Brian is outside, he wants to see you."

Debra nods enthusiastically.

Upon hearing his name, Brian enters the room. He rushes to Debra grabbing her hand and kisses it. "I've never been so scared in my life. Amber told me you're okay. Are you really okay?"

Debra's heart skips a beat the second she sees Brian's face. Her Prince Charming—the one she loves.

Tears instantly stream down her cheeks as the flood-gates holding back her pent-up emotions open up. "I'm okay, and Little George is okay too. Bed rest for the next few weeks, or until Little George decides it's time. Oh, Brian, I made a mistake."

Brian leans over, hugging her as best he can while she's lying down. "I know, and I'm sorry. You've had a lot to deal with, we—I never meant to cause you any stress."

"I picked the wrong one...I'm in love with you."

Brian smiles. You can see the mutual affection in his eyes.

"Brian, I said yes to Roberto today...I told him I would marry him."

For the second time today, Brian's face turns pale white. Luckily, he's standing right next to a chair, one that makes a loud noise as he falls into it, scraping across the floor.

Amber, who was watching this all unfold from across the room, rushes over to catch him should he miss.

"I knew it was Roberto asking me, but when we kissed, and I pulled back to gaze into his eyes...I was startled it wasn't you. I knew in that instant, I made the wrong choice. That's when I started bleeding," she says, hopeful it's a mistake she can make right.

"Excuse me, I think I need to take a walk," Brian says as he rushes from the room.

Brian, his face still white and staring into space, never saw Roberto coming at him...not until his fist was an inch from his nose.

Chapter Three

Zya brushes a few strands of hair away from Ashanti's face, so grateful she's okay. This day could have taken a 180-degree turn for the worse.

Ashanti, looking up at her mother, feels ashamed and sorry for not telling her about the bullying. They've never kept secrets or told lies to each other…she felt this time she had to, or her mother would give up everything she's worked so hard for just to keep her safe.

As Zya goes to kiss Ashanti on the forehead, the door opens, and two police officers enter.

The male officer says to Zya, "Excuse us, we need to ask your daughter some questions."

"My daughter is exhausted, and as you can see, still in a lot of pain. Can this wait?" Zya answers back a little harsher then she would have liked.

"No, this can't wait. A young man is fighting for his life —we need answers," the male officer responds more jarring than Zya.

Ashanti's eyes flash wide, and she starts to cry hard into her hands. The female officer turns to face her male counterpart and places her hand on his chest. "Mike, let me handle this. Your brute strength might not be what we need here, okay?"

Mike nods his head and leaves the room in a huff, and stops outside the door.

The female officer comes up to the side of Ashanti's bed and touches her arm. "I'm so very sorry about that." Her voice is warm and comforting—so nurturing. Ashanti begins to take control of her emotions.

"Mike isn't mean...his bark is much worse than his bite."

Ashanti lifts her head and sees a warm, beautiful face looking back at her. The officer looks over at Zya, without taking her hand off Ashanti's arm. "Ms. Monroe, again, I'm very sorry. We understand how upsetting this day has been, and I can promise you, we wouldn't be here if we didn't have to. We still have no idea what happened at the park, and we need to piece this all together."

Zya, looks down at Ashanti and asks, "Are you up for this?"

Ashanti nods, while fresh tears threaten to fall.

"Ashanti, we'll go nice and slow. Anytime you need a break, you just let me know, okay?"

Ashanti nods.

"If it's okay with you, I'd like to record this; my shorthand is a little rusty."

Zya and Ashanti both manage a chuckle. The officer's warm demeanor and pleasant personality put them at ease.

Ashanti begins to tell the officer about walking to the park but gets confused—not sure where to start. "I tried not to duplicate how I came home every day. I changed my routine as much as I could because I didn't want them hurting me any-more."

Zya's eyes flash.

The female officer urges Ashanti to go on. "Who's been hurting you Ashanti?" she asks in a soft tone.

"Kids in school. The school bully Mitch and his bud-dies—he's mean to everyone. He started picking on me the first day of school. He would call me *Terrorist,* and yell I wasn't wanted, and I should just go back to my dirty, bomb-making country." Ashanti can't control the tears.

"Let's just take a quick little break."

"I'd like to talk to your mother for a moment outside if that's okay?" Ashanti responds with a nod and grabs a tissue to blow her nose.

"Is this really necessary right now officer…"—looking at her badge— "Sanderson? Can't you see how upset she is?"

"Please call me Micki…I'm sorry, but I must get a statement as soon as possible. The young boy Ashanti referred to as Mitch is currently fighting for his life. To protect Ashanti, if this was self-defense, I need to find out what happened to-day. This is in her best interest."

Zya nods as her eyes fill up. Micki puts her arm around Zya's shoulders, comforting her.

"I know this must be very hard, and I'm gathering from your reaction, some of what Ashanti is saying is news to you. I know you must have a lot of questions, but please, try to refrain and let her get everything out. If she's worried about how you'll take this, she might clam up and not tell us everything, and it's crucial we get all the details."

Zya pulls away as she dabs her eyes.

They reenter the room to see Ashanti talking on her phone. She quickly says, "I gotta go," and hangs up. "Sorry, Mom, that was Stacey. They're in the waiting room, and she was really worried about me. I told her I was okay and I'd let her know when they can come up and see me, is that all right?"

Remembering what Micki said outside, she answers, "Yes honey, that's fine."

"Ashanti, did Mitch ever physically harm you?" Micki asks.

Looking sheepishly at her mom, Ashanti replies, stuttering, "Yes...I mean no...well—HE never actually laid a hand on me, but he would tell his goons what to do—they did the physical stuff."

"Have you been hurt by his friends at Mitch's instruction?" Micki rephrases the question.

She looks down into her hands, answering in a tiny voice, "Yes."

"Can you tell me about that?" Micki asks, gently urging her.

"The first time, about four months ago, they pushed me back into the girl's bathroom at the homecoming game. They made all the other girls get out, and then they locked the door. There were five of them—I was so scared."

Still looking down, Ashanti keeps staring at her constantly moving hands. Taking a deep breath, she continues, "Mitch yelled, 'She must not understand English. Let's teach her a lesson we know she'll understand.' Then they brought out switchblades and snapped them open—I screamed so loud—it happened so fast. I didn't know I was hurt. They grabbed me and ripped my clothes, so I screamed, one of them sliced me with the blade, then they unlocked the door and ran out. I thought I scared them away by screaming. I sat in the bathroom stall and cried for a while; I don't know how long. I heard girls coming in and out of the bathroom; some of them were saying mean stuff about me. They kept saying my dad was probably a terrorist and blew himself up with a bomb so he could be with his seventy-two virgins. They said I deserved it."

Ashanti starts crying again, remembering the hurtful things she heard the girls—girls she thought were her friends—say about her and her family.

"When did you know they had cut you?" Micki asks.

"I could tell the game was over, the yelling and cheering had died down. I was hoping the coast would be clear for me to run home. I stood up and noticed there was blood on the toilet seat. I looked at my shirt in the mirror and saw it. It wasn't deep, but I was definitely cut."

"The next school day, did you tell anyone? A teacher? Did you go to the office?" asks Micki.

"No, I didn't."—lifting her head to meet her mother's eyes up at— "I begged my mom not to say anything, to please let me handle it. Being a tattletale is the worst thing you can be. I was always told just to ignore them, and they'll go away."

Zya, unable to help herself, asks, "Who told you that honey?"

"My friends at school. They said their moms had told them to ignore the bullies. Don't let them know they're bothering you, and they'll leave you alone. They said their dads told them never to be a tattletale—it will only make matters worse."

"Did you get medical attention, of any kind, from this injury?"

Looking into her mom's eyes, "Mom, please don't be mad at her? I made her swear she wouldn't say anything to you. Promise me you won't be mad? She did it for me," Ashanti begs.

Zya cocks her head at her daughter, not saying a word, and motions her to continue.

"When I came home, Stacey was there with Tina—my mom's girlfriend."

Micki glances over at Zya with an amused look on her face.

"I couldn't reach it, so I asked her to please clean it and put a band-aid on it for me...so she did. We went to babysit that night for my mom's friend Debra. When we got there, I winced when she hugged me. She grilled me until I finally showed her the cut."

She was looking at her mom, pleading in her eyes. "She was really adamant about telling you. She was very upset with me—I made her promise. You said you wanted to pack up everything and go back to Africa. You were going to leave everything behind that you worked so hard for. You're so proud of your Made in the USA label—the land of the free—home of the brave, you always say. You've built something here, something you feel in your heart. I couldn't let you throw it all away. I couldn't let you, Mom; I won't let you."

Zya grabs Ashanti's hands. "Honey, yes, I did say that, and that is how I felt at the time. I understand why you didn't tell me about this, but I need you to know, without any reservations, you can talk to me about anything, I promise I'll listen and try not to be judgmental. Please don't ever keep any secrets like this from me again." She grabs her and hugs her tightly, forgetting about her dislocated shoulder.

Ashanti cries out—Zya quickly pushes back, forgetting her dislocated shoulder. "I'm so sorry honey. I just can't imagine you going through this alone—without me."

Not sure how there are any tears left, both Zya's and Ashanti's eyes begin streaming again.

"Okay, Ashanti, any other times these young men were physical with you?" Micki asks once the tears subside.

"About a month after they cut me, they cornered me on the landing between the second and third-floor stairs in the hallway. Mitch told them I couldn't take a hint, so they pushed me down the stairs. Luckily, the wall stopped me from falling all the way down. I bruised my shoulder, my hip, and my knee."—she glances up at her mom— "That's the day I told you I was riding someone's bike and fell off...I'm sorry I lied."

Zya kisses Ashanti on the forehead and says, "No more apologies, okay? I'm going to step out and grab a cup of coffee if that's all right with you both?"

Ashanti nods.

Zya exits the room with Micki in tow.

"I know this is hard, but we need to get everything out. We can't stop now."

Zya leans against the wall. Afraid her legs are going to give out—her hand on her chest, trying to catch her breath.

"I know, I just need some air. Keep going, I'll be right in. Just give me a moment," Zya pleads.

Micki nods and reenters the room. "Your mom will be right back. You okay to continue until then?"

Ashanti nods and continues, "After that, they never really had an opportunity to get me in a position to hurt me. I came to school early one day, then late the next. I always changed my route, making sure to stay where there were people or traffic. I took different ways to my classes every day. Some days I would find a reason to leave early. Others, I stayed late. I started volunteering at a nursing home down the street to keep me away from the usual hangouts. I guess I finally felt like it worked, and they were going to leave me alone, so I started cutting through the park again. It saves me twenty minutes of...," Ashanti's voice trails off.

"I know it's hard, but I need you to tell me what happened today," Micki urges.

Looking up, she sees her mom standing inside the door. "I was thinking about tonight on my way home. Stacey and I were going to the movies. As I passed by the tunnel, two of Mitch's goons jumped in front of me and tried to grab me. I heard Mitch yelling for them to get my hands and feet. They were going to get me gone one way or another. He yelled for them to get my backpack, and that's when I remembered what Stacey gave me for Christmas in the front pocket."

Ashanti glances up at Micki, and she nods for her to continue.

"Stacey gave me a carpenter's tool card. It's got tools you can use, but it's the size of a credit card. I have to leave it in its sleeve because one long edge—it's a razor blade—it's very sharp. I grabbed it out of the pocket and somehow got my other hand to pull the sleeve off. Mitch yelled for them to get whatever I had in my hand, ...it all happened so fast." Ashanti's eyes start to water again.

Micki places her hand on Ashanti's and says, "It's okay. Please continue; it's important."

Clearly upset, Ashanti continues, "Mitch lunged at me to grab my hand while one of his goons pulled my elbow backward. I didn't know the blade was facing out. I never had the chance to see how I was holding it. My shoulder hurt so bad and then I heard them all screaming and blood spurting up in the air—I thought it was coming from me. I thought I was going to die. That's when I heard Mitch's voice repeating, 'Please don't let me die. Please don't let me die.' I looked up and saw the blood was coming from him. It was coming from up high on his hip. I grabbed my T-shirt out of my backpack and tried to stop it. I couldn't use my right arm—it wasn't hanging right. I couldn't call 911 and keep the shirt on him at the same time. I kept screaming for help, but no one came out. His buddies were all gone; there was no one but Mitch and me. I used my knee to hold the shirt in place and grabbed my phone. I put it on speaker as quickly as I could—I'm right-handed—it was hard with my left hand; I was shaking so bad. The blood just kept spurting out of him and then less and less. I thought maybe it was clotting. Mitch's skin was all gray, and he was so cold." Ashanti's voice gets smaller and smaller as she described the look of death. "That's when the ambulance arrived. I saw it, and that's the last thing I remember until I woke up here. How is Mitch, do you know?"

"He's in surgery last I heard. I'm sure they are doing everything they can for him. I have to say, I'm quite impressed. Staying to help him after all the pain and anguish he caused you. That was very brave of you. Do you know who Mitch's friends are—the goons as you call them?"

Zya walks into the room and sees Micki giving Ashanti a gentle hug. She overhears her saying how proud she is of her. It melts her heart to see a complete stranger be so kind and loving to her daughter. Exactly what she and Ashanti need to see and feel in this world that can be so cruel and mean and yet so beautiful and glorious at the same time.

Helpless is how she feels, but that word just doesn't cut it. She's so angry and seeing redder than Lucifer's eyes. So hurt, her heart shattering into a million pieces. On a scale of one to ten, her pain level is twenty. She would kill for her—she would die for her. Helpless doesn't even begin to describe how she feels.

❦

She sits and watches her beautiful girl sleep, wishing so hard she could make it all go away; the pain, the fear, the betrayal she felt from her classmates. She's cried out all her tears, but she's still hurting; they hurt her baby.

How did we get here? In a world of such opportunity, a place to be all you can be, where dreams do really come true. How did my baby end up in the hospital after being harmed by a boy...a child?

She met Doug, Ashanti's father, one day at her dad's office in Africa. Doug was walking out of her father's office when she saw him for the first time. So handsome and worldly—dashing in his silver-gray suit. She fell in love with him that day...or what she thought was love.

She gave herself to him after he promised they would marry one day, then he was gone. He left for New York without saying a word. She told herself all kinds of stories, finally settling on going to America—New York, and find him.

When she turned sixteen, she asked her dad for permission to go. She thought he would be reasonable, but he yelled at her, "How can you be so selfish after everything your mother and I have done for you? Why leave us and go to America?"

She tried to reason with him, told him how much in love they were, but he was so mad. Things were said—words she can never take back.

Not sure if it was defeat, rage, or hurt, that made him go completely mute. Suddenly, he stopped yelling and silently signed her form. He said, if she was going, she was to leave at once. He did not want to see her again. She disappointed him—disgraced him.

Her father never came home that night. His secretary found him the next morning, curled up on his couch. When she tried to wake him, he was cold to the touch. Her father died from sudden cardiac arrest—she broke her father's heart.

Once she arrived in New York and got settled in school, Doug occasionally answered her calls taking her to some fast-food joint around campus, always ending up in the back seat of his car with him tearing at her underwear. He was busy; he had an important job.

She found out much later, that important job was providing the upper-class socialites with their drugs of choice. When he wasn't fucking them, he came to see her.

The one great thing that came out of it all was getting pregnant with her beautiful daughter. Ashanti was born just three months after she graduated from Parson's…with honors.

When they put Ashanti in her arms for the first time, she made her a promise. One she couldn't keep…one that almost cost Ashanti her life.

Chapter Four

"We're not going anywhere, Dom. You're probably right, and you're just tired. You've done a great job battling your anorexia, but you still haven't been eating right, so let's just make sure. Let's wait for the blood tests and chest X-ray results to come back first...peace of mind, okay?"

Reluctantly, she agrees.

Tad looks lovingly into her very red eyes. "I love you, Matilda Dominque Patterson," he kisses her.

"Did you have to go there? Matilda? Really?" She laughs.

The doctor comes into the room and introduces himself.

"Hi Matilda, my name is Dr. Harris."

Tad is quick to correct him. "She goes by Dominque, not Matilda."

"My apologies, Dominque, I'm sorry to keep you waiting for so long. I know the emergency room is not the Ritz Carlton."

Tad and Dominque both smile. A doctor with a sense of humor? That helps ease the tension.

"Do you have any of my test results back yet?"

"Not all of them, Mrs…"

Dominque can't help but snicker. "We're not married, and it's Miss Patterson."

"Wow, I'm batting a thousand here. Let me fix your file now so you'd don't have to correct any of the other egomaniacs here," the doctor says in a teasing manner.

"According to your blood tests, you're a bit anemic. That does worry me a bit seeing how you coughed up blood earlier."

Immediately thinking the worst, Dominque's chest suddenly feels very heavy, and her breathing becomes shallow.

"According to your chart, you've had some other health issues recently, so it could all be related…aftershocks, so to speak." The doctor smiles, trying to alleviate Dom's obvious distress.

"Your file says you had a mammogram recently?"

"Yes, but it was fine. They gave me my blue card and told me it was good," she says firmly.

"Great, we'll get the copies of your films."

"Is there a reason you need them?"

"I'm just going down my to-do list, making sure every box gets checked." He shows her the chart as he makes a big checkmark.

"On a good note, you won't have to sit around in this room much longer. I'm upgrading you to one of the hospital suites. The pillows are much more comfortable."

Dominque and Tad both chuckle, then it hits her…*why am I being admitted?*

She grabs Tad's hand, squeezing it. "We can't go home?"

"Not just yet, we're still waiting for the rest of your blood tests and X-ray results. It's just procedure, but we'd like to make sure nothing serious is going on before we release you. I think you'd be much more comfortable in your own room than laying on this concrete mattress."

Dominque nods as she unconsciously rubs her lower back.

He puts his hand on her shoulder to reassure her. "Try not to worry. I'll see you in your suite when the results are back." He winks and then turns to leave.

As he exits her room, she thinks, *there was something in his eyes, she's sure of it. He knows more then he's telling.*

Her eyes start to glaze over as she thinks about all the damage she did to her body over these years. She hopes— prays, she hasn't done irreversible damage.

"Do you believe in God?" she asks.

Tad looks up, completely caught off guard. "Um, yes, I do…Is this a trick question?"

"No, I've just never really considered myself a Christian, but I've been praying all morning to him—or her."

"You weren't brought up with religion?"

"No, jumping from home to home, most of my…"— finger quotes— "temporary guardians, were in it for the money—not really to give us any structure or guidance.

"There was one woman; she was a fanatic. Her husband, on the other hand, was an atheist. They decided early in their marriage they would agree to disagree when it came to religion. They had many discussions where she would try to convince him God created everything, and his retorts were about evolution and how we came from apes. Listening to their direct but calm, and opposite arguments, led me to believe neither of them was right, or wrong, they were just exercising free will. Although they had a difference of opinions, they stayed happily married. Of course, that didn't stop her from preaching to us every chance she got. I stopped listening to her at some point and was more interested in what he had to say."

"Do you want to join a church? I'm happy to if it helps."

"I'm not sure I would even know where to start. I hear so much about churches being more like businesses—some telling you what to believe and how you should live your life. If you haven't noticed already, I'm not too keen on being told what to do. Maybe we can just start with the Bible?"

"Can I ask, what are you hoping to get out of this?"

"I don't know, peace of mind. If there is a higher power, I certainly could use their support right about now."

"Dom, hon, I'm not sure that's how this all works. Pray to him—or her—but by just being a good, loving, kind person, you're already doing his bidding. You should pray, everyone who believes does. But don't think because you don't go to church, or you don't read the Bible, you're not worthy. He loves you, and he's here for you. We don't know why these things happen; they just do. Now, do I believe in fate...that's a different subject."

"Fate? Like me getting sick?"

"Hopefully, this is nothing, let's not worry just yet. What I mean is, I believe in free will. We can make changes in our lives. You decided to stop damaging your body and taking much better care of yourself now. That was you; that wasn't fate. If—big if—we are dealing with anything serious, I don't believe you did anything to make that happen. But you can decide on how you'll handle it. Will you just lie down and give up? NO! You'll fight it head-on. You'll do everything within your power to get through. And you will. You'll be better and stronger from it."

Although not at all romantic, that is one of the sweetest things a man has ever said to her. "Tad, I love you. How did I get so lucky to find you?"

"Fate?" Tad answers with a chuckle.

☯

Dr. Harris taps on her door and enters after just minutes since his last visit. His cheerful manner now replaced with a more serious demeanor. His attempt at smiling fails.

Dominque feels as if she's going to vomit—this isn't good.

Tad squeezes her hand.

"Ms. Patterson…"

She sits up straighter, trying to appear strong. "Please call me Dominque."

"Dominque, we've just received the films from your mammogram last year. We'd like to do an ultrasound and an MRI to compare them with."

"But they gave me my blue card. I was good to go until I turn forty. It was a baseline; she told me it was normal."

"It's just precautionary—mammograms with implants can be tricky. We'll get that ordered right away." He turns and exits without saying goodbye.

Tad hugs Dominque and says, "It's going to be okay. Please don't jump to conclusions."

"Jump? I'm leaping. How can I not?"

Tad looks out in the hallway when he hears the Doctor's name called. The file he was making notes in, left sitting open on the nurses' station counter.

He slips out, looking side to side, to see if anyone is around. Finding the coast clear, he grabs her file and brings it just inside her room. He opens the file, trying to be quick.

Dominque watches as the color drains from his face.

Chapter Five

"I understand, and I can't tell you how sorry I am this happened. There is a 4.4 cm solid mass showing on your films. I need to schedule you for a needle biopsy first thing in the morning to see exactly what we are dealing with. I'll have the lab rush the results," Dr. Harris explains.

"Cancer? Do I have cancer?" she asks, afraid of the answer.

"I need to get your biopsy results before I can answer that. It could be a calcification, a fatty deposit, or even scar tissue. Try not to worry yourself. I know it's not easy, but stay calm until we know more. On the other hand, I did get your chest X-ray's back, and there's nothing there. I was concerned since you saw the blood in your napkin. I'm happy to report, your lungs are clear."

Tad breathes a small sigh of relief. "So what made her cough up blood?"

"There are many possibilities. I'd like to do a sputum test in the morning to answer that for you, hopefully. It's noted in your chart, you've been coughing a bit lately?"

Dominque nods, still unable to speak.

"It's possible you broke some small capillaries. Mix it with saliva, and it looks worse than it really is."

He squeezes her shoulder just before he leaves. He doesn't say anything, but the look of pity in his eyes, register more than his words would anyway.

"Yeah, don't worry unless you need to worry. Easy for him to say." Dominque sits in the bed, staring off. So many words are spinning around: *cancer, death, chemo, sick...don't worry, he says.*

"Do you think I have cancer?" she asks Tad.

"Dom, I don't know. Let's try to stay positive until we have answers. I know that's tough, but let's try, okay?"

"I'm trying, really I am, but how can I possibly not think about it? It's a possibility."

"I get it. What can I do to help take your mind off it?"

She laughs. "Really, you want to have sex now—here in the hospital room?"

His eyes go wide...this must not have been one of the options. "No, of course not, but hey, it made you laugh."

She nods.

He jumps up off the bed. "I've got an idea."

Amber's phone vibrates while she's with Debra. "Deb, it's Tad, he's probably calling me with an update on Dom."

"Dom? What's wrong with Dom? Don't answer me, answer your phone!"

"I'm sorry I didn't tell you sooner, so much going on..." she says as she hits the answer button.

"Tad, how's Dom?"

"She's okay. We don't know a whole lot but, she could really use a good friend right about now."

"Tad, I'm here at the hospital, I'm with Debra."

"Debra? What's wrong with Debra? Is Little George okay?"

"She is…they're both okay."

Debra motions for the phone, so Amber puts it on speaker and holds it up. Debra yells out, "Tad, we're fine. We had a little blood scare. I just have to stay off my feet, but we'll be okay. Why is Dom here, and what room are you in?"

"They're admitting her now and moving us to a room. Fill you in when you get there."

Amber puts the phone back to her ear. "Okay, I'll get the room number. I'll be right there."

"Deb, I need to get to Dom."

"You mean WE need to get to her."

Upon Debra's insistence, Amber finds her a wheelchair in the time it takes to get Dominque moved.

When they enter her room, Amber senses the somberness—the darkness. Whatever is happening is not good. Her eyes are red and swollen with deep circles.

Her face brightens up when she sees them. "Debra, what are you doing here? Tad told me—you should be in bed, resting."

"I cleared it with the nurse. So long as I stay put in the wheelchair and promise to be back in bed within fifteen minutes, it's okay."

Amber leans over and kisses Dominque on the cheek. "You okay?"

Dominque shakes her head, and the tears start flowing again.

Debra wheels her chair over to the other side of the bed and grabs Dominque's hand.

She explains what the doctor told them. As she recites word-for-word, Amber starts to panic inside, scared for her friend.

"It's starting to sink in. The more I say it, the more I realize this is happening—to me!"

Neither Debra nor Amber says a word...speechless.

"They said there's a silver lining?" Amber asks.

"Yeah, coughing up blood. We still don't know why, but it's a good thing it happened."

Tad adds, "Once we have the biopsy results back, we'll know more."

Dominque stares out the window. "It's cancer; I know it is."

"We don't know that yet," Tad responds.

"It's okay, honey...it's better if I start wrapping my head around it now."

"What do you need us to do? How can we help?" Amber asks.

"I don't know yet, but you do know how much I need you both...and Zya too. Just when I thought my life was making a turn for the better, this happens—I'm not ready to die."

"You're not going to die—you're too stubborn for that," Amber says with a smile and tears threatening. She reaches for Debra's hand, so they are all three connected. "We've got each other. Everything is going to be okay. WE are going to be okay."

Amber excuses herself to use the restroom. Tad offers the one in the room, but Amber declines. She's looking for an escape—her emotions held in check as long as possible. She's always the strong one, the one to keep it together. But right now, she's about to fall apart.

Once safely behind the hallway restroom door, Amber slides down to the floor and lets it all go.

My sister was released from jail when she had another five years to serve. How did that happen?

Patrick, oh, I can't even think about him right now. I'm not sure I even know what to think about him—about us, if there is an us, right now.

Zya and Ashanti, I hope the boy makes it. He can't die. If he dies, I'm not sure Ashanti or Zya will ever recover.

Debra, I need to make sure Debra takes it easy. I have to help her out of this mess. No stress! She needs to keep Little George safe.

Dominque, oh, Dom...No, you can't die, it's not your time! I won't let you.

I just need to sit here and let it all out for a few minutes. They are my family; they are my sisters. They take priority.

Amber's phone rings. Tempted not to answer it, she turns it over to see who needs her now.

"Christoph, now really isn't a good time. I know I was not very nice to you last time I saw you, and I'm sorry, but honestly, I just can't handle anything else right now."

A thick French accent on the other end says, "Mon Chéri, I do not know why, but I have urge to call you. You pooped into my head."

Amber chuckles, then let's go with hilarious laughter. "I'm sorry, I'm not laughing at you, wait a minute—I might be —It's popped, not pooped."

"I'm so glad I make you laugh, Mon Chéri. Seems I call at just the right time, no?"

Her hysterics begin to calm down to a giggle. "Oh my gosh, yes, I really needed that, thank you. Where are you?"

"I am home. I have to tell you Mon Chéri, I've thought of you often, are you still in love?"

Christoph, the sexy Frenchman Amber met while in St. Tropez last year, has been playing it cool since his surprise visit a few months earlier. Amber told him she was in love with someone else. After urging her to call her so-called 'love' to find out if they were exclusive, they had one last tryst together before she broke it off completely. As he had hoped, Patrick was caught off guard and did not answer her question correctly, giving him the chance to make his visit very memorable—very memorable indeed.

Amber stutters a bit as her mind goes back to their last time together. "Yeeesss—Ummm, I mean noooo—Um, yes? Wait a minute, I am in love with Patrick, but I don't know about us. I don't know—I'm sorry, I shouldn't be dumping this on you, I just really don't know how to answer that question right now."

"Oh, Mon Chéri, I wish nothing more than to be with you right now. He does not deserve you. You need a man to always let you know you are loved, to never make you doubt. I cannot be there with you physically, but I can be with you an-other way if you like?"

"What way would that be?" she asks, confused.

"Are you by yourself, where no one can see?" he asks.

"I'm in the bathroom at the hospital."

"Hospital! You all right, Mon Chéri?"

"I am—it's not me—my friends…never mind, how can you be with me?"

"Remember the last time we were together in the back of your car, yes?" he asks.

She nods but doesn't say a word. That night was so hot and intense—she immediately starts to feel moist…she remembers.

"You are wearing skirt?"

"Yes."

"Close your eyes, and remember how my hand went between your legs and stroked you. Lightly remember, teasing you—just barely brushing over your silk panties. You tried so hard for me to press harder, but I keep pulling back. Now touch yourself the way I touch you."

"Christoph, you want to have phone sex with me right now, while I'm in the bathroom?" she asks while her hand, having a mind of its own, does precisely as commanded.

Amber has never been one just to have sex; all of her previous partners have been for love. With Christoph, it's different—he's pure lust. Ask her if she would ever have sex just for the sheer pleasure of it, and she'd quickly tell you, no way. Her time with him should feel wrong, but it doesn't. Being with him empowers her. He's helped her in so many ways. It's been worth it and now remembering the sexy—purely sexual encounters they have had, it just makes her want him more.

"Are you rubbing yourself as I ask? Remember, light-ly—I love teasing you. Keep going while I put my phone down, my shorts—too tight, I must remove."

Amber remembers how magnificent every inch of him is. With her eyes closed, she imagines him slowly undressing. Oh, that body! Phew! Those rock-hard abs! Big, tight quads! And that ass! OMG! She begins to breathe heavier—panting.

"Slow down, Mon Chéri, I like to tease, remember? Do not slip your fingers underneath your panties, you hear?"

"Yes," she whispers, painfully slowing her strokes.

"Oh, if only you could see the glistening on the tip of my cock. I remember you liked to tease me with your tongue. I imagine you, right now, tasting my sweetness. Teasing me, cir-cling, then sucking like a popsicle."

She moves her hand to her mouth. Imagining her thumb is Christoph as he brings back the memories of how much she enjoyed wrapping her lips around him. Her phone slides down into her lap. She can barely hear him, but then again, she doesn't need instructions; she remembers all too well how amazing he was—it was.

"Remember what it feels like to touch me? To put your hand on me? How you gasp the first time—your hand, too small, did not fit around? You want to imagine what it feels like to have every inch of me inside you?"

She nods as if he could see her respond.

Unable to control herself, her hand goes under her panties, slipping her index finger inside. Certainly no compari-son to his immense size, however, her vivid imagination brings all of her nerve endings alive as if he himself is filling her to capacity.

The only noise heard in the bathroom, and on the phone, is heavy breathing—and lots of moaning. Christoph is stroking himself, imaging her lips are working their magic.

Reliving that evening, Amber had completely let go because of the hurt she felt from Patrick's denial. She asked him if they were exclusive at Christoph's urging. They never said the words, but she was sure they were—he wasn't a player. Boy was she surprised when he couldn't answer the question. He wasn't as into their relationship as she was.

Working through the pain and betrayal, she let completely go. Their lovemaking was wild and hot—ripping at each other's clothes, not caring if they were destroyed beyond repair. Their animalistic sides took over. No regrets—hold nothing back—mind-blowing intensity.

She is interrupted by his loud groaning, hearing him climax into the phone. Afraid he might drop the call now, leaving her wanting more, she thrusts another finger in and uses her thumb to rub herself into oblivion.

He's talking to her, but she doesn't hear a word—she doesn't want anything to stop the fire. The sound of his voice suddenly getting through.

"I love to taste you. I can't get enough of your juices—so sweet. Your clit is so hard; I need to suck it."

He was an expert at giving oral sex. She'd let him live between her legs if that was possible.

"While my tongue is licking, teasing, sucking you, my fingers are inside, working their magic. I know just how to make you scream. Remember how I make you squirm?"

He was a very talented lover. He knew instantly where her G-spot was, causing her to writhe in delight. He could bring her to instant orgasm just by applying the right pressure and tempo. He brought her to multiples that way.

"I'm going to come again. Quick I have to be inside you. Spread your legs further apart, let me in!"

She covers her mouth just in time, so her screams aren't heard outside the door. She has no control over herself when she orgasms.

They sit in silence except for the sounds of their heavy breaths trying to slow down. She didn't think she would ever hear from him again. He made it clear he had feelings for her; it wasn't just sex for him. However, once her head cleared, she told him she loved Patrick. Amber wasn't sure where their relationship was going, but she wasn't ready to give up just yet.

Without saying a word, he hangs up.

She hears the click and ends the call, but has no desire to move. Unable to think straight—her mind and body—blown. *That definitely helped with the stress. Stewart and my crazy sister might be on to something.*

After ten minutes, Amber forms a plan in her mind. First, help Debra—Roberto has to go…have to find Brian.

After smoothing her skirt and washing her face, she flushes the toilet, in case anyone's been waiting. With her head held high, and a purpose to her step, she exits out into the hallway. That is until she sees the cops run past her down the other end of the hall.

Is that Brian? And Roberto? Oh my gosh, there's blood everywhere. Without hesitating, she runs after them.

Brian's face is a mess. His right eye is almost swollen shut. His nose looks broken—oh, it's definitely broken. His lip is split and oozing blood. The front of his shirt is crimson.

Roberto's face has a cut just below the eye—*good, Brian got in at least one solid punch.*

A police officer says, "Nurse, do you have a room where we can go and move out of the hallway here? This man looks like he could use some care too."

As they head into an empty room, Roberto sees an opportunity and reaches out, grabbing Brian's hair while yelling at him in Italian.

After breaking up the two men, once again, the officer asks Brian, "Want to tell me what happened?"

"Your guess is as good as mine." Wincing as he presses the cold compress, the nurse gave him to his mouth. "I'm walking to the elevators, then all of a sudden there he is, and he punches me in the nose."

Roberto begins yelling again in Italian, a police officer holds him back. "English, please—speak English."

"You cheat. We say we not sleep with her, but you did —you broke rule."

"What are you talking about? I didn't sleep with her. A deal is a deal; I don't operate that way. Why would you think I slept with her?"

"You two know each other?" one of the officers asks.

Brian responds, "Yes, we do; strange situation. We're both in love with the same woman, and we're trying to win her heart. We set up some rules, and then she decides who she wants to marry."

Roberto again leaps to get at him, yelling obscenities with raw anger and hatred in his eyes.

"Look, man, I don't know what you think, but I have not slept with Debra. You are the only one who has had that pleasure. I'm a man of my word. What on earth gave you the idea that I did?"

Amber would love to know the answer to that question as well. She watches as he stares at Brian. He's thinking about something…she can see the wheels in motion.

"She has accepted my proposal—she is marrying me. I forbid you to go anywhere near her, do you hear me?"

Brian hangs his head and drops his shoulders, looking defeated.

Amber, standing in the back, watching everything transpire and seeing the heartbreak on Brian's face, steps up. After loudly clearing her throat, she says, "Roberto, Debra asked me to find you, her accepting your proposal was a mistake. She's so sorry, and the last thing she wants to do is hurt you. But now, since she's had time to think about all this, she's in love with Brian."

Roberto's face turns beet red, his nostrils flare, and he leaps toward Brian, pummeling the air as the police, on either side, restrain him, "I kill you! What did you say to her? Why now she change her mind? I kill you!"

Chapter Six

She's been preparing herself all day for this, but actually hearing the words is still a shock. She feels like she's falling into a deep, dark hole. She can see his lips move, saying things she doesn't want to hear. *This can't be happening to me. What have I done to my body? I wish I could go back in time and change so many things. I don't want to die!*

Tad looks at her, trying to smile. He grabs her hand, pulling her back up from the bottomless pit.

"…there are several treatment options we can discuss. Due to the size of the mass…" Dr. Yen, the hospital oncologist, is explaining her diagnosis and treatment options.

Chemo? Poison my body? Surgery?

She looks over at Tad, her rock. Somehow, he gives her strength, more courage than she ever thought she would need. *I just found him. I want to grow old with him. I want to have a family with him.*

"…lumpectomy and radiation versus a mastectomy…"

I don't know what all this means. I don't want to know what it means! Someone wake me up from this nightmare, please SOMEONE WAKE ME UP!

"This is a lot to take in right now. Why don't you take some time and think about all this? Dr. Yen and I will come back in the morning. You're a fighter Dominque, don't give up hope."

"Did you get anything back from the sputum test?"

Dr. Harris responds, "Ah, yes, thank you for reminding me; nothing showed up. Must have been what we discussed, coughing probably broke some small vessels."

Earth to Dom...wake up. She thinks she heard something about hope?

"Any questions we can answer for you now?"

She hasn't heard most of the conversation. Yes, she has lots of questions, like: *'Why me?' 'I've had my string of bad luck, why is HE piling more on?'*

She imagines herself stomping her foot and decides. *I will fight this thing—I will win, I will survive.*

Looking up at Tad, "I'd...we'd like to have children someday. Will we still be able to?"

Tad squeezes her hand with a brilliant smile on his face.

"If you want to have children, we'll have our high-risk obstetrician come back with us in the morning. We'd like to spring you from here tomorrow morning after we meet with you if that's okay?" Dr. Harris says with a smile on his face.

Suddenly a reason to smile. "Yes, please let me go home. I'd love a nice hot shower and sleep in my own bed."

☯

After Tad fills her in on the details she missed when she was dazed, and a few more tears shed, she fell into a fitful slumber. She tossed and turned for over an hour before deep sleep took over.

Zya taps on the hospital room door and peeks inside.

Tad, sitting beside her bed, motions to come in.

She and Ashanti enter with a beautiful bouquet. "Hey, Tad, how are you holding up?"

"As well as can be expected. We're hanging on to hope and prayers."

Dominque's eyes flutter open. "Hi guys, I'm so happy to see you."

Ashanti hugs Dominque with her good arm, her right arm still in a sling.

"I'll be released tomorrow. I can't wait to go home."

"I bet. Has the doctor been in to talk to you yet?"

Her head still being in a fog; she's not sure what Zya knows.

"Yes, they're coming back in the morning, the high-risk obstetrician, to talk about my treatment options."

"Obstetrician? You pregnant girl?" Zya asks.

A faint smile appears on her face. "No, but I'd like to have that option later. Tad and I just found each other; I want us to have a future, and that future includes a family."

"Wait a minute...you said treatment options? What does that mean?"

Dominque's eyes begin to water again.

Tad says, "She has breast cancer, Stage II."

"Oh no! I'm so sorry." She hugs Dominque as she sobs into her arms. "I don't understand, we both had mammograms just a few months ago. Yours was good."

Dominque responds between sobs, "They screwed up, they mixed up the films."

Zya remembers the phone call she received shortly after her mammogram. They needed her to come back; they saw something on her films. When she had it redone, and it was all clear, it never dawned on her, it could have been Dominque.

❧

"Hi, Deb, how are you doing?"

"I should be asking you that question. I'm so sorry, Dom…you've got this!"

"Thanks, I had a feeling. We're waiting for the doctors to come in so we can go over the plan."

"That's kind of why I called…please make sure one of them gets me on the phone when they get there. I'm so sorry I can't be there in person."

"Your heart is here, that's all that matters."

"Mommy, mommy, see what I made you?" Tracey says in the background.

"It appears you have a little helper there with you," Dominque says, hoping one day for her own little person, or people in her life.

"Yes, and yummy Fruit Loops cereal…mmm, my favorite." She cringes, thinking about the amount of sugar drowning in milk.

"I better let you go. I promise we'll call you when the doctors get here. They should be in soon, and then hopefully they'll let me go home."

As she hangs up, Amber arrives with Zya in tow behind her on her cellphone.

"Sorry, I left a long message for Stan. He didn't quite understand my gibberish," Zya says with a big smile.

They hear a tap on the door just before three doctors enter the room. Quickly, she speed dials Debra.

"Wow, I see you have some company. We would like to discuss your treatment plan with you, would you all mind stepping out into the hall for a few moments please?"

"No, they all stay Dr. Harris. This is my family—they stay for all of it."

"And I'm here too," Debra says via the phone speaker.

"Okay, please allow me to introduce you to Dr. Clark, he's a high-risk obstetrician."

They all shake hands.

Dr. Yen is a brilliant specialist whose intelligence makes up for what his bedside manner lacks. He begins, "We need to discuss your options. You are young and healthy…"

Healthy? Did he say I was healthy? I have cancer!

"We'd like to get you started on a chemotherapy regimen as quickly as possible. The drugs we would like to use are Cyclophosphamide or Cytoxan and Doxorubicin or Adriamycin. Four cycles for sure, possibly six. We know you want to have children, so this will happen after you and Dr. Clark have finished your egg retrieval. We're hoping it will only take a few weeks. Dr. Clark, would you like to take over from here?"

A warmer, friendly face takes over the conversation. "I'm happy to hear you'd like to have a family in the future. The best way to ensure this is to collect and freeze some embryos before you start treatment, as Dr. Yen suggested. Are you menstruating regularly?"

"I am now. I wasn't for a long time because I was anemic and anorexic. I've resolved my eating disorders, so my body is regulating itself," Dominque says proudly.

"Wonderful and congratulations, I'm sure that wasn't easy. That certainly tells us a lot about how strong and determined you are. That will go a long way as you go through this. If you are regularly menstruating, we'll give you Clomid, a drug to stimulate ovulation and help produce multiple eggs. We'll track when you ovulate and retrieve as many as possible. Then we'll introduce your husband's sperm to your eggs and freeze them when they reach the blastocyst stage. That will help ensure the best possible outcome when it's time for implantation."

She doesn't bother correcting him; this is all so technical. However, talking about a future, a family with Tad keeps her head in the game.

"Isn't that a hormone drug? Is her breast cancer hormone-positive?" Amber asks.

"Clomid is actually an estrogen blocker, and Ms. Patterson's breast cancer is triple-negative—not hormone positive."

Dr. Yen impatiently interjects, "This is why the chemo cocktail we are suggesting is the best route. It's harsh, but it's the best chance of beating this."

"We can start right away if you're early in your cycle. We'll do a blood draw and test your hormone levels," Dr. Clark adds, beaming a big smile.

Dr. Harris says, "As far as surgery is concerned, you can have it before chemo, or after. I might suggest before in case you need another round of Clomid. This could give you another few weeks.

"Your surgery options are with a lumpectomy which would be followed by radiation or a mastectomy with no radiation."

Zya interjects, "Is one better over the other? I mean, do her odds improve?"

"Statistically, the odds are the same either way."

Tad asks, "Surgery after chemo? Why would you do that?"

"There were studies done twenty-plus years ago that show no difference in recurrence rate either way. Having surgery after chemo, seeing the tumors shrink, can have a positive physiological effect on the patient," Dr. Yen explains, softening up a bit.

"We know this a lot to digest, and you'll probably have lots of questions," Dr. Harris says gently touching Dominque.

"Probably not the smartest thing to do," Zya says, "but I did some research on the internet last night."

Dr. Yen groans.

The other two doctors are not affected.

She continues, "What's her recurrence rate based on your treatment?"

Dr. Yen, clearly agitated, says, "Stage II breast cancer survival rate is ninety-three percent or ninety-three out of one hundred women will not have a recurrence in the first five years."

Dr. Harris adds, "The odds are definitely in your favor, but it's going to be a battle. This is not going to be easy, but we're confident this is the best plan of attack."

"Okay, how soon can we start?"

Dr. Clark answers, "First, let's get that blood test and see where you are in your cycle. You'll take Clomid for five days. Hopefully, we can retrieve your eggs within the next few weeks?"

Amber asks, "I have another question, and I'm sure this probably is the least of her worries, but will she lose her hair?"

Dominque immediately sits upright. Amber's right—that thought hasn't crossed her mind. She's one of the few natural redheads left; her long, thick, lustrous mane, even more so now that she's been taking better care of herself.

Dr. Yen starts only to be interrupted by Dr. Harris, "I'm sorry, you will lose your hair, somewhere around two to three weeks after your first treatment. The hospital has a great support group along with a Look Good Feel Better program to help women lead as normal a life as possible while undergoing treatment. I'll make sure you leave with their brochure. Don't think you're vain; it's totally understandable." Dr. Harris removes his stylish cap to reveal a bare scalp. "Yours at least will grow back in."

☯

Nobody notices Ashanti slip out. She's been so worried about Mitch, but afraid to ask…her mom seems so angry. She shouldn't care—I mean, he was horrible to her! He disrespected her, talked down to her, even hurt her physically, but that doesn't matter, she needs to know if he's going to make it.

Ashanti makes her way up to the ICU floor, being careful not to let anyone see her and slowly strolls past the rooms peeking inside, trying to find him. Halfway down the hallway, on her right, their eyes lock. She stands frozen; she didn't want him to know she's checking on him.

He looks away, staring out the window, not wanting her to see the tears. After wiping his eyes, he turns his head toward her and motions her to come in. Her feet won't move. She continues to stand frozen, just staring at him.

A nurse walks by and looks to see what Ashanti is staring at and sees Mitch motioning for her. "It's okay, he's by himself, you can go in and see him. His parents won't be back for a little while. Looks like he wants your company."

Ashanti looks up at the nurse. "Thanks, ...okay, ...um, ...thanks."

She slowly makes her way into his room, not sure why or what she's going to say.

They just stare at each other for a minute.

Breaking the silence, he says, "Hi."

"Hi?"

Nervous, he fiddles with his hands. "Thanks. I know you stayed with me—you saved my life. If you hadn't, I would be dead." Embarrassed, Mitch turns his head as the tears begin to flow again.

Without hesitation, Ashanti moves to his bedside and puts her hand on his arm. "You would have done the same for me."

"That's just it—I wouldn't have. I'm mean, I'm disgusting, I terrorized you, and you saved my life. I meant to hurt you that day—bad. I'd never felt so much hatred for someone as I did for you. I wanted you dead, and you saved my life."

At hearing how much he hater her, she starts to cry and runs out of the room. Once outside, she runs into the arms of Mitch's father, Mr. Morris.

"Whoa, whoa—you okay?"

Unable to breathe, and now with Mitch's dad's hands on her shoulders, she begins to panic.

Mrs. Morris, Mitch's mom, comes up behind her husband. When she sees Ashanti, she goes nuts. "What is SHE doing here? Get that terrorist out of here!"

Now directing her attack on Ashanti directly, "Did you come back to finish the job? Did you come in while we were gone to kill him once and for all?"

Mr. Morris puts his hand out to stop his wife from getting any closer to Ashanti. "Agnes, that's enough!"

"What do you mean, that's enough, you're taking her side?"

"There is no side to take here. Our son was not innocent. He was mean—he bullied her. He hurt her, and she still stopped to help him. She saved his life."

"He would not have needed saving had her kind not been here to begin with!"

She yells at Ashanti, "Go home! We don't want your trash here stinking up our country!"

SLAP! Mr. Morris cannot contain himself; his hand connects with his wife's cheek. "That's enough! I've heard as much of your ugliness as I can stand. You're a racist!"

Holding the side of her face, in shock, her husband hit her. "Why did you slap me? Why are you protecting her? She tried to kill our son. She's a terrorist—they're all terrorists."

All of the nurses, doctors, and visitors are pretty much frozen where they are. They can't believe the exchange they're witnessing. The loud slap certainly gave everyone a reason to pause.

"Agnes, you are creating a scene, let's go."

Looking at Ashanti, Mr. Morris says, "Are you okay? I'm very sorry about all this. We don't all believe Muslims are bad."

Ashanti turns and runs down the hallway toward the elevators.

Agnes turns and runs after her.

A nurse, pretending to view a chart at the end of the hall, turns just in time for her foot to get in Agnes's way.

Chapter Seven

"Why you get me out? I not leaving. I fight for her," Roberto says firmly.

"Well, I'm betting on you not going anywhere. Otherwise, I lose my bail money," Brian responds.

They turn and walk out of the building together.

Brian continues, "This whole deal seems like something out of a nightmare, or maybe more like Hollywood. I don't want Debra to be hurt anymore. I'm worried about her and Little George. I just want her to be happy and healthy, so I'm stepping away and giving her some space. She needs time with her family and friends without stress. She's gonna have her hands full with Little George when he gets here, so I'm going to stay away, for now. I hope you'll consider doing the same. Us competing, fighting over her, has caused her a lot of pain, something she doesn't need right now."

Brian walks away, not waiting for an answer.

☯

Debra's doorbell rings, Tracey is quick to run and answer it. Before Amber can catch her, Tracey has the door wide open.

"Hi, you're my mommy's friend, aren't you?"

"Yes, I am. I'm going to be your mommy's husband—your new daddy," Roberto answers, entering the house and picking up Tracey twirling her around.

As Tracey squeals, Amber comes running up to him—the Devil in her eyes.

"Tracey, will you please go get your mom some water?" Amber asks.

"You just got her water," Tracey responds.

"Then go get her an apple please, she told me she was hungry."

"Okay. I'm happy you're going to be my new daddy. I need one," Tracey says as she turns and runs into the kitchen.

"What are you doing here? You can't be here. She doesn't want to see you. She knows what you did to Brian," Amber says in a hushed tone.

"I just spoke with Brian, water under bridge. He does not want her anymore—he told me she was mine." Roberto pushes past Amber knocking her to the side as if she was nothing but a feather.

"I'm calling the police. You need to leave now!" Amber says, pulling her phone from her pocket.

Roberto, in two giant steps, is beside her forcing the phone from her hand. "You will not interfere anymore! She is mine, and I will have her!"

Amber runs to Debra's room, trying to close and lock the door before he can get there. She's no match for him. He pushes the door open hard, sending her flying back, falling to the floor.

Roberto sees Debra's wide eyes—the fear instantly stopping him in his tracks. "Debra, I'm so sorry for the ah... what you say, confusion? Brian, he does not love you; he not want you; he gave you to me."

For a fleeting moment, Debra just wants to give in. Her heart cannot be any more broken than it already is. Then Tracey comes in with an apple for her. *This is not the lesson I want to teach my child.*

Tracey grabs Roberto's hand and says, "Mommy, thank you for getting me a new daddy. I like him."

"Tracey, honey, will you please go play in your room. Mommy needs to talk to Roberto and Amber for a few minutes. Grown-up talk, okay?" The fear has now turned into anger.

"Okay." She turns to Roberto and says, "Will you come play with me in my room after you talk to Mommy?"

Amber turns to Tracey and ushers her out of the room before Roberto can answer.

"Roberto, I'm very sorry if I hurt you. I didn't really think this through when you and Brian decided to compete for me, but someone was always going to get hurt—someone had to lose. I never imagined it would be me, but here we are," she says sternly and controlled.

"Mourning George's death was something I never did. You two wonderful men came into my life and wanted to care for me the way my George would have. And for that, I'm eternally grateful."

"While I do have feelings for you, it is Brian that I love. I choose him. You say he doesn't love me—he doesn't want me

—that hurts, but he's my choice. But right now, I need time to grieve for my husband. I need to spend some time with Tracey. I just need time. I'm very sorry, but I would like you to please leave my home now."

"Mia Bella, I do as you wish, but I not leave here. You will love me more than him, I am sure. I have started for green card, you will sponsor me, as they say, so I can stay here for you?"

It wasn't easy telling him she loved Brian. She tried to tell him as gently as possible. But now, the anger returns, "No, I will not sponsor you. I wish you to return to Italy—I do not want you here."

Roberto's face flashes red, and he takes one big step toward the side of her bed.

Amber watching his nostrils flare and his fists clench, reaches out to stop him.

He pushes her hard into the chair, causing it to tip over.

Looking directly over her, his face red with rage. "You have done enough! You say you're friend, but you get in way!"

Fearful for her life, Amber quickly reaches inside her purse, which is on the floor next to the chair and pulls out her weapon.

Aiming it directly at Roberto, she stands up. "I'm an excellent shot, don't try me. Leave this house at once, or I will shoot."

"You not shoot me. Child is here; she likes me," Roberto says as he takes a step toward her.

Amber cocks the gun. "Try me."

"Well, joke on Brian. He pay for me to be free. Now he lose if I go home," Roberto says as he walks out of the bedroom.

Amber is close behind with the gun still pointed at him.

As Roberto walks to the door, he sees a picture of Debra, George, and Tracey on a table. He knocks it off, shattering the glass as he walks out.

After locking the door behind him, Amber returns to Debra's room and puts the gun away. "I'm sorry I should have told you. The safety is always on. If Tracey finds it, she won't hurt herself."

"Amber, when did you get a gun?" shrieks Debra. "You know how I feel about them." Without giving Amber a chance to respond, she continues, "But in this case, I don't know what he would have done to you—us! The hatred in his eyes. How could I have thought I ever loved that man?"

"Scared the shit out of me too. I'm just so glad I had it —and I didn't have to use it."

"So why do you have a gun? I thought you felt the same way I do?"

"I do—I mean, I did. I'm getting these creepy texts, and they're getting scarier and scarier. It's like this man knows exactly where I am—what I'm doing—who I'm with every waking moment. It's freaking me out."

"Did you call the police?"

"I did. He's going through burner phones. He only uses one each time he texts me so they can't track him."

"Oh my God, Amber, who would do this to you?"

"I don't know. I don't have a clue, that's the scariest part. I think he wants to hurt me, and if he knows where I am at all times, he can whenever he wants to. I just need to try and protect myself as best I can."

"Bodyguard, you need someone protecting you."

"I thought about that, and it's not out of the question, I'm just not there yet."

"Amber, he can hurt you anytime he finds you alone. You need a bodyguard. I get the gun, but that might not be enough."

"I've been very cautious—never anywhere alone, I promise. I don't walk out to my car alone at night. No one can get into my condo parking lot or my building. There are cameras everywhere, and John, our front desk guy, is always looking out for me. I promise I'm taking precautions."

"How is it possible he knows where you are at all times? I mean, what does he say?"

"Here's the latest text. They come from a whole bunch of different numbers, and I know I should delete them, but they keep me on my toes and keep me afraid just enough to be careful."

"I love the suit today. Nice and slim, just like you."

"Who are you, and how do you know what I'm wearing?"

"I know a whole lot about you, Amber. I know your routine. You walked right past me this morning. Your perfume is intoxicating. I'll make sure to pour some on you when I finally get you."

"Get me? Why do you want to get me?"

"You play little Miss Sweet & Innocent, but we know better, don't we? You may not know why now, but when you see me, it will all become clear."

"Amber! That's some scary shit!"

"Listen, enough talk about me, Roberto just came in here and tried to attack us. He told you Brian doesn't want you. You need to talk to me about this," Amber says, changing the subject.

"Actually, talking about your stalker took my mind off all that. I'm still trying to make sense of all this. Roberto just tried to attack us…he was going to hurt us! Seriously, I don't know if I trust myself to judge anymore. I was with George for so long, I forgot what it was like to be with another man. I was too trusting!

"What was I thinking? Was I really that numb—that lost—to let those two men compete for me? I was supposed to marry one of them? Wow! That was really stupid! I'm glad it's over now, I feel better; hurt, but relieved. I'm not happy Roberto came in and tried to attack us, I'm just glad it's over. Do you think he was just using me to get his green card?"

Chapter Eight

"That bastard! I swear I'll kill him! Give me your gun. No, never mind, I'll get my own—one that can't be traced. That creep will never make it back to Italy!"

"Calm down, Zya, Debra, and Tracey are napping, let's not wake them," Amber says as she motions Zya to take a seat on the sofa.

"Okay, wait a minute, why do you have a gun again?"

"Long story, but first, I'm worried about Debra. You should have seen Roberto—the fire in his eyes—the hatred. I'm worried he's going to come back. That was a close call—too close. We need to make sure he leaves the country, but how?"

"Leave it to me. I'll call Micki and see if she can expedite his exit."

"Who's Micki?"

"She's the police officer that interviewed Ashanti at the hospital. She's also part of the No-Tolerance Bullying program in the school system; she's the Broward County point person."

"Think she might be able to help?"

"I don't see why not. She's very nice. She's like a member of the family already. Anyway, I'll call her and see what she can do about getting the creep on his way."

"Okay, well, let me know if I can help. How is Ashanti doing?"

"That child is as strong as an ox and just about the nicest young lady you're ever going to meet. I'm not just saying that because she's mine. She went to see how Mitch was doing in the hospital when we were visiting Dominque the other day."

"My turn, who's Mitch?" asks Amber.

"The kid who was bullying her. Calling her a terrorist, yet he was the one doing the terrorizing. She went up to his room to see if he was okay. Can you believe that?"

"Wow, how did that go over?"

"His mom is one mean bitch, all right. She's pressing charges against Ashanti. Micki called me yesterday and told me. She said not to worry about it; she was there when the witch came in screaming, wanting to see the Chief. He called Micki into his office to get more information. He, too, has a no-tolerance policy when it comes to bullying. Once he heard the story, he told Micki to ask me if I want to press charges against Mitch for harassing my daughter. Monster Mom grabbed her purse and stormed out of his office, threatening we'd be hearing from her attorney. I'm just waiting for the letter. Micki said to let her waste her money; no judge is going to convict Ashanti for trying to protect herself. The tool she has, it's legal; she didn't do anything wrong. Well, except maybe saving that boy's life."

"Zya! You don't mean that! A life is a life. It sounds to me like his mom brainwashed him."

"You're right, I didn't mean it. It's just so hard to find out my child has been going through all this, and there is nothing I can do to protect her. Except for putting her in a plastic bubble for the rest of her life."

"Come here," Amber says, stretching out her arms.

"What? You think a hug is going to make this all better?"

"No, but maybe it will help your aching heart."

Resting in Amber's arms, Zya lets out a sigh and relaxes a little. She didn't realize just how tense she was until now.

After a few moments, her heart stops racing. "Okay, okay, so you have the magic hugs. Thanks, I needed that."

"For you girlfriend…anything. I'm sorry, but I've got to run, I have some things at the office that need tending since Dom hasn't been in. One of the girls in my office told me Mr. Brettinger's office called for me."

"THE, Paul Brettinger? People Magazine's sexiest man? Oh, he's a hunk and a half," Zya says as she fans her hand back and forth.

Chapter Nine

"Tad, can you come here please?" asks Dominque from the bedroom. She's been home two days now, and with Tad's expert care and attention, she's feeling much better—much stronger. The sudden crying attacks are coming farther apart. His strength is what's getting her through it all.

"Hey babe, what can I get you?"

"Do you really want to make me happy?"

"Of course I do. You kidding, I'll do anything for you."

Dominque's eyes water as she looks at the concern and love on his face. "Come here, come lay next to me."

"Are you sure that's a good idea?"

"I think it's a great idea."

Tad does as asked and crawls into bed next to her. It's then he notices—she's naked.

"Dom, please don't tease me."

"Oh, I'm not going to be the one doing the teasing."

Tad smiles and even blushes a little. "Are you sure?"

"I'm sure I love you. I'm scared to death about my future—our future, but right now, I know I need you more than anything."

Tad touches Dominque's cheek then runs his fingers lightly across her lips. He kisses her gently, their lips barely touching.

After a few moments of soft, loving kisses, Dominque tries to kick up the passion.

"I thought I was the one doing the teasing? We've got all night, my pace, okay?" Tad said.

"Okay. I'm all yours…do as you wish."

He pulls the sheets back so happy to see she's looking healthier than the last time he saw her without any clothing. He drinks her in as he runs his fingers down her creamy soft, porcelain skin. Her long silky ginger hair is sprawling out across the pillows.

Her nipples perk up, either from the cool air or in anticipation of the promised teasing.

He intentionally brushes his hand across her chest, as he pushes a strand of hair away, tucking it lovingly behind her ear.

She jumps a little, the light touch sending shivers all over; her body now covered in goosebumps.

"I hope you don't mind, but I intend to make this last a —very—long—time."

Breathing heavy, Dominque says, "If you must. But please remember, I'm very sick, so you mustn't tease me too much."

"Nice try, beautiful. As I said, I intend to make this last."

Starting at her shoulder, he places tiny light kisses in a row down her arm. When he gets to her hand, his lips press into her palm. He turns her hand over, moving his lips to the tips of her fingers, one by one. When he gets to her index finger, he wraps them around it, sucking gently, pulling it ever so slowly, in and out.

Dominque's body quivers.

Once he's played popsicle with her appendages, he pushes up on his elbow, gently stroking her leg, starting at the hip, then slowly gliding down to her knee.

He moves further down her body, replacing his fingers with his lips. He starts at the side of her knee, working his way down to her ankle—to her instep—then down to her toes. He gently sucks on each one, giving each the same attention he did to her fingers. He knows sucking on her fingers and toes, gets her very aroused.

She becomes fidgety, squirming in anticipation.

"None of that, or I'll stop," he playfully warns.

"Sorry, sorry...okay...I'll stop, I'll try to stop," she replies.

Smiling to himself, he can't believe he's in complete control of this beauty. Pleasuring her is an aphrodisiac for him. Watching her squirm and moan, knowing it's because of him, is his foreplay.

He positions himself between her legs, picking up the foot he was caressing so lovingly with his mouth and begins tracing the inside of her leg with the tip of his tongue. When he gets to the top of her thigh, his lips gently brush over her pubic hair, again giving her tremors.

He strategically begins tracing his tongue on the inside of her other thigh, moving south until he is sucking on the toes of that foot. He is taking his time—teasing her. Hearing her beg and plead is music to his ears.

He decides to play it out as long as he can by moving to her other side, picking up her hand and begins sucking those fingers. After artfully circling the circumference of all five, his kisses trail up her arm.

When he reaches her shoulder, their eyes lock. The lust and desire clear on both of their faces.

Her lips pout as he moves her hair away from her neck. He proceeds to trail light, delicate kisses down to her cleavage. He's trying so hard to remain in control, but his own desire is making it very har—literally!

Dominque moans—the fire growing in intensity.

He kisses her ear lobes, his hot breath causing her to squeeze her legs together. She wants so badly to touch herself, but she doesn't dare.

His kisses are now covering the front of her neck, slowly moving down to her small, yet perfect breasts. He kisses all around her firm peaks, teasing, making sure to blow out as he moves over them.

The hot air causes them to stand more at attention. Her hand moves up to it, pinching it, as she moans.

He sits back, watching her.

While her hand continues to caress her breast, her hips rock back and forth. Her other hand reaches down between her legs, rubbing her index finger between her lips.

He watches as her head rolls back and forth. Her hair is covering her face.

Tad has never witnessed a woman masturbate, but he knows that's exactly what she's doing—so, he lets her play anyway. Just when he feels she's about to peak, he engulfs her other breast in his mouth, sucking hard on her nipple, sending ripple after ripple of ecstasy through her body.

"Someone's not playing fair…" Tad teases after she comes down the other side.

"I think it's you who's not playing fair," says Dominque, still out of breath.

"I am going to have to punish you now?"

"I've been a bad girl, haven't I?" she says with a sweet innocent look and the tip of her finger in her mouth.

"Yes, you have, and I think I'm going to have to take you over my knee."

Tad has no idea who he is right now, but he's thoroughly enjoying this game. Never having done this before, he's going on instinct. "Come here, my dear, and lay across my lap."

Dominque gladly obliges and lays across his legs, positioning herself, so the bulge in his pants, is in the perfect spot.

He begins to rub delicate circles across her butt cheeks. Each time, his rings get bigger, and bigger, until his finger slips between her legs. He's not going to spank her; he's going to make her orgasm, over and over again.

His finger slips between her lips—feeling the heat—the moisture. She squirms every time he slips, grinding herself into his erection. She parts her legs, allowing him to reach in further, sliding his finger into her hot pussy. She's so wet.

Without realizing it, his pinkie is rubbing up against her swollen bud, sending her over the edge. Her body is spasming as she climaxes for the second time.

Tad gently pushes Dominque over on her back. Looking into her eyes, he says, "You have no idea what you do to me. I love you so much. I never thought I would ever feel this way about anyone. You are mine, and I fucking love that."

He positions himself on top of her, kissing her passionately. Although he's still dressed, he grinds into her anyway as if there was no fabric between them. He pulls back on his knees and spreads her legs far apart. "Shall we go for number three?"

He dives in, smelling her earthy aroma, he takes long, deliberate licks.

She's so sensitive from orgasming twice, he immediately sends her over the top—again. He tries to keep up his part, but her hips thrashing about make it impossible, so he slips his finger in while she crests again, and again.

She opens her eyes with a devilish grin on her face and reaches for him. "Now, please take me. I need you inside now!"

"Who am I to disappoint a damsel in distress?"

Tad hurries and removes his clothes, but he doesn't enter her right away. He rubs himself up and down where his tongue has just been.

Her hips match his tempo until she tilts her hips just enough so the tip slips inside. His body takes over, and with one swift thrust of his hips, his penis buries inside, drowning in her fluids. The heat—the tightness all around him...he can't hold back. He tries to go slow, but after a few thrusts, he loses control.

One final push and over the edge he goes...falling, falling into the abyss. His orgasm is so deep—his body shakes all over like an earthquake inside.

He doesn't realize she's climaxing again until he feels her twitching all around him. The sensation as she pulses all around him sends him further out until they both come crashing down.

They lay in each other's arms for a while, trying to slow their breathing. Although they aren't virgins, it feels like their first time. The depth of their feelings taking them places neither has ever been before.

Dominque's insecurities and self-doubt had caused her to use her body to get attention and love before she met Tad. She was always hooking up with the last hot guy she just met, hoping for true love.

Jumping from foster home to foster home, she never had a reliable mother or father figure. The other kids liked to tease her, making fun of her flaming locks, freckled nose, and long, lithe body. Little did they know, those looks were exactly what she needed to work the runway.

At the age of sixteen, and after being molested by her then so-called father figure, she decided to leave and make a name for herself. She wanted to be a model. She was gorgeous, and with that fiery red hair, she got noticed.

She was cast for a few catalogs and ads but never anything significant. Little did she know, the girls that got those opportunities were the ones that didn't sleep with the photographers and agents. She thought, by having sex and performing her oral duties, they would open doors for her. They just kept promising her and keeping her coming back for more, or rather, them getting more.

One thing she noticed about the more successful models, they didn't eat. On the rare occasion she saw one of them take a bite, they would run to the bathroom obviously to barf it back up. That's when she realized, or at least thought, she needed to lose weight. That was why she didn't get any callbacks. She was fat—she needed to be thinner.

She continued not to eat and took every job that came her way. When they asked her to remove her top, she complied—no argument. When they asked her to remove her panties, off, they came. The more clothing she removed, the fewer callbacks she got.

With what little savings she had dwindling to almost nothing, she had to make a choice, go all the way and get into the adult film industry or look for a real job. She opted for the latter…that's how she met Amber.

She continued with a long line of one-night stands eating less and less looking for the right balance to find happiness.

Her friends staged an intervention one day telling her matter-of-factly, she looked sick and needed to get help. She accepted and got introduced to a social worker at the hospital. She not only helped her with her eating disorders and self-esteem issues, but she also started putting a medical history together for her, searching for her parents and other family members. Just as she began to show some progress, she received a notice…she was being audited.

That auditor ended up being Tad, Mr. Tad Johnson. A name that still makes her giggle. Knowing he was not the type she would go for, Tad became her secret admirer, sending her poems, flowers, and encouragement as she fought the anemia and anorexia beasts.

No, he wasn't her type at all; he wasn't what she wanted—but he was exactly what she needed.

Chapter Ten

"Ms. Sanders, please get me coffee," he says, a little harsher than he would have liked.

Brian has had a challenging time trying to concentrate since his run-in with Roberto. It's proving to be very difficult, but he knows it's the right thing to do. Still, he can't get her out of his head. This morning's last three patients have poured their hearts out to him, yet he can't remember a single thing they've said. Good thing he got permission to record their sessions.

Ms. Sanders comes in with his dark elixir. He closes his eyes, breathing in the heavenly aroma. He opens them just in time to see Ms. Sanders hurry out the door.

"Julie, wait, please come back in," Brian asks, motioning her into his office as he comes out from behind his desk. He knows he's been a jerk; he feels terrible.

She can't meet his eyes—she's flustered, cheeks pink.

"I'm so sorry; I don't mean to bark at you. I've just been in a bad place these past few days. The last thing I want to do is take it out on you. I'm really sorry."

As Brian touches her elbow to reassure her, she yanks away as if his fingertips were weapons. *I guess I've been a real prick.*

"Julie, we don't have any appointments left for the day, so why don't you go home. I'm sure I've been tough to deal with lately."

"Are you firing me?" she asks.

"Oh, God, no! I can't do this without you!" Brian exclaims, shaking his head.

Ms. Sanders breathes a sigh of relief.

"I've been a monster. Maybe it's time I go see a shrink."

Brian retreats behind his desk, putting his head in his hands and elbows on his desk. *I've got to get a handle on this. It's driving me crazy not knowing what's happening in her life.* He breaks down and reaches for his phone—he has to know.

"Brian, is that you?" Amber asks.

"Hi, Amber, yeah, it's me. I'm sorry to bother you."

"You're not bothering me. I'm happy to hear from you. You know Debra would love to as well."

"That's what I'm calling about, how is she?"

"Why don't you call and ask her?"

"I'm not sure I can do that right now. I think this is what's best for her, and I don't want to put her through any more pain."

"Brian, Debra sent Roberto packing. She sent him home —back to Italy. We had a...for lack of better words, some drama with him last week. Zya called in a favor, and his ass was deported back home."

It takes a moment for Amber's words to register. *Back home, Roberto's not here? Drama?* Those words keep playing over and over in his mind.

"Brian, you there? Hello…earth to Brian…"

"I'm sorry, wait, you said drama—with him, what did you mean by that?"

"Debra and I both saw who he really was, and we didn't like him very much. It was a little scary."

"Did he hurt her? Did he hurt Debra?"

"Oh no, not on my watch. I did have to pull my gun out on him, though—to get him to leave."

Brian sits straight up in his seat when he hears the word *gun*.

"GUN? Why do you have a gun?"

"Long story…I'm just thankful I didn't have to use it. Brian, Debra loves you so much. She messed up—she knows she messed up. If you have any feelings for her at all, please call her, she really misses you."

"I miss her too. I'm just confused about all this. Is she okay? Is Little George okay?"

"They both are doing great. Debra's on bed rest, so she's stuck at home. We've been taking turns going over and staying with her and helping with Tracey. She's become quite the little card player, by the way. She's taken us all for more than a few quarters."

Brian laughs as he imagines his sweet Debra, a hustler. "I'm glad to hear both of them are all right. You think I should call her?"

"Do you love her?"

"Very much."

"Then, I have a better idea."

Brian knocks on the door, palms sweating, and very nervous. Not sure he's doing the right thing, but he knows he can't stay away any longer. Brian smiles when he sees Zya's face peek behind the curtains.

"Hi, it's great to see you. Surprised—but pleasantly."

Debra asks from her bedroom, trying to be funny, "Who is it? Tell them I already bought at the office. If it's Avon, tell them to stop calling."

Brian can hear Debra and laughs. "Amber thought it might be a good idea if I take her shift tonight. That is, of course, if it's all right with you—and Debra."

She responds to Debra, "Well, it's not Avon, and you definitely did not buy THIS at the office." Zya steps back, allowing him to step inside. She puts her finger up to her lips, signaling for him not to say anything, then motions for him to follow her.

Brian stops just outside her bedroom room as Zya enters. Debra looks up at Zya, intending to ask who it was when she sees him. Her jaw goes slack as her eyes try to focus. Her hands instantly go to her hair, trying to smooth it, while her eyes stay glued to his. She can't believe he's here—right in front of her.

"Hi Deb, I spoke to Amber today, and she suggested I come to see you tonight. She told me what happened with Roberto. Well, some of it at least. You'll have to explain about the gun...I'm completely lost."

Debra doesn't say anything. Her heart is beating so fast. *He's here—he's really here. Maybe I didn't blow it after all.*

The waterworks start streaming down her cheeks. She opens her mouth, then closes it. She's surprised and speechless.

Brian feels she's happy to see him; however, he becomes uneasy when she doesn't say, 'Hi' or even smile at him. "I'll leave if you want me to...I wasn't sure. It's okay, Amber is waiting by the phone for me to call, and she'll come right over."

Debra still says nothing; her heart is pounding. The tears are continuously trailing down both cheeks with a dazed look in her eyes.

"Deb, are you okay? Deb, you need to say something," Zya says, prompting her out of her stupor.

Debra pulls out of her trance and puts her hand out toward him.

He grabs it.

She pulls him to her and hugs him tightly. She's crying harder now—she won't let go.

His lower lids pool with tears as he drops the roses on the bed, lowering himself next to her and wraps his arms around her tightly.

"I'll take that as a yes—you're glad he's here—and no Zya, you don't need to stay. I'll just show myself out. If you need me to pick up Tracey tomorrow morning for you, just let me know. Okay, bye..." Zya waves to an uninterested audience as she backs out of the bedroom.

Brian pulls away to gaze into her eyes.

Debra lovingly peers into his. "I can't believe you're here. I thought I lost you forever."

"I couldn't stay away. Debra, I love you. I've always loved you. I backed away when I saw how stressed that stupid competition was making you. I didn't want to hurt you—I wanted to save you."

Debra looks down into her hands, thinking about the horrible mistake she made. "And then I said yes to—him! Oh, was that ever stupid of me; I wasn't thinking. I was so over-whelmed and confused, trying to make a decision. I thought I had to make one, so I started praying for a sign, then my door-bell rang. It was the sign I asked for; I was supposed to be with him. I'm so sorry. Please forgive me?" The words are tumbling out as fresh tears threaten.

"I won't lie, it hurt, when you picked him over me. Then I realized how stupid it all was. There's nothing to for-give. If anything, it's I who should be apologizing to you. It was so juvenile of us to compete for your hand. We didn't even give you a chance to tell us what you wanted. It never dawned on us you might not want either of us. Talk about egos...I'm a therapist with a big head case."

Debra giggles. "Brian, I do love you, but I need to mourn George. I didn't do that, and I know if you and I have any chance at all, I have to say goodbye—in my own way, in my own time."

"I know, I'm here as your friend. You've been such a big part of my life; I just can't let you go. I don't want to inter-fere either. George was a great man, and obviously, a great husband. He deserves this time with you and your family. I won't interfere, you take all the time you need."

Brian drops back down on the bed and hugs her shoul-ders. Of course, he wants more than friendship. However, his years of training have taught him how important it is for Debra to go through this. She's right, they don't stand a chance if she doesn't deal with her grief. She's worth the wait.

He says as he pulls out of their embrace, "Okay, so I guess I'm your person tonight; what do you want to do?"

"Are you any good at gin rummy?"

"Only the best," he replies as he shakes his head no.

Debra says while giggling, "Come on, I'll teach you. Jump up here."

Brian sits on the bed, facing her as she shuffles the cards, the fancy way—like a Las Vegas dealer.

"Uh oh, is money involved in this game? If there is, I think you might be a hustler."

"No, we won't play for money, I'll just teach you."

For the next two hours, Debra attempts to explain the object or goal of gin rummy and how to play.

Brian concentrates and even does an excellent job of pretending to have fun—he hates cards.

Debra yawns and stretches.

"You must be tired. Would you like me to make you a bite to eat, it's getting close to dinner?"

"No, I'm not hungry, but I am a little tired…maybe just a little cat nap. Would it be bad if I asked you to lay with me while I sleep?"

Brian gulps, he's not sure if he can maintain the friend distance if he's that close. When he first hugged her—felt her in his arms, parts of his body had an agenda of their own.

She fluffs the pillow next to her, where George used to sleep. She's not thinking about that, just lying in his arms knowing he's there will give her comfort.

He can't deny her, he turns around and lays on top of the covers on the pillow, arms crossed.

She turns, so she's lying on his shoulder, keeping her hands between her knees. Within minutes, she relaxes against him.

He lets out a big sigh once he hears her steady breathing signaling deep slumber. He turns his head to kiss her lightly on her forehead. Her hair smells of coconuts and pineapple, a tropical paradise.

He closes his eyes and images himself lying on the beach with her in Hawaii. He loves it there although he's never been. It's so romantic...or, so he's been told. How can it not be with scantily clad bodies, sunscreen being rubbed all over you, the sounds of the ocean crashing in the near distance? He falls asleep to the lull of those waves...

He feels her hands on his shoulders, slathering coconut oil all over him. Her hands are so soft. It's relaxing as she takes her time, making sure to cover every inch of his muscular back, starting at the top, working her way down to the top of his shorts. His body is sun-kissed to a dark bronze—hers, lightly tanned. As her hand slips below the waistline, his heart begins to race, waking him from his laze.

The beach is deserted, except for a few birds chasing the waterline as the waves slap across the shoreline with fierce intensity. The sun is setting, leaving the sky a dark rusty orange, reflecting onto her skin.

Her breathing becomes shallow as she continues to move her hands along his well-toned body. A fire lit within, causes her to press her chest into his back, letting her breasts take over the rubbing. She kisses his neck. Her breathe hot in his ear, causing a physical reaction further below the waistline.

Having to touch her and taste her lips, he abruptly turns over. He pulls her close to him, kissing her neck, nibbling on her lobe, he blows hot bursts of air with each exhale. Her breath catches as she watches his mast become full and upright. The sudden desire to reach out and touch it gets the best of her.

As her fingertips brush against it, he moans, and it lurches with the sudden unexpected touch.

She giggles as he pulls her on his lap. The sun glistening off her sun-kissed hair blinds him temporarily as the wind blows towards them. The air mixes with the smells of the ocean and the tropical oils glistening on their bodies.

Smiling, he positions her perfectly, so even the fabric between them can't hide the urgency they both feel.

After pooling the oil in his palm, he returns the favor, rubbing it all over her chest, making sure to reach under her top as he slowly covers her skin.

Unable to control himself, he pushes the triangle pieces of fabric along the string, exposing her. His hand reaches for one of her breasts, gently squeezing while his thumb flicks across her hard nipple. Her breath catches while he presses and pinches gently.

Her lips taste like the last sip she took from her Mai Tai —cold and inviting—tasty and sinful.

His kiss deepens while his hand travels down, inside her barely there, bottoms.

She moans against him, without her lips leaving his.

His finger slides between her moist lips intentionally rubbing against her swollen bud.

Shock waves reverberate each time his fingertip presses against it.

He allows his fingertip to dip slightly inside, slipping further and further, with each stroke. Slow at first, then matching her tempo, fast and urgent.

In one swift plunge, he buries his finger as far as it will go.

She breaks from the kiss, her head now thrashing side-to-side.

Just as he senses, she about to peak, he lifts her, swinging her around, so she's straddling him. His lips find her again, more urgent than before. His intentions, as he pulls the side of her bottoms over, is to bury himself inside her quickly. However, his finger, once again, finds itself plunged deeply, instead.

She pushes her hips into his hand, willing it to take her over the edge. Once again, she's so close, he pulls his hand out and sits back, breaking their kiss.

Her eyes full of lust and yearning watch as he takes the finger that was just teasing her inside his lips, tasting her juices that are currently overflowing.

He wants more. He pushes her back, so she's lying on the lounge chair. He spreads her legs wide, teasing her through the fabric, running his finger lightly, up and down.

She pleads and begs him to touch her.

Following instructions, he pulls the fabric aside and runs the tip of his tongue the same trail his fingertip explored.

Her head is again thrashing side-to-side as it hangs off the end of the chair.

His tongue begins to work its magic against her ultra-sensitive clit; Flicking back and forth, sending her into ecstasy.

As her orgasm rips through her body, her legs wrap around his neck. Unconsciously, she thrusts her hips in the air, pumping with his wave. Without giving her a moment's rest, his finger plunges inside, while his lips and tongue pull out another series of hip raising thrusts, and screams.

Once she's ridden the wave to its end, she sits up and grabs him behind his neck, pulling his face towards her, kissing him with urgent abandonment.

She pushes him back as she breaks their lips apart, straddling him as he falls into a seated position. The sun glares across her face, almost blinding him.

He doesn't need to see her; he can feel her as she releases the struggle in his shorts.

Within an instant, she pushes her hips down onto him, taking his full erect length. The sensation as every nerve ending comes alive, sends her into another spiral.

He takes over—hands on her hips, her pumps her faster and faster, feeling her quiver all around him.

Just as she plummets back down to earth, he explodes.

He hears the waves crashing along the shore, matching his same tempo and intensity.

As the last wave crashes, her head blocks the rays of the sun, revealing her beautiful face.

"Shit!" He wakes with a start, breaking the spell. One so real, it has left him wet and spent.

He turns to roll off the bed, embarrassed by the situation. He tries not to wake her--too late.

"Are you okay? What happened?" she asks wide-eyed.

Brian, now on his knees, pops his watch off his wrist. "I somehow dropped this." Showing her from the safety of the floor trying to hide the wetness his recent dream caused.

He pulls his shirt out, feeling it, willing it to be dry. It is, for the most part, except the corner.

He has to get to the bathroom and quickly without her knowing, so he decides to fake a limp. "I must have hit my knee." This allows him to lean over hiding the evidence more efficiently.

"Are you sure you're okay?"

"It's an old racquetball injury...no big deal. I'll go get some ice," he says as he rushes out of the bedroom.

Debra lies back on the pillow, begins to fan herself. Her body is glistening with a light sheen of sweat.

"Boy, was that close..." she says aloud to no one.

Chapter Eleven

"Tina, I don't understand what you're getting so worked up about."

"That woman has been over here three times this week. She calls you almost every day. It's strange. She wants you!"

"She's the officer assigned to Ashanti's case. She's concerned about her. She's seen so many kids get messed up over this, kids committing suicide because they were bullied. She's not coming on to me, she cares. Besides, she's not gay."

"And you would know if a woman is gay or not, right?"

"Come on, she's not masculine—she's too feminine to be gay."

By the look on Tina's face, Zya instantly regrets her words. Tina is a stunning woman. Zya watches men fall all over themselves whenever she enters a room. Tina is all woman from head to toe. She exudes so much confidence and sex-appeal; she makes women stop and watch her when she walks by.

"I'm sorry, I didn't mean you, you're beautiful. No, you're more than beautiful, you're drop-dead gorgeous." Shaking her head, Zya continues, "She's not gay, Micki is not gay. I'm telling you, she's never hit on me."

Zya's cell phone rings. It must be karma because Micki is on the other end. Zya turns away from Tina. "Hi Micki, can I call you back? I'm right in the middle of something with... Ashanti, helping her with her homework."

Zya doesn't see Tina turn and walk away. She doesn't realize she's gone, not until she hears the front door close.

"Micki, I'm sorry, now is not a good time."

Micki can sense the pain in Zya's voice. "Are you okay? Is Ashanti okay? Something happen?"

"No, Ashanti is good. She's upstairs doing her home-work." Zya pictures her daughter upstairs doing just that, caus-ing her mind to shift gears. "That kid amazes me. With every-thing she's been through, she's okay. She goes to therapy three times a week, even though she doesn't think she needs it. Did you know she's friends with Mitch now? His mother, of course, doesn't know; she'd freak if she found out the *terrorist* that al-most killed him was now his buddy."

"I'm glad to hear she's okay. Are you okay?"

The argument between her and Tina back in focus. "Yeah, I'm fine, thanks. It's nothing; it will work itself out."

"I'm a good listener, or so I've been told," she says, laughing. "Tell me what's on your mind. Maybe I can help."

Zya hesitates. Micki has always been helpful, always knowing exactly the right thing to say, but this is about her. Deciding to throw caution to the wind, she blurts out, "I think Tina is a little jealous of you. It's my fault; I haven't been pay-ing enough attention to her. She's great! She's been at our side through everything and hasn't pressured me, or been demanding in any way. She's my rock. I need to spend more time with her, and we'll be just fine."

"She told you she's jealous of me?"

"Well, not exactly in those words, but she thinks you have a thing for me. She thinks you're gay. I told her she's way off base. You're definitely not gay…you're not into me."

She hears only silence on the other end of the phone.

"Micki, you there?"

"Yeah, I'm here. I've never been a home-wrecker, and I don't want to start now, but she's right."

"She's right? What do you mean, she's right?"

"Zya, I am gay, and I think you're one terrific and very sexy lady. I very much have a thing for you."

Zya says, "Oh!" Her hand is over her mouth, and she starts to hyperventilate. She throws her phone to the ground

"Zya! Zya!" Micki yells through the phone speaker, "Pick up the phone, Zya!"

Zya begins pacing around the room.

"Zya, please pick up the phone."

After a few minutes, Zya picks up the phone but doesn't say anything.

Micki can hear her breathing. "Zya, I'm sorry, I don't want to hurt you, Ashanti or Tina. The day I met you in Ashanti's hospital room, I knew right then and there, you were something special. I can't help it."

"Micki, don't call me anymore, and please stay away from Ashanti." Mad at herself for not realizing, Zya prays her naivety doesn't cost her dearly.

Zya goes to hang up the phone, stopping when she hears what Micki has to say.

"I can't do that Zya, I'm assigned to your daughter's case. I'm the officer partnered with both of you until this is all settled. You need me. You need me to fight for Ashanti. She was defending herself, but she still cut Mitch real bad. His mother is pressing charges. I'm your bully expert. I'm yours, and Ashanti's future. You don't want me to go away."

Zya slowly hits the end button on her phone.

Moments later, Zya's phone rings again. Thinking it's Micki still, she says, "Please, don't ruin my life. I love Tina."

"Zya, it's me, Amber, what's that all about?"

Settling down on the couch, "Sorry, thought you were someone else."

"Obviously."

"It's nothing, how are you doing?"

Ashanti comes running down the stairs, all excited, not realizing her mom is on the phone.

"Mom! Micki is on her way over. She needs to talk to us." Seeing the phone up to her mom's ear, she apologizes, "Sorry, I didn't know you were on the phone."

"Amber, I have to call you back. I'm sorry."

The hair on the back of Amber's neck stands up. "What's up Zya? What's going on?"

Waiting until Ashanti is back upstairs, she explains, "Micki—the cop assigned to Ashanti's bully case—that's what's up."

"Micki? The cop that helped us get Roberto deported?"

"Yes, Tina told me today that Micki was calling and spending too much time over here. She's jealous of her; Tina thinks she has a thing for me."

"Oh, come on, really? Micki's not gay…is she?"

"Well, it turns out she is—I just found out. She called just as Tina and I were talking about it, or rather, arguing. I turned around one minute, the next, Tina's gone. She walked out the door, and I don't know if she's coming back."

"You have to tell Micki you're not interested. You're not, are you?"

"No, I love Tina."

"Okay, so what's the problem?"

"Ashanti just came down to inform me Micki is on her way over right now. This, after I just told her not to call me—not to come over here ever again."

"She can't do that, can she?"

"No, I know—trust me—she made sure I know."

"Do you think she's going to play dirty? She's not going to try and break you and Tina up, is she?"

"I don't know, but I won't let her. I'm sorry, I have to go. I have to find Tina. How could I be so stupid?"

"Where do you think she went?"

"Not sure, but I have to find her. I owe her an apology; she was right—I was wrong."

"You have to stay there and wait for Micki, though, don't you?"

"I guess I do. Do I have to choose between Ashanti and Tina?"

Amber senses Zya's conflict. On the one hand, if she leaves to find Tina, Ashanti will be hurt because her mom was not there when Micki comes over. If she doesn't go, Tina may come home and find Micki there again, and that could be the final straw.

"I'm free. I'll go find Tina, just tell me where you think she is," Amber says.

"Thank you. The library, I'd search there first. If she's not there, she's at the gym. She didn't have gym clothes with her, but she might have a bag in her car. She's probably at one of those two places."

"Okay, you play it cool with Micki, but make sure Ashanti stays in the room with you. I'll find Tina."

"Thanks Amber, not sure what I would do without you."

"Good thing you'll never have to find out."

After searching the places Zya suggested, and a few other possibilities, Amber calls, feeling defeated she couldn't help her friend. "Zya, Tina is not at the library, or the gym, where else would she go?"

"It's okay; it's all worked out," Zya whispers.

"Can you talk?"

"No, it's okay, really. How about I meet you at Jack's Bar in an hour? I'm sure we could all use a break," Zya says while smiling at Micki and Tina.

Sometimes things do work out. Just as Zya hung up the phone with Amber, Tina pulled back into the driveway. Zya saw her car and ran out to greet her.

"Tina! Please don't you ever walk out on me again." Zya threw her arms around her, so scared she had left for good.

"I'm sorry I shouldn't have left. I was so hurt when you told Micki you were helping Ashanti with her homework instead of telling her we were talking."

"This is all so new to me, you know. You're my second love. I was in love with Doug my whole life, and that was a sham. And then you come into my life, I didn't know I could love a woman—love you the way that I do. I want you to know, I confronted Micki, and you were right, she does have a thing for me. I asked her NOT to come here ever again, and to please stay away from Ashanti."

"She can't do that—she's your police partner for Ashanti's case."

"I know, I know! She's on her way over now. I'm not sure if she's playing a game, or if she really is coming over for Ashanti. Please, don't leave again; I need you beside me. I need her to know—we're solid. She doesn't stand a chance."

As Tina and Zya embrace, Micki's patrol car pulls up. Zya and Tina hold hands and turn to face her.

Seeing the defiance in their eyes, she waves her hands in surrender. "Zya—Tina, I'm not here to cause any trouble, I promise. Have you heard of the talk show, *Bullied Bullies*?"

Zya steps forward and says, "I have, what's up?"

"They want to interview Mitch and Ashanti for an upcoming segment. There's a lot of details; I think you probably want Ashanti in on this conversation. Would it be okay if we discussed it inside with her?"

They walk up the driveway temporarily forgetting about the love triangle mess they're in and focus their attention on the youngest member of the household.

Ashanti hears the door open and comes running down the stairs. Their faces are a mixture of emotions. Unsure how to read them, she asks, "What's up?"

Zya motions her to sit next to her on the couch. "Micki has something to discuss with us."

"*Bullied Bullies* has approached Mitch and his father about doing a segment on their show. They would like you to participate too if you want to," Micki explains.

"*Bullied Bullies*? Isn't that the show that targets the parents responsible for turning their kids into bullies?"

"It is. Mr. and Mrs. Morris are separated…he's filing for divorce. Mrs. Morris's father, grandfather, and going back quite a few generations, were racists. Some were KKK leaders. She was brainwashed, as was every generation before her. It was only natural for her to do the same with Mitch. He's decided he wants to live with his dad. His mom is crushed, so she's trying to get some help, hoping he'll change his mind."

The front door opens, and Stacey bounces in. She stops when she sees the serious faces looking back at her.

"Oops, my bad…sorry, didn't mean to interrupt," she says as she starts up the stairs.

"Stacey, come here, I want you to hear this just in case I need reminding later. This is kind of freaking me out right now," Ashanti says as she moves over, giving Stacey room to sit.

She fills her in then motions Micki to continue.

"The producers of the show are very impressed with the relationship, or friendship shall we say, you and Mitch are forming. Mitch is still recovering, but he's told his dad he wants to get involved with the school's zero-tolerance bullying policy, once he's feeling better. He's even considering running for school president. A bully who's changing his ways. What do you think? Something you might want to do with him?"

Ashanti looks over at her mom for direction.

Zya nods her head, okaying her to make her own decision.

"Stacey, what do you think?"

"Honestly? I still don't know how you can even think about being friends with that fiend, but maybe that's just me. I'll never like him, but if this is something you want to do, you know I'll support you. Just don't leave me in the room alone with him. I won't be as forgiving."

Ashanti gives Stacey a quick hug. "I love you."

Turning back to Micki, she says, "I'm in. If our story can help protect other kids from going through what I had to, then I'm all for it. When do they want to do the show?"

"Taping is on the fifteenth. They're going to fly you and your mom—"

"—and her sister," Stacey adds.

"—and you Stacey, to New York, if that works with your schedule."

"How can Mitch fly? It will only be two weeks since the…won't it be too soon?"

"They are going to fly you all on their private jet. They are even going to have a nurse on board with him. Because the attack made headlines, they want to get you on the show as soon as possible. The doctor has said he will clear him on the fourteenth if he feels he's okay to travel. He's young, so he's got that going for him."

Tina looks over at the troubled look on Zya's face. "You can't go, can you?"

Zya shakes her head. "I can't. I'm getting my resort line together for my show this summer." Looking over at Ashanti, she continues, "Honey, unless you really need me there, Tina can go with you…" Zya moves her eyes over to Tina. "Right?"

The love triangle mess immediately comes back into her mind as Tina thinks about leaving Zya here with Micki.

Feeling defeated, Tina's shoulders drop. "Sure, I'm happy to go."

An excited, bouncing Ashanti squeals, "Oh, this will be so much fun. Maybe we can stay for a few days and see the sights. I've never been to New York. Well, I was when I was little, but I don't remember. Oh my gosh, Stacey, we can run up the Empire State Building." Ashanti and Stacey hoot and holler as they run up the stairs.

Tina switches over to sit next to Zya, who is in front of Micki. Grabbing Zya's hand, she looks up at Micki. "This" — motioning between her and Zya— "is solid. Don't think just because I'm gone for a few days this gives you the opportunity to take my place…won't happen. Do you understand?"

Micki says, "I do. Don't you worry, if I go after your woman, you won't be out of town."

Chapter Twelve

"I love those black heels you have on today. Oh, when I get you, I'll make you keep them on after I rip every piece of clothing off."

"Who is this? Why are you doing this to me?"

"My precious, 'I'm so innocent little Amber.' You know me, you know me very well."

"I don't know you. But if I did, why would you try to scare me like this?"

"Trying? Did you say trying? I'm not trying, girl, I'm succeeding. I want you scared—convulsing with terror. Nothing will make me happier than when I see the horror in your eyes when we meet...again."

Amber sends another text but gets the same message she's received in the past. *This is not a working number.*

Amber's phone ringing startles her, she jumps.

"Hi, Patrick," she says, shaking her mind still reeling over the text. "I'm sorry I haven't returned your call. My phone's been acting crazy like my life is right now."

"So you're not still mad at me?" he asks.

"No, I'm not mad at you." She pauses and takes a deep breath. Shifting gears in her head to where she left off with him. "I know there's no way you could have known I had a twin sister…It was stupid of me to think you should have thought that was a possibility. It's just that, Brandy—UGH! She gets under my skin."

"Have you heard from her since that day at the hospital?"

"No, thank God. She's the last thing I want to have to deal with right now." Terror from the text has now been replaced with anger and hurt.

"What's going on with your phone?"

"It was freezing up. I had my tech guy take a look at it. I have no idea what he did, but it seems to be okay now."

"That's good; it's nice to have your own tech guy; getting an appointment there is murder."

Before he changes his mind, he blurts out, "Could we maybe go out for dinner sometime…soon? I'd love to catch up. I know your friends are very important to you and they've been going through some major ordeals. Who takes care of you? Who do you lean on? Who's your rock?"

"Thanks, I appreciate your concern, really I do, I can take care of myself. I do want to have dinner with you…eventually, but not right now. There's just too much going on, and I have this big interview I have to prepare for. I need my head in the game. You and I have not had the best luck in the romance department. I just can't right now. I'm sorry…not now." It kills her to tell him no. She does want to be with him, but she can't handle a distraction right now.

Patrick slumps his shoulders in defeat. "I understand. It seems like although we are perfect for each other, *Murphy's Law* has always been one step ahead of us. Please know I care about you—I'm here for you, even if you just need a shoulder. I've become quite fond of your friends, and I'd like to help if I can."

"Thanks, I'll keep you on speed dial."

On the drive into work, she thinks back on the past seven, eight months of her relationship with Patrick. When she got the request to interview him, he was known as not only *The Ethical Attorney* but also one of the town's most eligible bachelors. He hates being called by both names. Being ethical was something he expected all, or realistically most, attorneys should always be. The money was great, but his ethics and morals were never for sale. And as far as eligible, he made it clear, he had no desire to get married or fall in love—ever.

"What are you doing here? You should be home resting," Amber says when she enters her office to see Dominque at her desk.

"If I stay home, I'll drive myself crazy. I'm fine, really. I promise you, I'm okay. Besides, I was hoping we could go wig shopping this afternoon. I'd like to try and make it fun."

"Absolutely! I wish Deb and Zya could join us."

Amber turns and walks into her office with Dominque in tow. "Do you think Tad and I will get married?"

"Are you kidding, you two are talking about having little rug rats, I'm sure you'll be tying the knot."

"Who would ever guess, me with a nerdy tax auditor? Not my type at all, but the one that makes me happy."

"Zya is going to want to do your dress, you know."

Dominque's excitement shows as her hands go to her face. "I'd LOVE to wear the dress I wore at her show in Milan. I felt so beautiful in it! It would be incredible if I could wear it on my big day. Here I am planning my wedding before he's even asked."

"I'm sure he will, and I bet Zya would be honored if you wore her design."

"Let's call her…let's call her right now," Dominque says as she hits the button marked Zya on Amber's desk phone.

Zya answers after several rings. "Hi, Amber."

"Zya, I'm here with Dominque."

"Hi, Dom, how are you feeling girl?"

"I'm good, waiting for the drugs to do their thing so we can get my eggs cooking."

Zya laughs. "That's a visual I don't think is quite right. I'm glad you're doing good and still have your witty sense of humor, I can't imagine what you're going through."

"Zya, how would you feel about letting me wear that beautiful wedding gown I wore last year at your show when I get married?" Dominque asks.

"He asked? You're not going to be living in sin any-more?"

Amber interrupts, "No, Tad hasn't asked YET, but I think we all know he will. His parents are very religious, so there's no way he's going to bring children into this world without getting hitched first. We were just daydreaming…"

"Of course, Dom, you can wear—have that gown. Wow, it's a dream come true to see one of my sisters walk down the aisle in one of my designs. When the time comes, honey, it's yours."

"Thanks, Zya, I really appreciate it. I know I'm getting a little ahead of myself, it's a bright thought inside this scared shitless brain right now."

"Dream away, Dom, your fairy-tale ending will happen."

"I hope so."

Amber hugs Dominque. "It will."

Turning her attention back on the phone. "How are things on the home front…with Ashanti…and all…"

Dominque looks at Amber, surprised, thinking all was status quo on that front.

"Everything is great; we're all doing good. Hey, let's meet up for happy hour tonight. We can celebrate Dom's eventual, upcoming nuptials," Zya says, changing the subject.

"Actually, Amber and I are going wig shopping tonight. Want to come?" Dominque asks.

"Wig shopping—I'm in! Where and what time?"

"I'm not crazy about losing my hair, or going wig shopping, but somehow, having you both, and Debra by my side, makes going through this crap somewhat bearable. And Tad too, of course."

The girls make plans to meet later after work for a light bite then off to try on wigs. Their quest…find a ginger one that matches her beautiful mane.

After they hang up with Zya, Dominque says, "Oh, by the way, Mr. Brettinger's office called and asked if they could push your appointment back until three-thirty on the sixteenth?"

"Do I have any appointments that afternoon? Oh, never mind, if I do, move it, I can't blow this chance."

Dominque leaves Amber's office to confirm the appointment change.

Amber asks, "Will you shut my door, please? I have to make some calls."

Once the door clicks, she calls Zya back. "Okay, spill it, what happened?"

Zya explains to Amber about the *Bullied Bullies* show and updates her about Mitch's parents.

"Okay, and what about Tina and Micki?"

After what seems like an eternity, Zya fills the silent air and says, "Tina is taking Ashanti and Stacey to New York on the fifteenth for the taping. I'd love to go, but I just can't. Ashanti is so excited; she wants to stay a few days."

"Does Micki know this?"

"Yes, and she made it very clear she's going to play nice. Tina trusts me, and she knows how much I love her, but it's going to be uncomfortable. I don't put it past her to make up some excuse to have to see me while they're in New York. I just won't be available, in person, that is. I'm going to take advantage of the time and work with Stan to get the final samples ready for the show. I don't normally get in his way. He's usually one step ahead of me telling me what I need before I do, but I need the distraction, I hope he'll understand."

"I'm sure Stan will be okay; he is your assistant, you know."

Zya chuckles. "You're right, and a damn good one too. I'd hate to piss him off."

"So then you and Tina are okay?"

"Yes, we are. We're meant to be together. I can't believe I'm saying this about another woman. I know I need to get over this hang-up, but it still surprises me. Oh, and Doug somehow found out Ashanti is going to be in New York, so he wants to see her. Can you imagine that? After all these months with no contact, now he wants to spend time with her. I hope he doesn't try to fill her head with ideas of us getting back together. That is never going to happen."

"Ashanti is a very smart girl. I bet she knows how much you and Tina love each other. Besides, you know she's not giving up her BFF Stacey. I wouldn't worry about it, that's the least of your concerns."

Zya, Dominque, and Amber make quite the evening of wig shopping. They even video chat with Debra so she can be involved. Brian wants to participate too. It's supposed to be just the girls, but he can't help himself.

Although vanity is the least of her problems, she can't stop looking at herself in the mirror, imagining all her hair gone. She's trying to plaster a real smile on her face, but her friends see right through it. So they do what any great friend would do, they create some fun by finding wigs of their own.

"Amber, what do you think of this one?" Zya asks, putting on a bleach blonde bob with chunky purple streaks.

"Wow, girl, that looks amazing and freaking awesome on you. Here, let me take a picture."

Dominque giggles as Zya makes faces into the camera lens.

Zya grabs one like hers but with blue streaks and puts it on Amber's head. With their arms around each other, giggling, they pose for Dominque, who has now taken over as the photographer.

Amber grabs one with pink streaks and puts it on Dominque's head. The wig fitter takes pictures of the three of them together, making silly faces, and laughing to the Madonna song, "Vogue."

They glance at the phone with Debra and Brian, where they get a surprise of their own. It appears Debra has a few wigs in her closet, being modeled by them. Debra's looks gorgeous, the one on Brian…let's just say, he'd never make it as a drag queen. Mission accomplished!

"I'm laughing so hard I'm going to pee my pants," Dominque says as she runs off to the bathroom.

Zya and Amber take the wigs off their heads and hug each other.

"Brian, that was perfect! Oh my—my stomach hurts from laughing so much," Amber says.

"So I didn't pull it off?" he asks.

"Oh, no, you looked great!" Amber says while rolling her eyes.

"Who is she kidding, you looked horrible in that wig, don't you ever put it back on again. Well, unless you want to turn Debra off totally," Zya interjects.

Just then, the wig fitter says, "Wait, I think I have the perfect wig for her," as she runs off to the back room.

She comes out, combing her hands through a wig she just took out of its bag. It's a beautiful bronze color, a little darker than Dominque's natural shade, but the waves, the length, the fullness…it's perfect.

Dominque comes out of the bathroom, wiping her eyes, "You guys made me laugh so hard, thanks, I needed that."

She catches sight of the wig in the fitter's hand…a big smile crosses her face. She walks quickly toward her with her eyes glued on the dark auburn wig in her hands.

"Come sit down, let's see how it looks."

The fitter turns Dominque around, so her back is to the mirror. "Now, mind you, it just came in today. I still need to style it, but…" She turns the chair so she can see her reflection.

Dominque is ecstatic to see how wonderful it is. It will be like she never lost her hair at all. Hopeful tears threaten to fall as she looks at Zya and Amber.

"Oh, Dom, it's amazing…It's you," Amber says as she hugs her.

"Damn, girl, I'd say it might even be better than you."

They all laugh.

"Let me see, let me see," squeals Debra from the phone.

Dominque looks at the video feed, turning her head from side to side. "What do you think?"

"Oh, Dom, it is perfect."

"I'll take it!"

The fitter touches Dominque's shoulder. "I'm so glad I remembered I had it. Can you give me a few days to style it for you? I won't cut it, but it does need a little special attention. I want to adjust it for you too, so it fits perfectly."

"Yes, of course, I can pick it up this weekend." Dominque pulls out her wallet as Amber puts her hand over it. "This is a gift from your sisters…the three of us are buying this for you."

"You don't have to do that."

Zya adds, "We don't have to—we want to."

"We feel so helpless, there's not much we can do for you, this is just a little something to remind you, we've got your back. Whatever, whenever, we're here for you," Debra says.

"So you'll bring some funny wigs over to my house when I'm feeling down, and make me laugh again."

"If that's what it takes, consider it done. Brian, you game?" Amber asks.

"Will I make you laugh, or make you sick?" Brian asks.

The girls chuckle.

"No need…just coming over and holding my hand will be enough. Although, they do say laughter is the best medicine. I don't know who 'they' are, but 'they' may have something there," Dominque says, making finger quotes.

The wig fitter pushes the invoice over for Amber to see. She gulps at the price, not realizing just how much a real human hair wig costs. "Do you take Amex?"

After saying goodbye to Debra and Brian, Amber says, "Dominque, you look exhausted…you must be, your first day back, and already we have you out past dark."

"I guess it is past my bedtime. I'm going to call it a night, see you tomorrow."

"You know you don't have to come in if you're not feeling up to it."

"Thanks, Amber, trying to keep my life as normal as possible is the best thing for me right now. It helps me take my mind off it. I do promise, though, if I need to, I'll take the day off or better yet, take a nap on the couch in your office."

"Deal." Amber hugs Dominque, then she and Zya watch her drive off.

After Dominque drives away, Amber turns to Zya. "You sure everything is okay with you?"

"Yeah, I am. Doug called me the other day, wanting to see Ashanti. He doesn't call for months and now all of a sudden, he's got to see her. I need this like I need a hole in my head. I'm still trying to deal with Micki."

"If there's anything I can do to help, please let me know."

"Even pull a gun on him?"

"Him or her? Him no problem...her? She's got one of her own and probably is a better shot than me. Maybe we should mull that one over a bit more."

"Him...ha, ha, ha, you know I'm just kidding...or am I?" she says with a big grin on her face. "By the way, any more texts from your stalker?"

"Every few days...they're the same thing, over and over. I'm starting to think he's just trying to scare me. If he wants to hurt me, he knows where I am all the time, wouldn't he make a move by now?"

"Maybe, just please be careful and go straight home, your stalker might be waiting for the perfect moment," Zya begs.

"I am—straight home—promise," Amber replies as she crosses her heart.

As Amber begins to back out of the parking lot, she changes her mind and puts her car back into park. *Maybe I should see what Patrick is up to tonight?*

Reaching for her phone to ask him for a late-night rendezvous, she realizes her phone is gone. "Damn!" She looks all around her car for it to no avail. *Must have left it on the counter.*

Reluctantly, she turns her car off and heads back inside. She hadn't realized how dark it was when she came out. It's pitch black now—shadows are everywhere. The hair on the back of her neck stands up while a shiver runs down her spine, pushing her to run back into the shop.

At the same moment, the wig fitter, having found Amber's phone, is racing outside to catch her. They almost collide in the doorway. "I believe this is yours," she says, her heart racing from the near impact.

"Yes, thanks. Glad I realized it now and not when I got home."

Amber, still contemplating her booty call, uses the light outside the door to search for Patrick's number. She begins her walk back to the car lost in her thoughts, debating whether to call him, forgetting for a moment all about the threatening texts piling up in her phone.

As she opens her car door, a man comes up quickly behind her, wrapping his arm tightly around her chest. She starts to scream, but it's muffled by his other hand covering her mouth as he tries to turn her around. He's strong—and his scent. *I know that cologne...*

118

"Wait a minute? Christophe, is that you?" she asks as she's spun around, entrapped in his arms.

"Mon Cherie, I cannot surprise you no more?" he says in a thick French accent.

Amber breaks down into gut-wrenching sobs. She can't stop. She let her guard down for just an instant, a second too long, exactly the opportunity her stalker would need to get to her.

"I'm so sorry, I only want to surprise you," he says, trying to comfort her, feeling terrible.

Still shaking, thinking about what could have been, yet relieved it turned out to be Christoph, "It's okay. Wait a minute —it's not okay! You scared the crap out of me! Stop doing that, will you?" she says as she playfully slaps his arm.

"Promise, no scaring…surprise yes, scaring no. I never want to make you cry."

"You didn't make me cry. I've just been on edge lately—a little stressed out. I guess your timing was off. But then again," —thinking about that phone call she was about to make —"maybe your timing is perfect."

Amber grabs Christoph by the back of his head, kissing him deeply, passionately before he has a chance to react. "Who's full of surprises now?" she asks, catching him off guard. "Last time was amazing, but do you think we could go somewhere else this time instead of the back of my car?"

In the car parked one row over from hers, HE is watching and taking pictures. *Oh, you are going to pay for this. You think you're safe—not within my reach. Good thing your Frenchman appeared, he saved you, this time…*

Chapter Thirteen

"Mommy, is Brian going to be my new daddy?" Tracey asks, seeing him snuggled up on the bed.

He wakes at hearing his name.

"Tracey, honey, come here." Debra motions for her daughter to come on the bed with her.

"Brian is a really good friend of Mommy's."

"Like that other guy? The one that talked funny?"

Brian and Debra both stiffen up at the mention of Roberto.

"Not exactly, honey, Roberto, the man that talked funny,"—poking Tracey in her belly, making her laugh— "won't be coming around anymore."

"But he said HE was going to be my new daddy."

"I'm sorry, sometimes these things don't work out."

"So, Brian is going to be my new daddy!"

"Honey, let's just say he's our friend, for now, okay?"

"Okay. But he's here all the time, does he live here now?"

"No, no, Brian doesn't live here, he's just keeping Mommy company."

A weary Brian walks over and bends down to talk to her. "Tracey, your daddy, was a great man, he can never be replaced. Will you be my friend?"

"Okay," she says matter-of-factly. "Want to play school with me again?"

"Can I be the teacher this time?" he asks as Tracey leads him out of her mother's room.

Debra takes this time to try and catch up with Amber. Her big interview is next week.

Amber answers on the first ring, sounding very chipper. "Hey girlfriend, how are you?"

"I'm great, and you sound great too. Do I dare ask? You and Patrick?"

"No, not Patrick...my handsome Frenchman decided to surprise me last night, and oh boy did her ever."

"Christoph? WOW! He flew in to see you?"

"Kind of—but not totally, he had a stopover on his way to Cali."

"Well, you sound like you got a lot off your chest."

"Off my chest, off my thighs, off my...never mind. PHEW is that man a great lover. He is an expert in the language of love—or lust at least."

"Glad to hear you sound happy...it's been a while. You've got your big interview on Tuesday, spending the rest of the week prepping?"

"I don't know how to get ready for this. He wants to meet me first before we do the interview. I don't know what to expect; I am excited though. I'm so honored he wants ME to interview HIM. Patrick is a fine specimen, but Paul, I mean Mr. Brettinger, he's out there. I've seen pictures of him standing next to *The Rock.* Put bags over their heads—they're identical. Not that I'd ever want to cover those beautiful faces."

Silly school-girl giggling ensues. "I'm so proud of you. You've come so far. Who would have thought, my friend, the school journalist who would one-day interview kings, queens, Fortune 500 CEOs, and now, gods!"

"Haha, you're so funny! I do keep pinching myself, though. With all the crap—or better yet, shit I've had to deal with lately, I'm pretty proud of myself too."

"Have you heard from Brandy?"

"Not a peep, and I like it that way. Why would you bring her up?"

"I'm really sorry, I know you play it cool, but I'm sure it must hurt like hell to have your own flesh and blood hurt you like that."

"It does, but I'm a big girl. I don't need her, I have you, Dominque, and Zya. I've got all the family I need. By the way, how's it going with your shrink? You're not mad at me for giving him my shift, are you?"

"I should be, shouldn't I!" Debra laughs. "Of course I'm not. I love him, and he loves me. You know he's spent every day with me since."

"Where is he now, waiting on you hand and foot?"

"He has been taking excellent care of me, however right now, he's playing school with Tracey."

"School? Is he for real?"

"He's genuine all right, and Tracey has asked him to play school every day since he's been here. He loves her—he loves me."

"I hate to ask…"

Debra interrupts her, "No, no sex. He's my friend, and that's all for now. It's perfect."

"I'm glad to hear that. I don't mean to pry…never mind, yes I do!"

Debra laughs at Amber. "It's okay; I know you only ask because you care."

"And, because I'm nosy." Amber laughs this time. "Everything with Little George all right?"

"He's doing great. He definitely knows Brian makes his mommy happy. He flips and rolls around when he's in the room."

"Like your heart, when's he around?"

"Yes, he does make my heart go pitter-patter."

"Back to the sex thing…he hasn't made any passes at all at you?"

"Oh no, definitely not. I think he may have had a wet dream one afternoon when we both fell asleep. I had one too."

"Is that safe?"

"Probably not, Doc said no orgasms, didn't say anything about keeping me hanging. I get it now when you had those fantasy dreams about Patrick, but you never got a release. I'm sorry for you…I had no idea; It's a living Hell. And I'm not even allowed to use a vibrator, or Buzz, whatever you call them."

"Oh, girlfriend, I do feel for you. I'm so sorry. Did you dream about Brian?"

"My lover doesn't have a face…and they're so vivid."

"You've had more than one?"

"Yes, I think it's because Brian is here. Even though I'm not dreaming about him."

"It's possible. If the doctor says you shouldn't orgasm, you're playing with fire; maybe you should send him home."

"You're probably right, but I don't want him to leave."

"You have to think about Little George. I'll swing by in about thirty minutes and take over for him. At least we know you won't be having any dreams about me."

Amber ends the call just as a text comes through.

"How was your Frenchman last night? You have fun fucking him? You play like you're such a good girl, but you're not. You're just another slut—a whore. I can't wait to make you scream..."

She throws her phone down, trying very hard not to let it get under her skin. She's getting these regularly now. Each one hits a different, deeper chord in her. She shivers.

Since Debra is only ten minutes away, she decides she has time, and right now, she needs something to calm her nerves. So, she pours herself a half a glass of red wine from the bottle sitting on the counter. After looking at her watch, she fills it to the rim.

Eyeing the newspaper on the table, she sits down and skims the pages.

After one large gulp that drains half the glass, she sips the remainder giving her heart time to slow down. *He's just trying to scare me, but I can't let him.*

The headline on the next page catches her attention:

WANTED: Roberto Antonio Paulucci. Age 45. Approximately 6'3" and 210 lbs
Armed and considered dangerous.
If you see him, or someone who resembles him,
please call 555-TIPS.

Amber immediately runs to find her phone. *I've got to warn Debra.* Finding it under the couch where she threw it, she sees the rest of the text.

"*I am going to take so much pleasure in breaking you. I almost got you last night, but your Frenchman interrupted me. I won't hesitate the next time...you're mine. Do you hear me, YOU'RE MINE!*"

Another shiver runs through her body as she reads it. She has to push past this; she has to speak to Debra.

Ring, ring, ring, ring, ring, ring. Debra isn't answering. *Hi, this is Debra. Thanks for calling...*

Chapter Fourteen

The flight to New York was uneventful. However, Tina can't get this nagging feeling out of her head. She trusts Zya… it's Micki she doesn't trust. *Would Micki try to take advantage of her using her badge?*

Ashanti breaks Tina's thoughts as the flight attendant welcomes them to New York. "Come on, Tina, let's go. There's a big city to see."

"Yeah, Mom, let's go!" Stacey adds.

"Okay! Okay! Just let me get our bags first."

Mitch smiles over at Ashanti. He and his father didn't say much on the flight. He's unsure how this is going to play out between them. The nurse was great and managed to make him as comfortable as possible, but the pain on his face proves the incision still hurts, a pain the doctors told him may never go away.

Once they're off the plane, the girls run ahead down the breezeway; they are so excited to be in the Big Apple.

I wish I was as excited as they are.

Tina was told a driver would meet them at the airport to pick them up. Exactly as seen in the movies, an older, tall gentleman wearing a suit and hat is standing with a sign that reads, "Ashanti's Team."

"That's us!" Ashanti squeals in front of him.

The driver beams at her as he offers her his elbow. "Well, Ms. Ashanti, shall we?" He even has a British accent.

Mitch and his dad catch up just as they are turning to leave.

They gather their luggage then proceed to the curb where a long, black stretch limousine is waiting. He opens the door for Ashanti bowing and motioning for her to enter. She hesitates, then looks back at Tina, "I wish Mom was here to see this."

"Me too, sweetheart...me too," *If only you knew how much.*

Their driver takes them the long way to their hotel, pointing out different sites. As they cross the Brooklyn Bridge, they get a glimpse of Ellis Island, where the Statue of Liberty stands in her elegant grace.

"Wow! Can we go there? Huh? Can we Mom?" Stacey asks, tugging on Tina's arm.

Tina is once again brought back to the present. That last scene continues to play in her mind when Micki left; she can't make it stop. Was she wrong to react the way she did? Zya has never given her any reason to be jealous, but she just can't help it. Zya is finally coming to terms with her new sexuality. It shouldn't, but somehow it makes her feel insecure. Every lover she's had in the past knew what they wanted. This is new territory for her.

The hotel had Tina in the same room with the girls; however, she opted to get a room by herself. The same floor, just a few doors down, next to Mitch and his dad.

Unable to stop herself, she dials Zya's number but gets her voicemail. "Zya, love…I just wanted to give you a little good night kiss, over the phone, before we turn in. Filming is first thing in the morning, so it's going to be a long day. I love you…I love you so much. I miss you. It's only been a few hours, but it already feels like forever. Can't wait to get back into your arms and kiss those luscious lips. Love you, good-night."

As Tina hangs up, she hears a knock on a door down the hall. Checking outside, she sees an elegant, black gentleman, knocking on the kids' door.

"Excuse me," Tina asks, "can I help you? My kids are in that room."

"Oh, please forgive me, I was looking for my daughter Ashanti, I must have the wrong room."

The door bursts open in front of him, and Ashanti stands there staring at him—her dad, Doug. Her hands are on the knob and door jamb, just staring at him. "Dad?"

Although Ashanti has been in some contact with him, she hasn't seen him in years. When she was younger, he would call regularly. As she got older, those calls came fewer and fewer in frequency. Now, as a teenager, he hasn't called in months—eighteen to be exact.

"Ashanti, my beautiful girl…wow, look how grown up you are." Doug hugs her. When he looks up, he sees a young girl behind her.

"Oh, this is Stacey, my friend. She's mom's girlfriend's daughter."

Doug's eyes go wide. "Mom's friend?"

Tina walks up to their room, now standing beside him. "Yes, Zya's friend. She didn't tell me you would be coming by this evening. It's kind of late, and Ashanti has to be at the studio bright and early in the morning."

"Oh, Tina, can he come in, please? I haven't seen my dad in a long time. Thirty minutes, that's it, I promise," Ashanti begs.

She grabs Ashanti's chin and says, "Who am I to say no to such a pretty face…please, let's all get acquainted."

Doug lets Tina enter the room before him. Looking at her rear as she passes by, he rubs his crotch and files in behind her.

As Tina turns, she catches his groping hand. He didn't move it—he meant her to see him! *SHIT!*

Ashanti sits in the chair waiting for the director to go, *'Lights, camera and action,'* but that only happens in the movies.

Ashanti can tell Mitch is really nervous. Even though he's told his story many times, now it will be on television. He told her he feels sorry for his mother, while still blaming her as the reason he got into this mess in the first place. "She's working on it," he said. "And it appears she's making some progress. " Ashanti was happy to hear his mother encouraged him to do this—tell his story.

Rose, the interviewer sits down between them, on stage, ready for the cameras.

"How are you two holding up?"

Ashanti shrugs; Mitch grunts.

"You are going to be great. I know the lights are super bright—and annoying—but before long, you'll forget they're there. Speak from your heart, and you'll be just fine."

And, 3, 2, 1…

"Good evening America and welcome to *Bullied Bullies*. We are honored this evening, to have Ashanti and Mitch here with us to share their story."

"Thank you so much for flying here and joining me on set this morning. I know it's a little scary up here, but I'm sure not as scary as January the third was, now was it?"

Ashanti is a little startled the interviewer went right there. Nothing about what lead up to it, just right into the infamous day in the park.

Ashanti takes a deep breath to try and calm her nerves. "That day was terrifying, I feared for my life!"—looking over at Mitch— "But I bet not as much as it was for Mitch…he almost lost his."

She realizes the host intentionally opened with the most vicious of moments. It startled her, and it showed.

Rose then backtracks, taking them through the details, emotions, and thoughts, through each of her attacks. During the second commercial break, Rose asks Ashanti, "What does your father think about all this?"

"He just found out last night. He knew some of it, but we filled him in with all the details; he's up to speed now."

"We? Who's We? Your mom's not here, right?"

"My mom had to work. She's a fashion designer, and her resort line show is coming up, so she stayed back. Her girlfriend, Tina, came with us instead."

"Girlfriend?"

"She's more than a girlfriend…more than pals. They live together…that kind of girlfriend."

And, 3, 2, 1…

"Welcome back, everyone. If you're just tuning in, we're joined tonight by Ashanti, the victim, and Mitch, the bully. Ashanti, do you think your mother being gay could have had something to do with why you were bullied?"

Chapter Fifteen

She pulls out her black Louboutin pumps and thinks about the advice her mother gave her years ago. 'Amber, invest in a quality pair of shoes, a high-quality suit, and at least one designer handbag. Sometimes you have to play the role of being highly successful while you're climbing your way to the top.'

She decides to wear her hair down even though she usually wears it in a bun when she's working. *Oh, screw it,* she says to herself. She reaches in on each side of her bra and plumps up her breasts, and she pushes her hair up a bit to give it more body. As she goes to the front door, she picks up her black Chanel handbag. *It's the new me.* She thinks as she strolls confidently out the door.

As the elevator doors open, she turns and runs back to her apartment...today is not the day to get daring. She grabs a long black pea coat and throws it on. She looks at herself in the mirror, her shoulders once high with confidence, now hanging. She sees a pencil on the table and uses it to secure her hair into a bun. She turns back, heading for the elevator; this time not so self-assured.

She arrives at his office fifteen minutes early and is motioned to a waiting area. She tries to hide her nervousness, but her palms are sweating, and she can't stop fidgeting. Unconsciously she keeps crossing and uncrossing her legs. The last picture she saw of him was six months ago, and of course, he had two beautiful women on his arms. For some reason, a hunky, successful man gives her butterflies. Not that she would ever want to be with him, no way...he's a player, she just gets nervous around them. And of course, this one, in particular, can help skyrocket her career.

"Ms. Fiore, Mr. Brettinger will see you now," his secretary calls out to her.

Amber consciously takes small steps to the large double doors. *Why did I wear these things? I can't even walk in them!*

As she reaches the door, she realizes she left her portfolio on the seat. The door opens just as she turns toward the chairs, and Mr. Brettinger comes out to greet her.

Oh my, she thinks to herself, *he could be Dwayne Johnson's gym partner. Not only is he very handsome, but OMG looks at those biceps...and those thighs.*

Mr. Brettinger watches as her eyes scan him from top to bottom. "Ms. Fiore, leaving already?" he asks with a smirk on his face.

"Oh, no, I left my portfolio on my seat," Amber replies, flustered.

"I'll get it." He swaggers over and picks it up. On his way back, he takes her by the elbow and leads her into his office. "Shall we get started?"

He steps back at the threshold, motioning for her to enter first. As she passes him, he reaches out for the collar of her coat. "Here, let me take that for you. It's pretty warm outside for this today, don't you think?"

Amber blushes as he takes her coat to hang it on his coat rack. His hand brushes against the pencil in her hair, knocking it out, so her full, long locks spill down. Amber quickly reaches down to grab the pencil.

"No, leave it out. I like your hair down."

Amber blushes again, hands locked in front of her, eyes down as she heads to one of the two chairs positioned in front of his desk.

He stays behind, watching her hips sway with each careful step. "Let's sit over here, shall we? I'd like to get to know you a little better on a more personal level."

Amber stops in her tracks, and her body immediately goes into full alert mode. The hair on the back of her neck stands up, and she freezes in her spot.

"Come on, I'm not going to bite you. I'd just like to know the person behind this interview. In my last interview, I didn't really connect with the writer, and I'm sure the piece could have been so much better if we had. You understand," he says as he again takes her elbow, walking her over to his black leather modern sofa.

Amber sits as far left as possible, pulling her dress down to cover her thighs.

He walks—no her strolls—over to his fully stocked wet bar and pours two glasses of whiskey.

"Here you go, Amber. Can I call you Amber?" he asks as he hands her a glass.

"No, thank you."

"What, you don't drink? Are you an alcoholic?"

"No, no," she stutters. "I just don't drink when I'm working. I save that for socializing only."

"Well, let's see, it's 3:30 in the afternoon. I'd guess to say you won't be going back to the office, right?"

Amber shakes her head with a shy smile.

"All right then, we're socializing. Go ahead, try it, you'll like it. It's very smooth."

And so are you. This man doesn't take no for an answer. Amber pulls her portfolio onto her lap and begins to open it. She feels flushed and uncomfortable. The hairs are still standing up, and now a cold shiver runs through her body.

Part of her wants to run for the door. The other part of her is telling her to toughen up. *This guy is nothing. You are so much smarter and wiser than him. Now take a deep breath and just chill.* Amber not sure where the voice is coming from, complies, feeling some relief.

Just as Amber looks up and decides to take charge of this meeting, he starts waving his hand around.

"No, no, no, not yet, I'd like to ask you some questions, get to know you a little better before we start talking business."

He slides over, halfway down the sofa to close the portfolio on Amber's lap. As he grabs the end of the leather-bound book, his hand catches the hem of her dress, pulling it up high.

She quickly grabs it and pushes it back down, clamping her legs together. She looks him in the eye, unsure if it was accidental or intentional—with that smirk on his face, most likely intentional.

136

The fight or flight instinct kicks in, and Amber stands up to leave. Once on her feet, he comes up in front of her putting his hand over her mouth. In one swift move, he puts his other arm around her waist, picks her up, crushing her body against his, then pushes her down on the sofa.

Amber's eyes are wide with fright. Her 110-pound frame is no match against him. She tries to wiggle free—she can't! She tries to scream—she can't! All she manages to do is sink further down into the couch, causing her dress to ride up, allowing him to get between her legs.

With little effort, he reaches up between them and rips off her panties. His fingers are inside of her, roughly pushing in and out. Tears streaming down her face, she can't move, he's too heavy—too strong.

With all of his weight on her, he thrusts himself into her. He's too big—the pain is excruciating. He's going to rip her in two. She can't move because he somehow was able to pin her arms underneath her. She tries to scream, but his hand is tight across her mouth. His arm across her chest is pinning her down.

His face ugly now, beet red, he wildly plunges into her. Slamming hard, making sure she takes every last inch. "You like that, don't you, you little vixen? See, before I can let you interview me, I have to know what you're really like. You play the shy little girl, then come in here with your four-inch stiletto heels and your breasts spilling out of your neckline. I know your type. You're just begging for someone to throw you down and fuck your brains out. Damn, you feel so good. You're so tight."

He grabs the top of her dress and frees her left breast, squeezing it hard. He starts biting her nipple so hard it draws blood. Amber stops fighting and just stares at the ceiling. It's no use; she can't fight him. He's shoving himself into her faster and deeper and biting her like an animal.

She can't feel it anymore—she goes numb.

"That's right, baby, don't fight it, you like it rough. You should feel lucky. Do you know how many women would love to be in your place right now?"

He continues to pump faster and faster, suddenly shoving in so deep, she feels her insides rip.

Once he's finished, he rolls off her. "That went well, don't you think? I guess I'll grant you that interview after all," he says as he gets up moving into his private bathroom. "Clean up and make that appointment before you leave. Maybe we can have a repeat…thanks for socializing Amber."

She's unable to move; she can't peel her eyes away from the ceiling. She's in shock; her brain in a fog. She hears the shower turn on. His whistling is what finally gets her moving.

Slowly, she pulls herself up and fixes the top of her dress. The threads are ripped around the neckline, making it pucker out. She picks her panties up from off the floor, intending to put them on before she realizes they're in tatters. She tosses them in the trash by the mirror. She looks up at her reflection, not sure what just happened or what to do next. Seeing the pencil behind her, she gets it and twists her hair to put it back up. She's numb—in shock—she just going through the motions.

She puts her hands on the table in front of the mirror, dropping her head and starts to cry. *Are you going to let that man get away with it? You aren't, are you?*

"What can I do?" she asks out loud to the mirror.

She looks around the room, her eyes stopping at the wet bar, focusing on the ice pick. She quickly knows what has to happen—what she must do.

She opens the door to his bathroom, the rage boiling inside.

"Come back for more already?" he asks.

Fear overtakes her anger causing her to drop the ice pick and leave. She hurries to the door, stopping in time to smooth her dress. She tries to fix the neckline, settling on the use of her coat to hide it. She takes a long, deep breath, then slowly opens the door.

As she walks out, his secretary asks, "Ms. Fiore, would you like to make an appointment for the interview before you leave?"

Amber stops and turns slowly toward her. She's probably been his victim as well. The pity in her eyes says it all.

"I'm not sure...I'll call you," Amber responds then turns hurrying toward the elevator. She has to get out of there —NOW! Once she's inside, her phone chimes. She shouldn't answer it, but it's automatic. She's not thinking clearly.

"You'll do anything for the next big break, won't you?"

Amber, in shock, doesn't respond.

"Cat got your tongue. You must have liked it rough. That's good to know. I can make you scream."

Her hands shaking, she answers, *"Just leave me alone!"*

"Oh, I can't do that. This is so much fun..."

Amber is visibly shaking with tears streaming down her face. She is unaware if there is anyone in the elevator with her. Her mind, in overload between the attack and the texts, shuts down.

After what seems like an eternity, the elevator stops on the lobby floor. She needs to get out of there. That's when she remembers...she left her portfolio upstairs. Once the doors open, her brain says, 'Go back and get it,' but her legs take her in the other direction.

She's nauseous; she's going to vomit. Rushing out, she gets turned around and goes toward the wrong doors, correcting herself after a few steps. Her brain and legs are still waging war over the portfolio, while the bile inches up—she must get outside and fast.

As she rushes out the door, she goes through a group of people entering. She doesn't wait for them; she pushes herself through.

The elevator doors open on the sixteenth floor. She strolls down toward the desk in front of his office.

"I didn't expect you back so soon. Would you like to make that appointment?"

"Yes, I would, that would be great, thank you. Anything available next week?"

"Let me check his schedule for you." The secretary says, looking surprised.

"While you do that, honey, I've left my portfolio in his office. Is it okay if I go retrieve it?"

Without waiting for an answer, she lets herself in. After removing her dress, she goes into his private bathroom.

She sees the ice pick on the floor and picks it up, intending to put it on the vanity.

"Well, now aren't you just one red hot siren. I guess you've had time to think about it. Come on in, and I'll give you round two. I knew you were all heat under that cool exterior. Get in here and wash my back," he demands.

She stops mulling over his words. She decides to join him after all and begins to soap up his back. She knows what she has to do, and she came prepared. She pulls her hand out from behind her back, and in a flash, he's going down, blood everywhere.

He turns around in shock—arms out to grab her.

She slides her foot under his, sending him crashing to the ground in the corner of the shower. After calmly rinsing the blood off her hand and arm, she leaves the water running. She looks down at his lifeless body—his eyes bulging in panic. "Piece of shit!" she says as she spits on him.

She purposely puts her dress and heels back on, smiling at her reflection in the mirror while she fixes her hair. Noticing a tiny drop of blood on her chin, she grabs a tissue and wipes it away.

She pulls the door closed behind with a big smile. She lifts the portfolio in front of her. "Thanks for letting me get this. Anytime next week good for him?"

Amber wakes up groggy, sitting in her car parked in her garage. That's strange, she thinks, *How did I get here?* The last thing she remembers was opening her portfolio on her lap in his office. *Why can't I remember?*

Shaking her head, she gathers her purse and portfolio and heads up to her apartment. Her body hurts all over, and she's throbbing. Finally, getting into her place, she pours herself a glass of wine. *I hope I'm not catching the flu.*

She tries to recall what happened...who loses track of time? She stands there for a few minutes trying hard to remember. "What happened?" she asks out loud.

She goes into her bedroom, taking a long drink from her wine glass, *Wow, what a week.* Suddenly, she gets the urge to shower; she feels dirty for some reason. She takes off her dress and only then realizes—she's not wearing her panties.

"What the hell..." She turns and sees her naked body in her full-length mirror. She has red marks all over her arms and legs. She sees a bite mark around her nipple caked with blood. It all comes back to her as she crumbles to the ground.

Knock, knock, knock. "Ms. Fiore, Fort Lauderdale Police, ma'am, we need to speak to you."

Chapter Sixteen

Stewart can't believe she's calling him. "I wasn't sure I'd ever hear from you again. You're one, naughty girl."

"I thought you liked bad girls," Brandy responds.

"Oh, I do."

"I guess the cat's out of the bag now, you've seen me—wanna screw?"

Almost choking, he replies, "Uh…yeah, sure, um…okay. No wining and dining?"

"You don't need to feed me—just fuck me."

Stewart hesitates—a moment too long.

"Never mind. I guess the cat wins."

Stewart hears the click as she hangs up the phone.

They had so much fun having phone sex together. Now that he's met her, he wants more. Not phone sex, no, not even sex.

Her contact name was Phone Fun. How his body would instantly respond when he saw that name flash on the screen, just thinking about it would make his body react. What are the odds, he would misdial a client's number, and end up with his roommate's, on-again, off-again, lover's identical twin sister? Identical in looks only—totally different personalities.

He remembers the night in Jack's Bar when he saw Brandy walk up to him in that tight red dress. He couldn't believe his eyes; he thought it was Amber, the woman Patrick was madly in love with. The one he just purchased an engagement ring for. Was she Phone Fun?

She played coy for a few minutes, letting him believe she was Amber. She almost had him convinced. But then, she laughed. It was actually more like a cackle. It was eerie.

A distraction, walking rapidly toward him, broke the trance. He looked up to see Amber come up behind Brandy—Amber?

She explained everything and begged him not to say anything to Patrick. She wasn't prepared to introduce her sister to everyone. But now, she'd be forced. She wanted to do it her way. The problem is, her way lost her Patrick.

Maybe it was the mystery of not knowing who she was or the excitement of having phone sex with her—and it was great fun—but he had hopes someone had finally gotten to him. He would finally settle down. No one affected him the way she did. She got into his head, doing things to him he never imagined.

He's a very successful salesman, but he found his mind wandering. He even totally ignored a drop-dead gorgeous, make cartoon eyes bulge out, receptionist at a new client's office. His buddies gave him a hard time back at the office when they asked if he scored her phone number. He had no idea why they were giving him such a hard time. He saw her; she just didn't register. That was it—that was the instant he knew he had to have her. Over the phone wasn't what he wanted—he needed her in his arms, in his bed, in his life.

Patrick enters the room and finds Stewart lost in his thoughts. Snapping his fingers. "Earth to Stewart—Stewart— You there, buddy?"

"Uh, what? What do you want?"

"I just came in to see if you wanted to go have a drink with me at Jack's—you okay? You seem a bit lost?"

"Yeah...I'm okay. Brandy just called me."

Patrick jerks his head around."What? What did she want?"

"To have sex, ...she just wanted to screw."

"You turned her down, right?"

"Well, yeah...I'm not a total sleaze-bag—not totally."

"I would have thought she'd have left town by now. Especially since Amber wants nothing to do with her. I wonder if she knows Brandy's still around?"

"Ms. Fiore, we need to ask you a few questions, if that's okay, please," the officer says as she lets them into her apartment. She's in a daze—functioning out of necessity—numb.

Amber nods and sits down on her couch. She's still playing it over in her mind. It's so surreal—a dream. No! A nightmare!

"Ms. Fiore, were you at Mr. Paul Brettinger's office this afternoon?"

Amber looks up, her eyes wild at the mention of his name.

"He raped me," she says quietly.

"Excuse me, what did you say?"

Replying to him louder, "He raped me. That son-of-a-bitch attacked me."

"Ms. Fiore, Mr. Brettinger, raped you? Are you accusing him of rape?"

The other officer says, "Is that why you killed him?"

Amber's head snaps around. "Killed? Did I kill him? No. No? No! I didn't kill him." she replies with venomous eyes. "He does deserve to die, though, that's for sure."

Amber laughs. A little chuckle at first until she's full-on in hysteria.

Amber's phone, on the table in front of her, rings, it's Patrick.

She picks up the phone, still laughing uncontrollably. "They think I killed him. Can you believe that? I wish I had, that bastard."

Patrick was calling to ask her out to dinner. He's totally caught off guard. "Amber, what are you saying? Who's asking?"

"These fine police officers here want to know if I killed Paul Brettinger."

"Amber, don't say another word—nothing. Put one of them on the phone, please."

"Here, he wants to talk to you."

"Officer—" Patrick prompts to get a full name.

"Officer Smith."

"Officer Smith, Amber Fiore is my client. I'm not sure exactly what's happened here, can you please fill me in?"

"She can fill you in herself at the station. We're taking her down for questioning."

"Can you please put her back on the phone then."

"Amber, please don't say anything until I can get there to the station, okay?"

Still giggling, and not all together. "Okay, whatever you say. Did I tell you he raped me?"

"Amber, please don't say another word, I'm on my way."

The officers allow Amber to get dressed. As she slowly puts her clothes on, the hurt and pain start coming back—physical, mental, and emotional. The reality of the situation becomes clear to her. *Did I kill him? I don't remember a whole lot. I think I remember getting in my car...forgetting my portfolio...vomiting in the grass...*

Amber picks up her purse as they exit the apartment. She pulls it up on her shoulder but misses, and it falls to the ground. Everything spills out—including her gun.

❧

Patrick sits across the table from her in the interrogation room. He clasps Amber's hands in his. "Are you all right?"

"I don't think I am. They think I killed him and I can't remember. I might have, but I don't think so."

"You said he raped you—Mr. Brettinger forced himself on you?"

Looking down at their hands, she silently begins to weep. "He did. I should have known better. I can't believe I put myself in that situation—especially with the texts. I was so stupid—it's all my fault."

"Texts, what texts? Amber, you're not making any sense right now. Can you please tell me everything? I can't help you if you don't tell me every detail."

"I've been getting these threatening texts. Someone is saying they're going to hurt me."

Patrick makes notes. "How many have you gotten?"

"I don't know…eight, ten, maybe?"

"Any idea who they're from?"

"No…he says he's going to destroy me; he wants to hurt me."

"He? How do you know it's a man?"

Her thoughts scramble as she's still trying to make sense of it all. She practically yells, "I don't know! I just assumed it! He talks about ripping my clothes off and doing things to me. It's a guy!" She puts her head into her hands and weeps.

"I'm sorry, one thing at a time. Can you tell me about what happened this afternoon?"

His image appears in her mind making her face turn red, and she clenches her fists. "Mr. Brettinger—Mr. Paul Brettinger, South Florida's most eligible bachelor! Women swoon over him—fall over themselves for him. He wanted me to interview him. I was so caught up in the honor; I didn't stop to think. I should have done more research and been better prepared." The anger drains away as she slumps over on the table.

"Amber, this is not your fault. If that bastard raped you, you did not ask for it. You did nothing wrong. I know this is very painful, but can you please tell me what happened?"

It's still too fresh; she's too raw. "I tried to get away, but I couldn't fight him. I couldn't win." Amber's cries turn into screams as she relives the terror.

Chapter Seventeen

"Oh, Zya, thank you so much...I just love this dress. You didn't have to bring it over so early on your way into the studio. I would have come and picked it up. Besides, he hasn't even asked me yet. Do you know something I don't?"

"If you're asking me if I know if he's going to pop the question, no, he hasn't said anything. And honestly, even if he did, you think I would tell you?" Uncomfortable, she quickly changes the subject. "I'm truly honored you're going to wear my gown when you do walk down the aisle."

Dominque replies while giggling, "Amber said you would say that."

"She's one smart cookie. You're going to be the most beautiful bride. I hope you don't mind me bringing it over now. We're clearing out samples from the last show, putting them away in storage. Trust me. You don't want this to go there; it will be a wrinkled mess. Do you have a place to hide it?"

"I do, he's afraid to go in my closet, he says it's too girlie for him. He'll never know it's here."

"Well, let's try this on, shall we? I had the seamstress make a few adjustments since you are much healthier now. No reason we can't play Princess today."

Dominque grabs the dress and runs into her bedroom.

She yells to Zya through the door, "Everything is just so perfect. Well, maybe not the cancer part, but everything else is."

Zya's phone rings, it's Patrick. "Hey, Patrick, if you're looking for Amber, she's not with me," Zya answers coolly. She is still a bit miffed at him. She knows Amber still loves him, but Zya doesn't give second chances anymore. She learned the hard way with Doug.

"Hi, Zya, no, actually Amber asked me to call you. No easy way to say this...she's in jail."

"WHAT?" Zya screams while jumping up from the couch. Dominque comes out with the wedding dress half on.

"It's a long story. I've bailed her out, just waiting for them to release her. She's had a rough night. She's been through quite an ordeal. I know she needs you, girls, around her. Think you can get Dom and head over to her place and open up a bottle of wine? I know it's only 8 a.m., but I think these might be extenuating circumstances. We can video chat with Debra."

"Can you tell me anything?"

"Amber was raped yesterday, and her attacker was found dead later in the evening."

"OH MY GOD!"

"We'll fill you in with the details later. Right now, I just want to get her out of here. I'll text you when we're heading over."

"Okay—tell her we love her."

"Will do."

Amber walks through the gates and stops to gather her belongings, everything except her gun, with Patrick beside her. She's still in shock, just going through the motions.

Once outside the door, Patrick puts his arm around her and pulls her close. She stops, turns to him, then faints, dropping to the ground. He's able to catch her with his other arm before she hits the pavement.

One of the guards stationed outside the jail exit door, runs over with a capsule, breaking it under her nose.

She wakes up instantly, taking a deep breath, staring up at Patrick. She breaks into get wrenching sobs hanging onto him for dear life willing him to make it all go away.

When the door opens to Amber's apartment, Zya and Dominque jump up from their chairs to greet her. They went there immediately, opening a bottle of wine, with glasses at the ready. What they weren't prepared for were her sunken eyes and swollen face.

"Amber, honey, what can I do?" Zya asks, walking to her, taking her hand as her eyes begin to water.

Amber looks up at her and just shakes her head. Nothing, there's nothing anybody can do.

Patrick says to Amber, "Would you like to go lay down?"

Amber nods.

Patrick moves toward the bedroom, keeping his arm around her should her legs buckle again.

"Patrick, please tell us what's going on?" pleads Dominque after he gets her settled.

"Amber had an appointment with Paul Brettinger yesterday afternoon."

Reality hits Dominque—eyes wide open. "You mean… He raped her? Paul Brettinger raped Amber?"

"She says he did." Looking down, not able to meet their eyes, "As her attorney, I'm privy to the case—and the pictures." The last part, he says in barely a whisper. Those images in his mind. The marks—the dried blood—what she must have gone through.

"It could be self-defense except his secretary claims she came back for her portfolio. Obviously, she was of sound mind enough to go back and get it.

"She does not remember everything. She recalls the first part of their meeting then leaving his office. She says he was very much alive and taking a shower in his private bathroom when she left. She vomited by her car, then the next thing she remembers is waking up, sitting in her car, in her parking space at home."

"Do you think maybe she could have gone a little insane and killed him?" Zya asks, although she's afraid of the answer.

"Did she use her gun? Did she shoot him?" Dominque adds.

"That's a whole other subject, one I just found out about; I had no idea she was carrying."

"I can't believe it. Amber wouldn't kill anyone unless someone she cares for were in danger," Zya adds.

"I agree. They have security footage from the hallway to his office. Of course, no cameras inside; he wouldn't want anyone to have proof of his abuse of power. It clearly shows Amber walking back up and going into his office. She even seems oddly chipper—totally at ease. Anyway, I'm going to persuade her to go with the insanity plea. I hope she goes along."

"Why wouldn't she? If she did kill him, it was because he hurt her. If she was chipper and happy walking back into his office, she had to have been in shock, she wasn't thinking straight," Zya says.

"She feels guilty. She thinks she asked for it. Maybe after some rest, it will all be a little clearer. She also told me she a stalker? Can one of you fill me in?"

Zya responds, "I don't know how much she told you..." Zya fills him in on the last few texts she remembers.

"If you get her phone, you'll see them. I highly doubt Paul Brettinger was her stalker." Zya's eyes get huge as she begins to digest what's just happened to her best friend. "I can't believe he raped her!"

"I know. And, she's dealing with this crazy as well," Patrick adds.

"How can we help? Is there something we can do to help catch him?" Dominque asks.

"First off, we don't know it's a man; it could be a woman just throwing her off."

"Oh, I didn't think about that," Dominque says.

"Keeping an open mind will help us find this person. We need to put a list together of anyone, male and female, who would want to hurt her, ruin her life…everyone."

"Roberto…"

"He's gone, he's back in Italy. It can't be him," Patrick responds.

"He's not gone. Amber saw it in the newspaper. She warned Debra and Brian."

"Okay, well, he goes to the top of the list, for sure. Who else?"

"She's always doing these special reports, trying to help the little guy. Just last week, she wrote an article about an apartment manager that was harassing one of his tenants. He kept telling her the rent was higher than it was, making her think up creative ways to pay him. Amber's story cost him his job and his home."

"How often does she do these types of stories?"

"One—two a month at least; it depends on what she feels needs attention."

"Dom, can you get me information on the last six months' worth of these articles? If he or she just started, I'd bet it would have to be a more recent report."

"Unless, of course, they were in jail?"

"Good point, let's start with the last six months for now. We'll go back further if we need to. Who else?"

"Her sister Brandy…"

Chapter Eighteen

"Deb, are you awake?" Brian asks as he quietly enters her room. Little George is almost ready to meet everyone. His constant moving is making a good night's sleep an impossibility.

Debra yawns, "Yeah—I think I'm awake." Looking at the clock, "I feel like I just got to sleep."

"I know I'm sorry, but I need to talk to you."

Debra reads the concern on Brian's face pulling her out of her slumber. "What happened?"

"Well, a couple of things," he walks over to the bed and sits down next to her. "This is tough...Amber was raped."

Debra gasps. "WHAT?"

"Zya and Dominque can fill you in. She's okay for now. She's home; Patrick and the girls are with her."

Debra throws back the covers and starts to get out of bed.

"Wait, wait, before you get out of bed, against doctor's orders, I've been assured they are on it, and taking care of her."

Sitting back down in bed, "I feel so helpless! I wish I could be there too!"

"That's what they told me you would say, and they assured me they would put you in the loop when you wake up."

"Give me my phone—I need to call them." Looking frantically all around the bed and on the night stand for it. "Phone! Phone! Where's my phone?"

Brian hands it to her. He raced over as soon as Zya called him. She wanted someone to be there with her when she found out.

"Zya—is Amber really okay?"

"As much as she can be," she answers wearily.

"What can I do? I have to do something."

"Can I put you on speakerphone? Patrick and Dominque are here too."

"Yes, of course...hi guys, Brian told me Roberto is the top name on your list?"

"Yes," Patrick answers, "he's still in town. Since Amber pulled a gun on him, he makes it to the top. You need to be safe, Debra—you and Brian both. I've spoken with the authorities, and he's been jumping around. They've had sightings of him from Miami up to Orlando. He's hanging around for a reason."

Brian adds, "That's the part that's got me most concerned. He's got a whole life back in Italy he worked very hard for. He is one of the best masseuses in all of Europe. He would have to be crazy to give that all up."

Debra's gaze travels to the window as chills run up her spine. The bush moves outside, and she jumps.

"What is it?" Brian's eyes follow hers.

"Nothing! I thought I saw something outside. You've just given me the willies."

Brian gets up, moving to the window.

"Don't go out there, please," Debra begs.

"I'll be all right. He wouldn't be dumb enough to do anything in broad daylight."

Debra says into the phone, "Guys if you hear me scream, call 911 right away. Brian is off to play the hero."

Just as they are about to ask where he's going, Amber walks out of her bedroom. Still in a fog but with a little more color in her cheeks.

"Hey," she says as she walks past them into the kitchen. Intending to get a glass of water, she sees the open bottle of red wine and fills her water glass to the rim. "It's five o'clock somewhere."

She sits down next to Zya on the couch. Nobody says anything; they just watch her.

Debra's focus on Brian outside is interrupted when she hears Amber's voice through the receiver.

"Whoever brought wine, thank you." Amber toasts her glass in the air.

"Amber, is that you?" Debra asks.

"Deb, are you okay? Everything all right with Little George?" Amber asks, temporarily forgetting about her problems.

"I'm fine—we're fine, how are you?"

"I don't know how to answer that right now. I'm numb, and that's probably a good thing. It's just so surreal…I'm having a hard time realizing this wasn't just a bad dream."

Patrick says, "Amber, we're working on a list of people who might want to hurt you. You may have been set up."

"Set up? You mean someone else killed Paul and is framing me?"

"Maybe. At first, I thought we should go with an insanity plea—self-defense. But now, after talking with Zya and Dominque about these texts, someone may be trying to tarnish your reputation—ruin you. We need to explore every avenue. I know the police are on this, but we need to work on it too." He shows Amber the paper. "Here's our list so far, can you think of anyone else we need to add?"

She looks at the list. "Roberto…I wish that bastard would just leave already!" Amber snarls as her eyes narrow.

Amber looks back at the list in her hand. "Brandy? You've got Brandy on here? I know she's bad, and she's done some cruel things to me, but she's not capable of murder. She wouldn't stoop that low."

"Are you sure?" asks Patrick. "What was she in prison for anyway?"

She sighs after taking a long drink of her wine. "Drugs—my sister was at the wrong place at the wrong time. Don't get me wrong, she's been in trouble since we were kids, but she didn't deserve to go to jail."

Zya interjects, "Honey, that doesn't make any sense to me. I'm sorry, but I have to ask, then why were you avoiding her? Why didn't you want her back in your life?"

"Brandy has always played the guilt game. Even when we were growing up, she always had to be the center of attention. I was a good student, mostly on the honor roll. I was on the cheerleading squad, debate teams, you name it, I wanted to be involved. Of course, our parents were thrilled. Brandy didn't do so well with her grades. She tried out for cheerleading, thinking it would be fun to have twins on the team, but she didn't make it. She wanted me to quit, but I wanted to be a cheerleader. That was when things really changed between us.

"She started hanging out with the druggies at school. She went goth at one point, dying her hair pitch black, wearing black makeup and clothes, the whole nine yards, she looked like a witch. Then she went to the other extreme, becoming blonde sporting peace signs and flowers—the hippie chick. That was probably the only point in our adolescence you could tell us apart.

"Once she realized our parents were okay with her expressing herself, she set out to look exactly like me, but act entirely the opposite.

"It was so hard, my last two years in high school. She'd start gossip and hit on boys pretending to be me. She even gave the quarterback a blow job under the bleachers. He went bragging around school the next day telling everyone how he got the *Ice Queen* to give him a blow job. I was devastated.

"One thing my sister did when she went goth was to get a tattoo on her back, right shoulder. It's a yin-yang symbol. I started wearing spaghetti straps, and other shoulder revealing tops, so everyone knew which one I was. She didn't care; she still stirred up trouble whenever she could.

"My parents tried to get her to stop. They even threatened to move her to another school. She just laughed at them and then stayed out all night partying.

"She got picked up for shoplifting at least eight times while we were seniors. The manager usually felt so sorry for my mom, so they let her slide. Finally, my dad put his foot down and told them to take her to juvie and lock her up.

"Brandy never came back home after that. She was already sixteen, so legally, she didn't have to. Mom and Dad, well, they were relieved.

"She still showed up at school sometimes just to harass me. I changed tactics, killing her with kindness, and she just took advantage of it. I started including her, asking her to meet me for lunch, or the library. She'd come, but only to start trouble. She was out to get me.

"When I graduated high school, Brandy was there. She wasn't sitting in the seats with our parents, but I saw her standing outside, across the street. I waved to her, but she just turned and walked away.

"We didn't hear from her for a few years, and then all of a sudden, like a cockroach, she came out of the woodwork. She promised she was better—grown-up, but she just used us. She played my parents one against the other, and me too. She told them lies about how cruel I was to her in school, and how I was the reason she didn't make the cheerleading squad or any other groups. She told them I destroyed her and made sure she was hated. They didn't want to believe it, but when you're fed this crap, day after day, you can't help but wonder if maybe part of it is true.

"I was stupid and naive. It hurt me when my parents started asking me questions. I should have known what she was doing. She planned to put a wedge between us, and stupid me, I let her succeed. I distanced myself from them in my late twenties—hurt they would doubt me. Then one day, my dad read an article I wrote. I think it touched a chord in him, and he reached out. We got together and cleared the air. They were so hurt to find out how she manipulated them. I was crushed to realize that once again, she got me too. Even as adults, she was hell-bent on destroying me.

"I didn't see her again until my thirtieth birthday cele-bration—our thirtieth birthday. Mom and Dad were there. Zya, you and Ashanti were there too. She was strung out. I realized that night, she was still my sister. She was mean and cruel, but I felt sorry for her—she needed help.

"I got her into rehab, even paid for it. She did really well. Her therapist said she made significant progress. She de-cided on her own to stay in for a full ninety days working there to earn a few dollars applying it to her bill. One of the steps you take when you're an addict is to make amends. She did her circle, genuinely asking for forgiveness, including her old deal-er. She was in love with him. I didn't know if I had, I would have gone with her.

"She asked me if I could take her somewhere, but I had to work that night for a big interview the next day. I asked her if it was urgent. Otherwise, I would take her the next day.

"I guess it was urgent enough to her. She thought she was strong enough, but when she met with him, she crumbled. She ended up in the bathroom with him, making up for lost time. He stuck his finger in her mouth after he had first put it in the little baggy full of coke in his front pocket. Once she real-ized, she started hitting him and yelling at him, so the manager called the cops. He had enough drugs on him to send him away for thirty years, and because she was with him, and had a long rap sheet, she was arrested as his accomplice. She tried to ex-plain, but they wouldn't listen.

"When I found out what happened, I went to the jail to get her out. She refused my help. She didn't want me to do anything. I tried to get her to reason, but in her mind, because I didn't go with her, it was my fault. She felt I wanted her to be a failure, so she wrote me off, again.

"I tried for two years to get her to let me help, but she just got meaner and meaner. I finally had to give up. My parents tried too, but they eventually couldn't take it either. My dad's heart was failing—the stress wasn't good for him.

"Brandy sent me letters every week faithfully. Oh, not the 'I miss you—I love you' letters, she wrote me the vilest, most offensive words you can imagine. It crushed me, so I finally stopped reading them. In the shredder they went—never getting opened.

"I gave up on her and promised myself, I'd never look back. I know how bad that sounds, but she deserved it."

"Why did she reach out to you when she finally got out then?" Dominque asks.

"She didn't really reach out to me. She started calling, trying to guilt me, saying they were letting her out, and it was time I made up for the misery I've caused her. I checked with the prison, and they told me they knew nothing about an early release, so I just let it go and refused the charges when the prison called.

"I had no idea she was out. And then, somehow, she became Stewart's phone sex friend. He explained to me how that all started, and I honestly can't think how she could have planned that since he was the one who dialed the wrong number.

"Then she shows up at my building, claiming to have forgotten her key. Her hair was cut just like mine; she was even dressed like me. John, our security guy, let her up and into my apartment.

"Imagine my surprise when I got home and found her sitting on my couch, drinking my wine. I was pissed! I demanded to know why she was there and what gave her the right to invade my privacy. I was nasty, but she just smiled at me and gave me a big hug. She was grateful for my help and apologized...she was making amends again. She even met this guy and thought maybe he was the one. I was speechless. If I didn't know any better, I would have thought I was looking at myself too. She was good—I mean she was really good. She had me fooled.

"The next thing I know, she kissed me on the cheek, told me 'no hard feelings' and that she was off to meet her true love at Jack's Bar. I just stood there, stunned. It took me a few minutes before it dawned on me—she was going to Jack's. I know a lot of people there. I couldn't let her go there; they'd think she was me."

Dominque adds, "That's the night I came looking for you. You told Patrick we were all going out that night."

Glancing over at Patrick, she remembers lying to him. "It is—I'm sorry. When you texted me, I was heading out the door. The only thing I could think of was I had plans with you all. How do I tell you my evil twin sister just showed up?"

After draining her glass, she looks at Dominque. "I saw you drive down my street, and I avoided you on purpose. I had to get to Jack's—I had to stop her.

"By the time I got there, she was already at the table with Stewart. I couldn't believe my luck, Stewart! I rushed over and explained everything to him—well, not everything. I think he was shocked when he first saw her. For a minute, he thought she was me. I guess you know the rest of the story. The next day you all met her at the hospital."

"Wow, um…that's one hell of a story and just reinforces why she's number two on the list," exclaims Patrick.

He moves over to sit next to Amber on the couch, taking her hand in his. "I'm so very sorry…you never shared any of this with me. I had no idea. I mean, we all have family issues, but your own sister—that's really harsh. I'm sorry you had to go through all that."

Looking into his eyes, she sees right through to his soul. She's been such a fool—this man truly does love her. As quickly as her heart feels warm, thinking about his love, her body turns ice cold. "I've been raped—I'm damaged goods…why are you helping me? You shouldn't want me!" she says through her hands sobbing.

Chapter Nineteen

Zya waits anxiously at the airport for Tina and the girls to arrive. Late, of course. Due to their sight-seeing plans, they had to fly commercial home. So much has happened over these last few days, it's so hard to comprehend. Before she gets too lost in her thoughts, she hears Ashanti yelling for her. "Mom! Mom!"

Ashanti jumps into her arms. "I've really missed you. We had such a great time, and it was so much fun!"

Tina comes up from behind Ashanti and walks into Zya's open arms. "I've been thinking a lot since I've been gone. I'm so sorry I didn't trust you. Shit! I'm a jerk. I should not have put that on you. It's my own insecurities—I love you. I don't want to do anything ever to jeopardize that."

Zya has been holding in so much emotion since, their discussion about Micki. She lets out a little moan which ultimately, turns into tears.

Tina pulls back, seeing her eyes. "Am I too late? Please tell me I'm not too late!" she begs.

"I'm okay. It's not you; I get it. You were right, and I was wrong. She—Micki—did come on to me while you were away. We need to talk about it, but not here, not with the kids around. Let's talk about it when we get home." Hugging Tina again tightly, "I'm so glad you're back."

"Me too."

Tina walks toward the airport exit, but Zya stays back. Tina turns around and walks back to her.

"There's more…Amber was raped, and now he's dead. They think she killed him. I'll fill you in later."

Ashanti interrupts them. "Mom, Dad wants me to come up and visit with him in New York some time, can we do that?"

"Can we talk about it later? Let's get in the car and get everyone home. You have all your luggage with you?"

All three nod.

Tina's eyes are wide from the news. She's visibly shaken.

"I want to know all about the taping of the show."

Stacey and Ashanti turn toward each other, then turn toward Tina as if to say, 'You tell her.'

Tina pulls herself together and turns to Zya. "Yeah, there's something we need to talk about too. Something you need to know about before the show airs. We had our own drama as well."

On the drive home, Ashanti tells her mom all about New York and the sights they saw. Every detail about the museums they went to, they even went by her old school, Parsons.

Zya gets caught up in her daughter's excitement giving her heart temporary reprieve. She's smiling; she hasn't done that in the last few days. She's just so happy to have her home.

They enter the house to a delicious aroma from the slow-cooked pot roast and potatoes—gotta love those crock-pots. Throw it all in at once and *voila*, a few hours later, dinner.

Tina pulls Zya aside. "What happened with Amber?"

Zya fills her in quickly with the details. She's not ready to have this discussion with Ashanti yet, so she asks Tina to keep it between them, for now.

As they are finishing up their last few bites, Zya asks, "So who wants to fill me in on the taping drama?"

Tina clears her throat, "Ahem…I think your brave, super-smart, witty, OMG,"—finger quotes—"incredible daughter, should be the one to share."

Ashanti blushes. "I'm sorry mom, I didn't think…I kinda spilled the beans about you and Tina. The host, Rose, asked if I was bullied because you two are more than just friends."

Zya, drinking from her water glass as she hears this, spits it out. "She what?"

"Just wait," Tina adds

"Anyway, I wasn't expecting it, but I decided just to say what was in my heart. You've always told me to follow it, so I did. I looked over at Mitch when she asked, and he was just as shocked as I was. It was actually a little funny. I told her my mom's personal life had not been a topic of conversation at my school—but it certainly will be now, thank you. In fact, I think my school is pretty hip when it comes to personal choices. Some kids are exploring their sexuality, while others do not doubt what gender they prefer. I said, by her asking me that question, did she realize that she was inviting those kids now to be bullied?"

Stacey jumps in, "It was so perfect, you should have been there. Of course, she wasn't trying to be malicious, but if she was, Ashanti stopped her right in her tracks."

"Mitch jumped in as well telling her that wasn't why he bullied me. I was his target because of the brainwashing from his mother, and she from her family before her. He got her back on track to the topic of discussion. I used to hate that kid. Now, I'm a bit in awe of him."

Zya reaches over and squeezes Ashanti's hand. "Wow, I'm so proud of you. Not surprised—and very proud."

"Thanks, mom. Even Dad said he thought I handled it pretty well."

"Your dad was there? At the taping?" she asks, looking up at Tina.

She nods.

"Yeah, he came by to watch. He was great, Mom...he's changed. Can we please visit sometime? He's got a cool place, and I love it there."

A bit uncomfortable, Zya shifts in her seat. "We'll see. Let me talk to him and see what's on his mind, and then we'll talk about it, okay?"

"Okay. Do you want Stacey and me to clear the table and do the dishes?"

She puts the back of her hand on Ashanti's forehead. "Are you feeling okay. Wait? Are you an alien? And if so, what have you done with my daughter?"

Laughing, Ashanti and Stacey start clearing the table. "Ha, ha, ha, you and Tina go spend some time together."

Once in the living room on the couch, Zya turns to Tina. "I haven't told Doug about us. He thought you were just a friend, chaperoning the kids to New York, while I had to stay behind and work. Was he shocked?"

"Honestly, I don't know. We were all shocked when the host asked the question. I didn't look at him—I was focused on Ashanti."

"So, he didn't say anything to you? He didn't mention anything at all?"

"Let's go out for a walk." Tina grabs Zya's hand, pulling her up from the couch.

Once outside, "I know he's the father of your daughter, and you were once very much in love with him, but that guy is a major piece of work—he's an asshole."

"Yes, he is, and he can be a very scary one too. I had no idea what he was doing until I got here. You have to tell me what happened."

"He insisted on taking us out to dinner after the taping to celebrate—all of us, including Mitch and his father. We had a lovely time. When we got back to the hotel, Ashanti invited him to come up. I tried to stop her, but you know how she can be. Anyway, once we got up in the room, he kept looking at me strangely. He made a crude gesture when I first met him when he thought I was just your friend, but this time, he creeped me out.

"The girls ran out to get some sodas from the machine in the lobby. I didn't want to be alone with him, so I went after them, but he closed the door before I could get out. I knew I had to stand my ground, I couldn't let him scare me, so I just stood there, praying for the girls to be quick.

"He ran the tip of his fingers down my neck, my breast, and down to my thigh." Tina struggles to speak. "He said, 'You must be one excellent lay to get Zya to switch sides,' then he grabbed me between the legs."

"Oh, Tina, I'm so sorry."

"While he was grabbing me, he told me he was going to get himself some of this pussy too, or maybe it would be better if Ashanti lived with him in New York. She needs a male influence. He doesn't think it's the best environment for his daughter to be raised in." Tina's eyes begin watering.

Zya hugs her tightly. *This shit just keeps piling on!* "Tina, it's okay, I'm so sorry he did that to you. I promise you, there's no way that jerk is going to lay a hand on you, or Ashanti, ever again. He doesn't know, but I accidentally caught one of his transactions on video a few years ago. I was filming a street performer in Manhattan, and he was in the background. I've never deleted it."

"Are you sure? He's got connections, and you don't think he'll try to hurt you—or me?"

"No, I don't. If he threatens, I'll make sure Patrick has a key to a safety deposit box, with instructions to collect a certain package, should anything happen to either of us. Don't worry about a thing. Honestly, Doug is not a worry to us. Micki on the other hand..."

Chapter Twenty

"Ms. Patterson, good afternoon," the doctor addresses Dominque as he enters the room. "I understand you've done your egg retrieval and everything is good, is that correct?"

"Yes, we were lucky with the timing. We've been successful at retrieving, and we've got a few viable soldiers ready to go."

The doctor chuckles. "That's great; I'm glad to hear that. Your blood test results are fine, so we are ready to go unless you have any questions for me before I take you to the Chemo Cafe?"

"How will I feel when the chemo is going into my body?"

"Many feel nothing at all. Maybe a little cold, but we have plenty of blankets for you. Otherwise, you'll feel pretty normal."

"It won't make me dizzy or make me feel weak?"

"Not immediately, you may feel that way later, but today you'll pretty much feel yourself."

Tad asks, "She won't be nauseous?"

"We'll be giving her anti-nausea medicine along with her chemo drugs. She'll go home with a prescription for more to combat any nausea she may feel after what she gets today wears off. She must take the pills as directed. If she waits to see if she gets nauseous, it will be too late, and she won't be able to keep the pills down. Any other questions?"

Dominque and Tad both shake their heads.

"Okay then, let me lead the way."

Dominque starts trembling. Surgery is one thing, but poison being injected into your veins to save your life...seems like an oxymoron.

The Chemo Cafe is nothing like what they imagined with nice comfortable reclining chairs and bright, cheery colors all around. Laughter can be heard from the other patients as they watch a comedy on the big TV screen. Most of the patients smile as they enter.

"Not what you expected, huh?"

"Not at all!" exclaims Dominque. "Everybody looks happy."

"We try not to be all gloom and doom around here. You're already scared enough as it is. If we can help make this any less traumatic for you, we will."

The doctor motions for Dominque to sit in one of the chairs closest to the far wall. There's a comfy chair for Tad right next to her. As Dominque is getting comfortable, a nurse approaches and introduces herself. She unfolds a slice of warm heaven and places it over her lap.

"Can I get you something to drink? Juice? Water?"

"Vodka tonic?" Dominque jokes, trying to ease the tension. Getting cancer sucks! Having chemo sucks! Watching a comedy under a warm blanket, sitting next to the man you love —sucks less.

Once the IV gets started with her chemo-cocktail, Dominque reaches across to Tad, touching his arm. "It's not too late, you know? If you want to run, now's the time, before my hair falls out."

"Leave? Are you crazy? Besides, if you don't have any hair, I won't have to hold it back when you're barfing."

Dominque gets a mental image of herself leaning over the porcelain god with no hair. An image that probably should terrify her, but instead, makes her burst out laughing.

It's contagious; the other patients are now either smiling or laughing with her.

Tad gets up, then turns to face her. "You think I would leave you because you've got cancer?"

Dominque's laughter stops abruptly, not sure where he's going with this.

"You are the love of my life. I've waited thirty-two years to find you. Okay, maybe not my entire life—I didn't even think about girls until I was fifteen—I digress. You're everything I always wanted, and more. Nothing, and I mean nothing, is going to send me away, got it?"

She nods. She's so in love with this crazy man standing next to her, making quite a scene.

"Good, then I have just one more question for you..." Tad removes the box from his pocket and gets down on one knee.

"Oh!" is heard from all around the room.

Dominque's heart skips a beat. *Oh, my God! Oh, my God!*

"I'm in it for the long haul Ms. Patterson. There's nothing too big we can't tackle together. You've already been called Mrs. Johnson a few times, how about we make it official? Will you marry me?"

With tears in everybody's eyes, including Tad's, Dominque nods. She's trying so hard to say something, but she can't find the words—she can't find her breath.

"Breathe baby; it's for real. We're for real."

"Yes! YES!" Dominque squeals.

The room erupts in applause.

Tad leans in and kisses her.

Holding the back of his head, with her lips right by his ear, she asks, "Any chance on you taking my name?"

"Hey, you."

"Hey, you, back."

"Is it okay that I'm calling you?"

"I won't tell if you don't."

Brandy laughs. "I'm sorry about the other day…that was pretty bad, I shouldn't have just called you for sex."

"So, you're saying you don't want to have sex with me?"

"Of course I do! I mean, yes, I do, but maybe we could just go out for a drink instead…first."

"Okay, I'd like that, but let's go somewhere quiet, not Jack's, too many people know me…and Amber there. Can we keep this between us?"

"Are you ashamed of me?"

"No, I'm not. However, Amber has a lot on her plate right now, and I don't want to be the one to pile on any more. I know you two have some issues, and that's between you two. I just don't want to add any more burden right now."

"What, she's busy climbing the corporate ladder getting to the bigwigs and CEOs?"

There is a long pause from Stewart. "I probably shouldn't be telling you this, but Amber was raped last week."

"Are you kidding me? Really?"

"Really, and to make matters worse, her attacker was murdered."

"Why does that make matters worse? It seems like he deserved it—karma is a bitch, baby."

"I agree totally, except they think Amber did it."

"Amber kill someone,"—laughing hysterically— "in what world? That would never happen—she doesn't have it in her."

"Again, I agree. But she was the last one to see him alive, so she was arrested."

"They have evidence she killed him?"

"No, they arrested her on probable cause. I think that's what Patrick said. I'm not the legal guy; he is."

"You know, we've had our differences, but that really sucks. Amber has never been the tough one; she's always been the delicate little flower. She'd never make it in jail. So, is Patrick defending her?"

"He is. Not sure it's a great idea, he may be just a little too close on this one, but he won't budge. He's determined to find out who set her up and who's stalking her."

"Wait…what? She's being stalked too?"

"Where are we meeting? Somewhere quiet, and I'll fill you in...literally."

Chapter Twenty-One

Beads of sweat are dripping down her forehead. Her hair is plastered to the back of her neck—it's all coming back. His hands are on her again, across her mouth, she can't breathe…

She runs, terrified, out of the bedroom into the living room, stopping suddenly when she sees someone asleep on her couch. She's about to scream but stops just in time when she realizes it's Patrick. Their relationship has been anything but conventional, and he's hurt her; in fact, they've hurt each other. Regardless of what damage they have done in the past, he's here for her now. He's been a rock. She's always so strong for everyone else; it's almost impossible for her to let her guard down. That is until now. She trusts him completely. Her life is literally in his hands, and she's okay with it. She knows he's doing everything within his power to help her. She can see it in his eyes when he looks at her.

Needing to feel safe, she crawls into his arms—protected from her demons—shielded from her dreams.

He wakes up, feeling her lie down against him. She's cold and shaking, crying silently. He wraps his arms tightly around her, "I've got you. No one is ever going to hurt you again, I swear. I've got you." She knows he's letting her lead. She'll decide when, and if, they once again become a couple.

They lay like that for hours. Although safe, the images of that fateful day—being forced upon, still haunts her. He's shared how frustrating it is for him, how helpless he feels knowing she was hurt—attacked. He told her he never understood how any man could ever force himself on another. He almost got physically sick when they talked about it.

The one good thing, if you could ever find one in this nightmare…they've come together again.

"Are you okay? You seem to be in pain."

"Well, if you must know, I am in pain—I'm in labor."

"Why didn't you tell me? You have a go-bag here somewhere, right?" Brian asks, obviously freaking out.

"Yes, Brian, I do. Don't go crazy on me; I've done this before. It's still too soon to go to the hospital."

"Is Little George okay? It's not still too early, is it?"

"I'm thirty-nine weeks, so he's considered full-term. My contractions are still six minutes apart, but they are coming regularly, so it's definitely labor."

"When do we go?"

Debra's eyes glaze over as another one hits her. Her belly tenses up, and she breathes through it, staring at a spot on the wall.

Debra looks down at her watch. "That one was five minutes since the last one. When they are about four minutes apart, that's when we go. Can you call my sister, Megan, and have her come stay with Tracey, please?"

Brian kisses her forehead. "You're so calm—how do you do that?"

Debra chuckles. "It's a beautiful and natural experience to give birth. Besides, as I said, I have done this before, I know what to expect. Now go call Megan, please."

As she watches him leave her room, she smiles. *I'm so glad he's here.* She panics a little when she thinks about Roberto and the biggest mistake she might have made in her life. She was so afraid she had pushed Brian away. *Brian is her forever.*

"Hey, sorry to wake you, Debra and Brian are on their way to the hospital. Little George's birthday is going to be today."

She's complained about being a little tired, and she can't get rid of the metallic taste in her mouth, but overall, it's not been as hard as she thought it would be. It's only been ten days since she made the mistake of not taking her anti-nausea medicine as directed. She told Tad she felt great; she thought she didn't need it. She was...right up until three in the morning when the liquid drugs wore off. She barfed continuously for four days straight, not able to keep anything down. Food, water, medicine, everything came up. They ended up in the emergency room, where they gave her a shot to break the cycle. She promised him that day, she would never defy the doctors again.

Dominque stretches like a cat. Getting to her feet, Tad is right by her side to help steady her if she needs him. She smiles and kisses him sweetly on the lips. "I'm good, thanks."

"I love you, Red."

Giggling, she responds, "And I love you more. Now come on, let's get dressed and get over there to meet that little man."

"I have a concern. Sorry, but I have to voice it."

"Okay."

"Hospitals are full of germs. Now, I know they try to keep everything clean and sterile, but there are sick people all over the place, do you think you should be there? You're midway between treatments; Isn't this the time when your white-blood count starts to drop?"

"Good point, think I can get by with a mask?"

"I'm not sure, but I'm happy to call your doctor and ask for you."

"That would be great, thank you. I'll jump in the shower while you call. Or, rather, you go call, and I'll wait for you in the shower."

She leans forward and kisses him passionately, pressing the full length of her body up against him, making sure to grind into his early morning erection.

"Okay, hold that thought, I'll be right back," As he turns and walks away, he mumbles, "I hope they don't put me on hold."

Luckily, they answered the phone rather quickly, and the doctor was available to approve the visit once Debra is closer to delivery to help protect her.

Tad slips into the bathroom and quickly undresses. The mirror is already cloudy from the steam filling the room. The shower enclosure is all glass, so he has a view of her womanly curves. The body she didn't have just a few months ago when she was fighting her eating disorders. One she may not have a few months from now after the effects from cancer. For now, she looks healthy and full of life.

She is going to be my wife. We are going to spend the rest of our lives together.

Tad's thoughts quickly turn somber knowing their future—her future, is not a promise. The sudden urge to hold her in his arms is overwhelming. He opens the shower door and envelops her from behind. The thought of losing her crushes him with a sudden pressure in his chest. He's never letting go —ever.

Caught up in his thoughts, it takes a moment for him to realize, she's crying. The sound of running water is drowning the echoes of her sorrow. Tad turns her around, seeing her face etched with hopelessness.

"Oh, Dom, what is it? How can I help?"

Throwing her arms around him, she whispers in his ear through her tears, "Just hold me; I'm so scared. I've never been so afraid in my life. I don't want to die—I'm too young. I've got so much to live for. We've just found each other, and I want to grow old with you; I want to have babies with you."

He feels so helpless, wishing he could take her fear away. "Dom, I'm scared too. But I promise you, I'll do whatever it takes—It's not your time. Look at everything you've been through and where you are—where we are today. If you've proven anything to me, it's how strong and determined you are. It's normal to be afraid, but please don't give up. Whatever you do, don't ever lose hope."

They hold each other in the shower for a few moments, both afraid of the unknown.

"They say that which doesn't kill you makes you stronger, right?" she asks with a slight smile.

Tad pushes a long wet strand of hair from her face. "You're already strong—stronger than you think. We've got this. Together, this cancer shit doesn't stand a chance."

His lips touch her mouth, but it's his heart that fuels the passion. "I love you, Matilda Dominque Patterson. You are my everything—you are my world."

"I'm so happy! I never knew love could feel like this."

The pure joy in his heart at hearing those words is all the encouragement he needs. He pushes back that same lock of hair to kiss her along her slim, swan-like neck while she leans her body into him. Their bodies fit together like two pieces of a jigsaw puzzle.

Her hands slowly roam over his shoulders, down his back, switching to her nails scraping across his firm cheeks, as his kisses leave a trail along the other side of her neck.

He whispers in her ear, "I never knew love could feel like this. I'm the luckiest guy in the world."

He's an accountant—a nerd, but one who works hard on keeping his body firm and tone. He has an incentive as well. She's never given him any reason to think he has to stay in shape, but watching the way her eyes light up, and how she licks her lips whenever she sees him naked, is all the motivation he needs.

She reaches for the shower gel, soaping up her hands with a mischievous gleam in her eye. She takes her sweet time getting a big pile of suds built up.

He watches her with lust, knowing full well what she plans to do with them. His mind is already imagining what her hands are going to do to him.

She goes slowly, making sure his chest is nice and clean, then works her way down his abdomen.

He tenses, giving her full view of his six-pack. He knows it excites her. His abs are one of her favorite parts. Her hands always find a way under his shirt or between his buttons.

She washes inside each crevice, between each rock-hard ab muscle—slowly—her expression showing full admiration.

Her diligence leaves him breathless. He tries to touch her, but she pushes him back against the wall. "I need to make sure you are thoroughly clean—I need to focus."

It's so hard for him to be the receiver—he's always been the giver. He's not sure what feels better…the joy in knowing you've helped someone or the feeling of being helped. Right now, it's the latter.

She stoops down and washes his ankles, slowly moving up to his calves. Her face is just inches away from his throbbing cock, pulsing, trying to get her attention. She leans in and brushes her lips against it.

He lets out a gasp.

She drops two folded washcloths on the ground in front of him then drops to her knees.

His mind immediately starts to spin when he imagines her intentions.

She wraps one soapy hand around him, causing his knees to buckle.

He catches himself as her other hand goes on his thigh…inside, up high, almost touching his scrotum.

"You're driving me crazy," he says as he grabs his head in frustration.

She's watching his face as she strokes his full length, gradually picking up the pace. When she feels he's close, she wraps her lips around him, sucking hard, while her hand continues its rhythmic strokes.

The sudden intense sensation catches him off guard. His hands quickly go to her shoulder to steady himself as his legs go numb, threatening to collapse under him. *Oh damn!*

She uses her lips just around the rim, while her tongue darts in the slit at the tip of his penis.

With his hands still on her shoulders, he begins to thrust his hips—faster and faster. She's no longer providing the momentum, he is.

His moans are getting louder and louder, signaling his imminent release. Just when he thinks it can't get any better, she moves the hand on his thigh, gently grasping his testicles. They're already pulled up tight against his body, but her touch catapults him leaving him light-headed and gasping for air.

Her lips still encircling him so she can get every last drop.

Once he's caught his breath, he looks down and sees her licking her lips. He's fully erect again in two-seconds flat.

He has to kiss her. His lips have to be on hers—it's urgent. He pulls her up while their lips stay locked and maneuver her to the other side, against the wall. The heat from the water, and their bodies, having turned it into a steam shower.

He doesn't bother with the soap. He urgent kisses move to her neck—to her ear, while his fingers gently pinch one of her nipples. He's not patient like she was—he feels slightly out of control, like an animal.

Urging her legs apart with his knee, he presses his thigh into her, rubbing, grinding commanding her hips to move while his lips continue their exploration.

"I've got to have you inside me. Please, I need to feel you inside me," she begs.

He pulls back, giving her a devilish grin. Had she not begged, he might have complied.

He drops on one of his knees, lifting one of her legs over his shoulder. His hands reach up behind to help steady her.

He looks up into her eyes, again with that same mischievous look, he kisses her on the knee then quickly buries his face between her legs.

The instant he touches her, she cries out, and her other leg gives out. He's got her. She's leaning into the wall, and with his hands cupping her ass, he keeps her steady while his tongue devours her.

Within seconds, her moans turn into screams. The louder she gets, the deeper his tongue goes, making her cry out louder.

Just as she's about to peak, she grabs the corner shelf and steadies herself.

Sensing her time of release, he stops abruptly.

She looks at him pouting.

With hat look again in his eyes, he reaches just outside the shower door and pulls in a plush bath towel.

Her eyes are now dancing mischievously like his.

She walks over to him and puts her arms around him. "What you do to me…I've never felt an orgasm like I have with you ever before. You take me places I've never been before." She seals it with a kiss.

"That's because you've never been loved like this. As much as I'm sorry for the hurt in your past, I'm so happy knowing I'm the one you're experiencing this with for the first time."

He stoops down and motions with his hand for her to lie down.

As she takes a step past him, he stops her kissing her ass cheek, while his hand goes between her legs.

She lets out a squeal and grabs the wall to her right to steady herself.

Impatient, he turns her towards him again, burying his face into her pussy.

With both hands supporting herself on the wall and up on her toes, she thrusts her hips into his face urging him to give her release.

His arms go between her legs so she can put her weight on his arms. It also allows himself to bury his face deeper into her—his tongue switching between being buried deep inside her to flicking and sucking her swollen bud.

Her hips begin to rock violently back and forth, pressing his head back into the wall as she screams through her orgasm.

He gently lays her down on the now saturated towel on the shower floor. Once she's comfortable, he starts at her toes, on his hands and knees, and crawls up between her parted legs. He stops midway, taking one long lick between her legs, visibly causing her to tremble before he stretches out on top of her.

He places his tip just inside, intending to tease a bit. He thrusts just enough, so the head, right up to the rim of his penis, ducks inside and out. He's able to do this only a few times before his plans get thrown out the window. He has to be inside of her—now!

He grabs her behind her waist and upper back and rocks up onto his knees, pulling her up with him.

With her arms around his neck, she plants her feet on the ground behind him and takes over. She sits down, pulling every inch of him inside her.

He's being swallowed up, drowning inside her…she so wet! It momentarily takes his breath away.

She rocks back and forth, slowly grinding into him.

He can feel her rubbing her clit against his pubic bone. Deciding to help, he licks his finger then places it between her legs giving her something more to stimulate herself.

Her eyes glaze over. "I love you. I love you so much."

Hearing those words come from her luscious lips, sends him once again, into orbit.

She cries in unison with each of his grunts. Their climax seems to go on forever.

Afterward, they stay in that position with her head resting on his shoulder. His thighs are screaming, from the position, and the hard tile floor, but he doesn't hear it. The feeling of her heartbeat against his chest drowns everything else out.

Brian asked Amber if it was okay to be there when Little George arrived. He didn't want to be in the delivery room; he just wanted to be there.

"Why don't you ask Debra?"

"I don't want to put that pressure on her. She's been pushed too much these last several months since George died."

"I'm sure she'd love to know you're waiting right outside. No worries." Amber is impressed by his caring and thoughtfulness. *Yeah, he's a keeper Debra.*

After several hours of waiting, Amber comes into the waiting area to update everyone on the baby's progress. "Mom and baby are doing great. She's eight centimeters dilated, so she'll be pushing soon. Next time I come out, he'll be here."

She walks over to Brian, "I told her you stayed. You should have seen her eyes light up. She's happy you're here."

Brian grins from ear-to-ear.

Tracey runs up to Amber and grabs her leg. "Can I see my mommy now?"

Amber picks her up. "I know your mommy would love to see you too, but you know, she's helping your little brother right now. I promise, as soon as possible, I'll make sure you get to see her, okay?"

"Okay. Will you give her a big kiss for me?"

"Sure thing, sweetie."

Amber puts Tracey down in the chair next to Megan, Debra's sister. "Do you want to come back in with me? Zya or Tina would be happy to keep an eye on her."

"Thanks, but no thanks. This is exactly why I'm never having kids. I don't need to see all that. I'll see him when he's all clean and wrapped in a blanket. Kiss her for me too."

As Amber stands to go back into the delivery room, she catches a sight down the hall. "He wouldn't dare," she mumbles to herself as she starts after the mirage.

Quickly, but not too urgently—she doesn't want to cause any alarm—she walks down the hallway and turns toward the elevators. They are closing, but not before she sees one of its occupants—Roberto!

There's a phone next to her on the wall. She picks it up and dials zero. An operator answers and is alerted of the wanted man on the premises.

Not thinking about the possibility of missing Little George's birth, she rushes down the stairs to the lobby. Just as she exits the door, she catches sight of two security officers approaching him just inside the sliders.

Roberto catches them out of the corner of his eye and makes a bee-line for the door. What he doesn't see is the security guard outside, coming in.

One hit across the chest with his billy club and Roberto falls backward right into the awaiting officers behind him.

They immediately turn and place him on the ground, face down. Once he's handcuffed, they help him to his feet. He's calm for a moment then lurches toward the doors, making a run for it again. He's caught instantly and, with his head hanging down, is escorted back inside.

As he passes Amber, he looks up—If looks could kill...

A shiver runs through her body. *Thank God they have him. He scares the crap out of me.*

Amber hurries back up the stairs. As she exits on the labor floor, she plans to go straight into Debra's room, but she turns to Brian instead. He has this perplexed expression on his face as if to ask, *Where did you just go?*

She goes to him and whispers in his ear, "They've got him. Roberto was here, but they got him. You don't have to worry about him anymore."

Just as she's inside the main door separating the waiting room from the labor and delivery rooms, a text comes through her phone. She's expecting to hear from Patrick. He's in trial today. He said he would call when he got a break.

Terror crosses her face as she begins to read.

"So your friend is finally delivering that curtain-climber, I see. Watch closely…all that blood will be no match for what will come out of you. But I do plan to play with you a bit first. Can't wait to see just how fast your blood clots. Ta-ta!"

She's trying so hard to keep it together since the attack; for her friends—for herself—for her sanity. The helplessness she felt after being raped comes flooding back. Her eyes widen as she begins to hyperventilate.

A nurse walking by stops and touches her.

She reacts and almost knocks her to the ground, then she crumbles, making herself as small as she possibly can, sobbing.

"Miss, how can I help?" the nurse asks.

Amber looks up into warm, kind eyes, her own wild from the memories. It takes her a moment to get a grip. "I'm so sorry. I didn't mean to lash out like that. I've just been through so much lately—I'm sorry if I hurt you."

The nurse hugs Amber comforting her. "I'm sorry for whatever you've been through. I know from experience, sometimes all you need is a good cry, so go ahead, I'll stay here with you as long as you need."

As horrible as some humans can be, there are those beautiful, giving people that seem to show up just when you need them. This interaction is precisely what Amber needs to help her get past the terror, warming her heart with the offered kindness.

As her heart slows down and her breathing normalizes, she wipes the tears from her eyes. "Thank you, you're so sweet. My best friend is about to give birth to her baby boy, and I need to be there with her."

"You sure you're okay?"

Amber stands and wraps her arms around the sympathetic nurse. "Yes, thanks to you. Thank you for caring, that truly means the world to me." Brushing herself off and straightening her clothes. "Now, I gotta go and get ready to be an aunt...again."

Amber slips into Debra's room just as the doctor says, "Okay, Debra, I need you to bear down for me. Keep pushing through the contraction."

Amber goes to the side of the bed and grabs Debra's hand. Debra squeezes it tight. Amber has to squeeze back, or she's afraid it will break.

Once the contraction ends, Debra asks, "You were gone so long, everything okay?"

"Everything's great, sorry, I didn't mean to be gone that long."

"Wait, have you been crying?" Debra notices her red eyes.

"It's just like you to worry about someone else right now. You're having a baby…this is all about you."

"I need a distraction, what's up?"

"I just got another text, and no, you can't read it."

Debra grabs Amber's hand. "I'm so sorry. Is Patrick any closer to finding out who this creep is?"

"He's working the list you all put together. We can scratch Roberto off it."

"We can? Why?"

"He was here in the hospital. I called down to security just as he was trying to leave."

Debra's eyes go wide at the mention of his name.

"They've got him. He's been arrested. I'm sure he'll be deported now."

"Oh…," she says at the start of another contraction.

"You've got this girlfriend. Bear down, I want to meet my nephew."

Things progress pretty quickly after the fourth pushing contraction. Little George's head peaks out. Debra is handed a mirror between contractions to see her son arriving. She's laughing and crying at the same time over the bittersweet emotions in her heart. The love of giving birth to her child—and the hurt, when the love of her life, George, is not here to experience it with her.

On February 1, 2018, at 2:36 p.m., George Baron Harris Junior entered the world. All six-pounds, three-ounces and nineteen and a half inches of him.

Chapter Twenty-Two

On Valentine's Day, Brian knows Debra is missing her late husband even more, which is why he needs her to know he cares...today and every day.

Amber answers the door. "Hi Brian, what a nice surprise."

"It's good to see you, you look good. How are you holding up?"

"I'm okay. Since Little George has come, I really haven't had much time to think about anything else. Taking care of them has helped keep me busy."

"I understand a newborn is a lot of work, so you're definitely in the right place, I think. I'm surprised she's letting you help, though."

Amber chuckles. "I know right! I guilted her—she didn't have a choice. Plus, she knows I need this."

"I won't keep you any longer from your domestic chores, is she up, can I see her?"

"Absolutely, she'll be glad you're here."

Brian follows Amber into the nursery, where Debra is rocking her new baby boy. He's sound asleep, but she just can't put him down. He's so perfect. Her face lights up when she sees Brian behind Amber.

She puts Little George in his crib and moves toward Brian, her intentions obvious. Amber scrambles to take the beautiful rose arrangement and gifts from him so he can wrap her in his arms.

He picks her up and twirls her around.

She giggles...Little George stirs.

She puts her fingers to her lips as they exit the nursery.

"Brian, I've missed you. Where have you been? I told you to come by and visit."

"I didn't want to intrude, but I want you to know you are on my mind. I couldn't let today go by without at least seeing your beautiful face and letting you know I'm thinking about you."

It has been nice to spend this time with Tracey and her new bundle. The girls have taken turns washing laundry, cooking meals, and helping out in any way possible. Having them around has helped her deal with the loneliness of bringing her son into the world, without his father by her side. She's been feeling rather raw lately. Brian distancing himself has been a good thing, but seeing him now, it's like falling in love with him all over again.

She notices Brian seems a little nervous—he's fidgeting, shifting his weight back and forth. His uneasiness makes her smile.

He picks up the rose bouquet and begins to explain. "The white ones are because I know how hard it has been for you, wishing you peace during this challenging time. Yellow, because I want you to know, no matter what, you'll always have a friend in me. Pink because come on, you are my sweetheart, and red, one red because I want you to know I love you, but I don't want to overwhelm you. When or if the day comes that we can be together, I promise you two dozen of the most beautiful red roses I can find. In fact, you'll always have them as a constant reminder of how much you mean to me."

As he's explaining the colors, she's can feel how heartfelt his choices are. Tears trickle down her cheeks as she looks lovingly at him.

"They're beautiful and so thoughtful, Brian." She picks up his hand and holds it. "I love you too. Thank you for being so patient with me. When the time comes, you won't need to send me red roses, I already know."

She leans up and kisses him lightly on the lips.

The kiss has visibly affected him. After a pause, he continues as if the kiss didn't happen. "This one is for Tracey, and this one is for Little George. I hope it's okay I brought them something. No candy...a pink and red bow for Tracey and a pacifier for the little guy."

She hugs him tight, "That's very sweet and generous of you, thank you. Thank you for everything. Knowing you're still in my life gives me comfort."

Dominque can smell something heavenly coming from the kitchen. Just two days after Chemotherapy treatment number two, she's feeling a bit tired. The anti-nausea drug they gave her to take after treatments gives her an awful headache. Today is no different. She'll take it over vomiting her guts out.

Her red and white blood counts were low—borderline. The doctor warned her if she doesn't start eating, they may have to push back her treatments until her numbers improve.

She makes her way out to the kitchen and turns the lights down.

Tad turns to her, seeing the lines on her forehead and her eyes like slits. "Headache, huh?"

"Yeah, but something smells wonderful. What are you making?"

"I've been doing some research. Since everything tastes metallic to you, and you need the calories and protein, I'm making you a spinach and bacon quiche, with extra cheese. I'm hoping your stomach is feeling okay?"

"Thankfully, my tummy is just fine, and I can't wait to find out the culprit of that delicious aroma. I haven't felt like eating anything in weeks. Mmm, it smells so good. When will it be ready?"

She turns to the table and sees the fine china placed perfectly with the elegant crystal glasses. A dozen red roses in a beautiful crystal cut vase sit in the middle with an envelope leaning against it, her name on the front.

"Oh Tad, the table is so beautiful. It's Valentine's Day, isn't it?" she asks, frowning. "I'm sorry, I didn't get you anything—not even a card."

"Really? I think you get a free pass this year. I'm counting on you making it up to me next year, though. And the year after that, and the one after that...," he says as he nuzzles her neck.

"I'm sorry—I promise I will make it up to you," she says with a wicked grin.

A knock at Amber's door makes her jump. She's been on edge lately despite knowing no one can get up to her condo without going through security. With everything that's happened, she doesn't trust anyone.

Looking through the peephole, she sees a bouquet staring back at her. She doesn't know who's behind them.

"Who is it?" she asks without opening the door.

"Flower delivery, ma'am."

"I didn't order any flowers."

Shock registers at her angry tone. He replies, "They're being delivered to you. Would you like me to read the card for you?"

"I didn't order any flowers—go away."

Pulling the card, he opens and reads it. "Ma'am, they're from Patrick?"

She sighs and goes to open the door, but then stops. It could be a trick. Her stalker knows everyone in her life. "Can you just leave them by the door and go, please?"

"I'm sorry ma'am, I can't, I need a signature."

"Take them down to security. John will sign them for you."

"Are you sure?"

She screams at him, mad at being so afraid. "Yes! Take them downstairs. John will bring them up to me."

Ashanti brings in the mail, sorting it at the kitchen island. "So Mom, you and Tina have any romantic plans for tonight?"

"Maybe…"

"Where are you going? Out to dinner?"

"Every restaurant is going to be so busy tonight, rushing us to get through our meal so they can turn the table, we've decided to do something a bit nontraditional."

Ashanti tears open an envelope addressed to her. She never gets mail—it's from Mitch.

"Mom, Mitch sent me a Valentine's Day card." She turns the card around, showing it to her.

"Let me see." Reading the card aloud, "Happy Heart Day,"—opening to read the inside— "My friend, my heart. *Ashanti, crazy how far we've come in such a short period of time. I want you to know how grateful I am that you stayed that day…you didn't let me die. I'm forever in your debt. I'm forever your friend, Mitch."*

"I have his heart? That's weird—that's nuts."

"Honey, I think his near-death experience is something he's still trying to wrap his head around. From the few times I've talked with him, it's hard to imagine him being so cruel. I can see how thankful he is every time he looks at you. I think it might be genuine. It is nuts, but I think he really does like you —as a friend."

Ashanti shrugs her shoulders. "Oh well…it's still weird to me. So what are your nontraditional plans for tonight?"

"We're going to the movies to see Fifty Shades Freed. First, we're going to watch the two Fifty Shades movies here, then head out to the movies. The movie starts at eight-fifteen, so our date starts at three o'clock sharp, right here on this couch."

"Mom, not like I want to imagine you ever having sex, but you know what those movies are like, right? You think you'll be able to make it to the movies?"

Zya flushes inside; she can't either.

"You're right. You should never envision me having sex, ever."

☯

"Miss Fiore, I'm sorry for sending him up. I thought you could use some cheering up by having them delivered to your door. I know Bob, the delivery guy, he delivers to this building all the time. I'm really sorry."

"It's okay, John. I'm just not very trusting lately. Can you put them on my table, please?"

Amber hands him a folded up ten-dollar bill. "No, no, I can't take that. I didn't mean to cause you any misery. It's okay. I'm glad someone is thinking of you today."

After John leaves, she pulls the card to read it.

> *Roses are Red,*
> *Violets are Blue*
> *I'd give anything in the world,*
> *To take this pain away from you.*
> *I can't wait until the day when my love*
> *replaces the fear and hurt in your heart.*
> *Always, Patrick.*

She picks up her phone to call him to invite him over. She's lonely—he makes her feel safe. That's when she realizes—she missed a text…must have been while she was showering.

"Happy Valentine's Day. Enjoy it because it will be your last. Your heart may pound today, but it will take its last beat soon. Forever yours, and you'll be forever mine."

Chapter Twenty-Three

"Play that again. Something doesn't look right."—Amber points at the screen— "There, right there, look at the time. It jumps from 16:03:29 to16:08:29. Where did those five minutes go?"

Patrick leans forward in his seat. "You're right, the three and the eight look so much alike, I didn't catch it the first time. Let's go frame-by-frame and see if anything changes."

After rewinding and replaying the feed several times, they're stumped—nothing changes—no discontinuity between the scenes at the beginning and end of that missing time.

"That's really strange, is it possible it's a glitch in the system?" she asks.

Patrick runs his fingers through his hair, confused. "I don't know. I'm not sure what else could cause this unless someone intentionally cut those minutes out, but why? Nothing seems missing."

"Let's play it further along and see if anything jumps out, proving it's not me." The woman on the screen looks happy, smiling with a spring in her step. "Well, I certainly don't swing my portfolio like that. It's not me—it has to be Brandy," Amber states.

Patrick frowns. "Maybe, but that won't convince a jury. We have to keep looking—there has to be something else." Patrick is in despair, worrying if he'll be able to prove her innocence. *She can't go to prison; it will break her. I have to find something.*

"Okay. I'm drugged, passed out. I'd have to be in the front seat, right? Where else would she put me? I don't think she's strong enough to lift me and put me in the trunk. Plus, someone might see her. It has to be quick."

"If you pass out behind the wheel, that could be what we see before the time jump. During that lost time, she opens the door, pushes you over on the front seat, and covers you with your jacket. She gets behind the wheel in the exact same position you were in when the time restarts."

"We've watched that over and over, nothing is different."

"Let's replay it, and maybe we can get a glimpse of you inside the car. That would be proof."

They watch the car door open and close twice: the first when she came back from the meeting, and then again when she left to retrieve her portfolio. She opened the door just enough to get in and out, her body blocking the interior. It appears intentional, planned out carefully.

"Nothing—I can't see anything." Patrick's hair now sticks up, in several places, from running his fingers continuously through it. He cannot hide his frustration; Amber takes notice.

"It's easy enough to figure out how she got you home and parked in your space. What time did you wake up again?"

"Around six—in a fog, I had no idea what happened. It was like I had been in a deep sleep."

"Does your parking garage have cameras?"

"I think so…I really don't know."

Patrick makes a note to talk to her building security. If there are cameras, he needs to see what's on them when her car arrived. "Did John, your security guy, see you come in?"

"He acknowledged me, but I was dazed. I went straight upstairs, trying hard to make sense of why I couldn't remember. I wanted to take a shower, my mind still spinning. When I undressed and looked in the mirror, that's when it all came back."

Patrick pulls her into his arms. "I'm sorry you have to keep reliving this."

"It's okay. If it keeps me out of jail, I've got to do it."

"Have you been hypnotized before?"

"No, and I've never been accused of murdering someone before either," Amber says, trying to use humor to calm her nerves. "Sorry, this is just all so surreal to me. I feel like I'm living inside a dream."

"I understand. This works better if you are open to the fact that you can be hypnotized," the hypnotist says. "If you have doubts, let's deal with them now—questions?"

"Okay, yes, um, will I remember what I say or do when I'm under?"

"No, you won't. Don't worry, I won't ask you to cluck like a chicken or bark like a dog."

Everybody laughs.

Amber continues, "Okay, just explain the process to me."

"I'm going to get you to relax and take you to a place of complete focus through my voice. Once there, I'll help you go back to the day of the attack asking you questions to help you remember better. Your mind is most likely keeping things tucked away to help protect you. I know today you're only in-terested in what happened to you after you left his office—I can go back earlier to help you work through the actual attack if you like."

She shakes her head, not ready to go there yet. "Let's stick with clearing my name for now. But I may take you up on that at a later date if that's okay."

"Of course. When we're done, you'll feel refreshed, as if you've had a nice long nap. Ready to begin?"

"Yes."

"You can sit or lay down, however you're most com-fortable."

"Sitting."

"Okay. Close your eyes and get comfortable. I want you to squeeze your shoulders, arms, legs, and feet really tight for me—hold it, hold it, hold it, now relax—relax everything. Your shoulders, arms down to your fingers. Focus on these body parts and relax them. Now move down to your legs, knees, feet, then toes—relax them all. Feel your body sink into the couch; imagine the impression your body is making. Now I want you to sink lower, lower as if you are riding down in an elevator. Take a deep breath for me, as deep as you can…now release it. Again, another deep breath sinking farther and farther down. I want you to keep breathing for me finding yourself so relaxed you feel like you're floating, you're floating inside that elevator."

"Are you okay Amber?"

She nods.

"Now, I want you to go to your favorite place in your mind, where you're most happy."

A big smile forms on her face as she imagines being at the beach. She's a kid chasing the waves as they roll up on the shoreline.

"Wherever you are right now, I need you to stay but be there this year. Enjoy this place as you are today."

Amber nods.

"Keeping those happy thoughts, I need you to move to the morning of Tuesday, January sixteenth. You're waking up that morning, turning off your alarm. What are you thinking?"

"After I turn off my alarm, I lay back down excited and yet nervous about my meeting that day. I've never been pre-interviewed before, and if I don't pass muster, I'll miss out on this opportunity."

She takes Amber through her morning, her dressing for her appointment. Once she gets Amber to where her hand is on the door handle to go into his office, she jumps forward. "Amber, you're leaving his office now and closing the door behind you."

Amber's mood immediately changes, her breathing becomes rapid, and beads of sweat form on her forehead.

"It's okay Amber, he can't hurt you now, he's back in his office."

Amber's breathing begins to slow, but she's still very uncomfortable.

"Can you tell me what happened once you left his office?"

"His secretary asks if I want to schedule my interview with him. I should want to, but I can't think. I tell her I'll call her back."

"And how does she appear to you?"

"She pities me? She looks ashamed. Why does she look sorry for me?"

"I don't know Amber, but what happens next?"

"I can't get to the elevator fast enough. I just want out of there. I keep pushing the down button wishing it would get there faster."

"When the doors open, there are people inside. I try to pull myself together and slip in, turning my back to their curious gazes. They know—they know!"

"Amber, they can't possibly know what's happened to you. Take a deep breath for me and just relax. Feel yourself going down with the elevator, away from his office."

"I remember, I forgot my portfolio inside. I don't know if I want to get it or leave it. It's important to me—all my work is in there."

"Do you go back in and get it?"

"No, I have to get out of there...I got a text too."

"A text from who?"

"I don't know. Someone wants to hurt me."

She glances up at Patrick with a questioning look.

He motions her to ignore it.

"When the elevator doors open, I jump out as quickly as I can, I have to get to my car."

"Tell me about your walk to your car."

"Well, first, I go the wrong way. It takes me a couple of steps to realize it. I turn and head for the doors. When I get there, there's a group of people, about six or seven of them coming in at the same time. I push my way through; I can't wait, I have to get out of there."

"One of them says I'm rude. Another says I must be in a real hurry."

"Anything else?"

"One actually smiles at me."

"A woman or a man?"

"Um, I don't know—I can't tell. I think it's a man, but he looks feminine—built more like a woman."

"How close is this person to you?"

"Right next to me. I think I pushed him—her out of the way."

"You're out of the building, past that group, now what?"

"I get to my car. I get in and I grab the steering wheel. I'm sick to my stomach, so I jump out and throw up next to the tire. I go back in, and I want to put the key in the ignition, but I can't move. I will myself to put the key in, but I'm still think-ing about my portfolio. I don't know if I can replace it—I have to go back and get it, but I just can't," Amber says, getting worked up again.

"Deep breath for me—let's take a few nice, deep breaths."

Doing as she's told, Amber starts to relax again.

"Your hands are on the steering wheel, and you're looking straight ahead, do you remember that?"

"I do. I was trying to reason with myself why I had to go back up there. The next thing I remember, I wake up in my car in my parking lot at home—two hours later."

"Can you remember anything else after you left his office, anything no matter how insignificant you might think it is?"

"No, but why did that person smile at me when everyone else thought I was rude?"

"I don't know. Is there anything else? Any tiny little detail?"

She shakes her head.

"I need you to go back to your paradise, the place you feel the safest."

Amber relaxes again with that sweet smile.

"Your toes are starting to tingle as are your fingertips. You're floating up, up now. Your legs and arms are waking up, wanting to stretch and move."

Amber stretches out her legs and arms and lets out a big yawn.

"See the light in your mind getting brighter and brighter. Slowly, very slowly, I want you to open your eyes."

She opens her eyes and yawns again. "Wow, you weren't lying, I do feel like I just had a long nap."

She peers over at Patrick with a questioning look.

He immediately asks, "When you left the building, you went through a group of people, and one of them smiled at you —do you remember that now?" he asks.

"I do. I was in such a rush to get out the door; I just pushed right through them. They were all really bothered by me except for him—her. What a minute…was it a woman or a man?"

"You can't remember. If it was Brandy, she was close enough to inject you. So assuming that's what happened, the drug would have to work quickly. You can remember about ten, maybe fifteen minutes, and then you wake up two hours later."

"So this crazy idea is actually possible? Brandy could have murdered him and set me up?" she asks, hurt and unsure.

"I'm sorry, but yeah, it's starting to appear that way. Remember, all we have to do is raise reasonable doubt. If there's a plausible explanation, you won't go to jail."

"Get off? Reasonable doubt? You won't be able to clear my name?"

Chapter Twenty-Four

After a long grueling day at the studio, Zya pulls up into her driveway to see Micki's car. She lets out a sigh…she does not need another challenge today.

Entering the house, she finds Tina and Micki sitting at the breakfast table, each with a glass of wine. Tina's not stressed at all—she looks calm.

Zya approaches Tina and gives her a full kiss on the mouth, making sure they have an audience. "Hi, honey, sorry I'm so late." Turning now, she briefly glances at Micki. "Officer—didn't expect to see you here."

Tina gets up and pours Zya, a glass of wine. "Here… looks like you need this."

Zya drains the glass in one gulp. Narrowing her eyes at Micki. "What do you want?"

Tina interrupts before Micki can speak, "She's here to discuss this," holding up a legal document.

Zya grabs the paper to see it's a petition from Doug. He's suing for sole-custody of Ashanti, stating Zya is an unfit guardian.

"WHAT THE FUCK!"

Tina pulls out the chair by Zya and motions her to sit down.

"The sheriff who was supposed to serve these knew I was working on Ashanti's case, so he brought them to my desk. I told him I would bring them to you—it might be better coming from me...but then again, maybe not. I've grown to care for your daughter. I'm not going to let this low-life do this to her—or you."

"Zya, you remember Cassandra, my ex, the child services counselor I met when I moved here?"

"Yes," Zya answers, a bit confused.

"She's an attorney now. She got her law degree after seeing how many kids get shuffled through the system. She's also very active with the no-tolerance, no-bully program."

It takes Zya a few seconds, remembering Tina's description of her ex before she connects the dots. "I've never met her, but you're right, I bet she would be a big help."

Tina dials her right away. "Cassie, hey girl, I know it's late, but I was hoping you might be able to help me out. My girlfriend needs a bad-ass attorney. Her ex is trying to take their daughter away from her. You may know her daughter—Ashanti?"

"Hi Tina, I'm great, thanks for asking—wait, Ashanti Monroe, the girl who's been all over the talk circuit about being bullied?"

"The one and only...interested?"

"Yes, of course I am! I'm heading out for the night. I can make an appointment to see them in the morning."

"Forgive me; I was kind of hoping you were available right now. Can you come over here tonight? I'm sorry, I wouldn't ask if it wasn't really important."

"Well, I was meeting a gorgeous woman for drinks tonight—or at least I think she's gorgeous; I haven't met her yet." Looking for an excuse anyway, she hates blind dates, she concedes. "Okay, send me the address…I'm on my way."

Within ten minutes, the doorbell rings. "Cassie!" Tina hugs her and motions her inside. Tina introduces her to Zya and Micki, who holds her hand a little too long…bingo!

Micki can't take her eyes off the gorgeous Asian woman in front of her. Her hair is long and thick in big black waves. It's so black—it shimmers blue. Her hands are soft and feminine, yet her firm handshake shows she's no pushover. She returns the smile to Micki with a sparkle in her eyes.

"Cassie, Officer Sanderson is Ashanti's police contact. Together, they've been working on the no-tolerance, no-bullying program here in Broward County."

"Is that right?" Cassandra replies, not taking her eyes off Micki.

Tina and Zya exchange looks.

Interrupting their gaze, Tina says, "Cassie, Zya's ex-husband, is suing for full custody of Ashanti. He doesn't approve of Zya's lifestyle, so he's claiming she's an unfit mother."

Cassandra chuckles. "Let me guess—big ego, right?"

"The biggest! Doug proposed to me last year, and I turned him down. We've been on-again, off-again the past seventeen years. I guess it took me that long to realize I'm better off without him. He didn't take it very well."

Ashanti and Stacey walk in the front door laughing between themselves. They stop as they see the four women staring at them.

Looking around, then at each other, seeming guilty, Ashanti asks, "What? What did we do?"

"Someone's a bit paranoid…," Zya teases.

Cassandra walks towards her, extending her hand. "Hi, I'm Cassie, you must be Ashanti."

"Hi," she replies. As she's shaking Cassie's hand, she introduces her. "This is Stacey, my best friend."

"Hi, Stacey."

Motioning the kids, Zya says, "Come sit down, honey, I need to talk to you."

"Uh oh—someone's in trouble," Stacey sing-songs.

Ashanti catches a glance at the paperwork on the table. Seeing her mother's and father's names on the first page, she picks it up.

Zya thinks about taking it away but decides to let her read it.

"Mom, what's this?"

"Your dad doesn't approve of Tina and I being in a relationship. He wants full custody of you. He wants you to live up in New York with him full time."

"What about what I want? I mean, I loved visiting, but I don't want to live there. Don't I have a say in this?"

"I'm sure your dad will want to hear what you want, but just in case, Cassandra here is an attorney. She's also very active with the bully program here in the county."

"He won't win, will he?"

"I don't have all the information, but honestly I don't see how he can, he's just trying to stir up some trouble. I think his feelings are hurt."

"His feelings?"

Tina responds, "Your dad came onto me in New York. I turned him down. After your mother turned down his proposal, and then I turned him down..."

"I get it. I probably didn't help matters telling him how much fun I was having there. He kept pressing me about visiting—maybe I should have known better."

"Baby, it's not your fault," Zya says as she hugs her. "You have nothing to be sorry about. He's your father, of course, you want to get to know him better."

Ashanti gets up from the table. "I'm not moving to New York. I don't want to live there."

"You're not going anywhere—I promise."

Cassandra picks up the petition and puts it inside her briefcase. "I'm going to head out and do a little research tonight. Ashanti, it's been a pleasure meeting you. I'm very proud of everything you're doing to help stop bullying. You've been very brave. I'd be honored to help you with this."

Ashanti and Stacey head upstairs.

"Before you leave Cassie, can I talk to you for a moment?" Zya motions her aside.

"Doug works for one of the powerful drug lords in Manhattan. I've got a video with some incriminating evidence on it...just in case, you know. I plan to put it in a safety deposit box for safekeeping. I don't trust Doug or his boss. I don't want anything to happen to Tina, or me...it will be my bargaining chip."

"You probably won't need any of that. However, if he tries to be tough-guy, it will help if he knows you have it. If he works for who I think he does, protect yourself."

Zya hugs Cassie before she walks her to the door. "Thanks, I really appreciate all your help."

Cassandra turns with her hand on the doorknob and says, "Okay, let me get out of here and see what I can dig up. Oh and Tina,"—thumbs up—"you did good girl, real good."

Micki comes forward, "I'm on my way out too. I'll walk you to your car."

Another sideways glance occurs between Zya and Tina.

Micki stops and turns around before she leaves. "Oh, I almost forgot to tell you, Roberto was returned to Italy this morning; however, there was an assassination attempt en route from the airport to the jail...he escaped."

"Someone tried to kill him?" Tina and Zya both ask in unison.

Chapter Twenty-Five

"Thanks for coming over, you guys. It's been too long since we've had any female bonding time."

"Way too long," Zya says as she fills a wine glass and hands it to Dominque.

Debra grabs the glass as it's passed, "I'll take that one —it's been way too long since I've had wine too!"

Zya asks, "Deb, are you sure it's okay? Aren't you breastfeeding?"

"I am, and I have enough milk pumped to last twenty-four hours. I figure I'm good for two glasses."

Dominque is surprised Debra is allowed to have alcohol.

"It takes twenty-four hours for alcohol to leave your milk?"

"Only about five to six, but you know how paranoid I am."

The girls laugh.

"Is Amber coming? I'm sure she could use some bonding time too."

"She is, but I'm glad she's not here just yet. I want to run something by you before she gets here. I love you all—we're all sisters—"

Zya interrupts, "You want to ask Amber to be your Maid of Honor…and you should!"

She wasn't expecting that reply. "Um—I do want to ask her, but I don't want to hurt your feelings."

Debra puts her arm around her shoulders. "Our feelings are not hurt—we're surprised you haven't asked her yet."

Dom takes a long drink from the glass presented to her. "Phew, that went better than expected. You both will be bridesmaids, won't you?"

"Only if you don't make us wear hideous dresses," Debra responds.

Dominque and Debra both turn toward Zya.

"I know that look…you want me to find our bridesmaid dresses, right?"

Both girls shake their heads.

"You want me to design our dresses?"

Now they nod.

"You don't need to design anything new. Your new collection has some drop-dead gorgeous evening wear. Since my wedding is going to be in the summer, anything from your resort collection will be perfect. Maybe we could get a discount too?"

Zya laughs. "Family discount, right?"

"But of course," Dominque replies.

Amber enters after a light tap on the front door. After hugs all around, she grabs a wine glass and fills it to the rim.

"I've been looking forward to tonight. Dom, thank you so much for organizing this. I feel like my life has been completely turned upside down. Being here with you all brings me some clarity."

"Amber, I'm so glad you're finally here, I have something I need to ask you." She takes Amber's hand and walks her to the couch.

"Should I be scared?"

"I hope not...will you be my Maid of Honor?"

"Me? Oh my gosh, of course, I'd be honored." Amber hugs her. "What does that entail?" Maybe she agreed too quickly.

"Not too much, Tad, and I don't want a big wedding. We just want our family with us. I want to wait until my treatments are over in June, but Tad wants to marry sooner. He's having a hard time with us living together; he hasn't told his parents yet. He was hoping he can tell them about the engagement, and getting married, at the same time. I hated to play the cancer card, but I can't imagine walking the aisle right now. This last treatment really kicked my butt. I have zero energy, and I still have at least one more."

"You have been a trooper. I don't know how you do it. You're past the hump, at least, on the downside of this mountain."

"Yes, and trust me, I count the days when this stage will be in the past. It's a residual effect...the next treatment will be worse. I'm hoping I won't need a fifth or sixth. They are trying to keep me from needing my lifetime limit."

"Lifetime limit?" Amber asks.

"Cytoxan is the chemo of choice for a lot of different cancers so, they'd like to keep that option should I need more in the future. I know you shouldn't get on the internet, but I couldn't help myself. The very drugs that save you can also give you cancer. Weighing it out, saving your life now is more important than the ramifications."

"Wow, I had no idea," Zya says, intrigued.

"It can also cause heart issues. One woman's heart was damaged from Cytoxan, for breast cancer, and it wasn't detected until she was diagnosed eleven years later with leukemia. She had the gene...jury is still out if Cytoxan activated it or if it did on its own. Anyway, Cytoxan was her best shot at beating leukemia, but they couldn't give her the balance of her lifetime limit because of the heart damage. Very sad...she was in her forties."

"That's horrible...they're checking your heart, right?"

"Yes, they've detected a murmur, but they aren't worried. It should go away on its own. But, we'll keep checking it just to be sure."

Debra goes to refill Dominque's glass with a questioning look.

Dominque nods. "Just half."

"I wish you had told us this sooner," Amber says.

"There's just been so much going on, and I pretty much sleep most of the day. Tad has been so wonderful. Chasing me around the house with food making me take a bite of something every ten minutes. He's even doing laundry...all of my whites are now pink, but I'm not complaining."

The room fills with laughter, imaging pale pink bras, and panties.

"We understand...please let us know what's going on— good and bad?" Zya asks.

Dominque nods.

Zya glances at Amber...her mouth is smiling, but her eyes are blank. "Amber, how are you holding up? And before you answer with, 'I'm doing great,' how are you, really?" Zya asks.

Amber replies, "As well as can be expected, I guess. Patrick has been a saint. I don't know why I have been giving that man such a hard time these past few months. He's proving himself to be more than I ever wanted—more than I ever thought I deserved."

"Any news on the investigation?" Debra asks.

"Nothing concrete, but it's all pointing back to Brandy as being the killer."

Amber brings the girls up to speed with the hypnosis and Patrick's thoughts.

Dominque asks, "You mentioned the secretary seemed uncomfortable. You don't think she had something to do with this, do you?"

"I don't know, she could be a victim herself. Patrick wants to hold a news conference tomorrow. In case there are any more of Brettinger's victims out there, we're hoping they come forward, it may help with my case."

Debra questions, "I'm sorry, I'm confused, how could other victims help your case? I get it if he raped or abused other girls that will help corroborate your story, but he was murdered—how does that help clear you?"

"It doesn't...Patrick wants to make sure we have reasonable doubt."

"You're not going to plead insanity, are you?" Zya asks.

"NO! I'm not insane—I didn't kill him!"

"I'm not trying to upset you, I'm sorry—I'm just not following this. How does proving he's a scum bag, help prove your innocence?"

Debra says, "Maybe establishing him as a creep will help gain sympathy with the jury?"

"But you didn't do it—you don't need sympathy, you need the truth," Zya adds.

"We're still looking for concrete evidence. We need to establish doubt at this point. It's already been in the news, I've accused him of rape, so that gives me motive. The defense is going to be all over that."

"So, you're going to accuse Brandy, your twin sister, to raise doubt?"

"I know—it sucks. We have no proof, but it's the only thing that makes sense. If we can prove I was drugged, there is no other explanation."

Debra says, "Sorry, this is all just so surreal. We can't believe you're going through all this. What can we do to help?"

"Just keep filling me up," she says as she drains the last bit from her glass.

"Your wish is my command," Debra says as she empties the bottle into Amber's glass.

Zya squeezes Amber's hand. "I'm sorry, it just gets me so mad how a total scum bag can be called a victim, and a great, honest person like yourself is already found guilty. This world is fucked up!"

"I know, and I thank you all for being here for me. It has been one horrible nightmare. Your strength and support are what's going to get me through it all. Knowing you've got my back, gives me hope."

Looking over at Dominque, she grabs her hand. "I'm sorry I haven't been here for you. If you want to ask someone else, my feelings won't get hurt."

Zya answers for her, "No, she will not! We've got your back, girl. You don't worry about a thing…and as far as titles, we're all her maids of honor, bridesmaids, whatever you want to call us, more importantly, we're sisters and family supports each other, no matter what."

Amber's eyes tear up. "I love you all so much. Thank you for your support and love. It gives me strength."

The girls come together in a group hug.

Zya grabs the tissue box and passes it around as each grabs one and wipes their eyes.

"I know it's personal, but have you and Patrick had sex?" Zya asks.

The waterworks threaten to fall again as she relives the abuse and violations to her body. It's her mind's instant reaction now when she thinks about sex. "No, he hasn't even tried. He's been so amazing and patient."

"Do you want to talk about it?" Zya asks.

"Will I ever feel like I can…I don't know? Right now, it's still too fresh. I don't want to give HIM that power over me to take away my happiness, but I'm not sure when, or if, I'll ever get him out of my head. I can still feel his hands on me," she says with a shiver.

"Patrick feels so helpless. He's doing so much, but in his eyes, it's not enough. If he wasn't dead already, Patrick would kill him with his bare hands. The anger I see on his face when he thinks about HIM, and what he did to me."

"You two deserve each other—you are perfect together. I'm just sorry it took something this horrible for you two to figure it out finally. It's cheesy, I know, but you complete each other," Dominque says.

"Guess we are all feeling a little helpless lately. Our sisters are hurting, and there's nothing we can do," Zya adds.

Dominque experiences one of the many hot flashes she's plagued with now as a side effect of her treatments. Without thinking, she removes her scarf.

She looks so healthy—almost aglow—with her makeup carefully applied, and her colorful scarf tied fashionably on her head. Seeing her bare skull with a few wisps of hair is alarming. The girls can't hide their expressions.

Reading the alarm in the room, Dominque puts her scarf back on and proceeds to tie it up.

Amber stops her. "No, leave it, it must be hot wearing that thing. A pact...you don't have to cover your head..."

"...or paint on your eyebrows," Debra adds.

"I don't think we were prepared. Let me see?" Amber asks as she proceeds to remove the scarf.

"I'm sorry, I'm so used to seeing myself I didn't think about how I must appear to you. These damn hot flashes..." she fans herself as the beads of sweat begin to dry from her lip.

Zya gently grasps Dominque's face. "You are beautiful. I agree, be comfortable around us—no facade, okay?"

The girls, from both sides and behind, hug Dominque.

"I guess I'm in charge of the liquid portion tonight," says Zya as she retreats to the kitchen and opens a new bottle of wine. She reenters the living room with the bottle ready for refills. "Can we talk about a wedding now?"

"Yes, but first," Dominque interjects, "I'd like to find out how Little George is doing?"

Debra jumps from the couch and runs to get her phone from her purse. "Wait till you see the pictures I took today."

They all groan.

Debra, looking at Amber says, "You be careful there Missy, you're his godmother…you better want to see pictures."

Amber scoots over so Debra can sit next to her. "You know we're teasing you; come sit here. Of course, we want to see my godson—our little nephew."

The girls pass the phone around, oohing and aahing.

"Is he sleeping through the night yet?"

"Almost—It's funny, I want him to sleep through the night, but I really enjoy waking up when the house is quiet to spend time alone with him. Tracey is so in love with him. She wants to be with him every moment he's awake. That's not selfish of me, is it?"

"Not at all," Amber answers. "How's it going with Brian?"

Debra's eyes glaze over, and she smiles.

"Before you answer that, I have a bone to pick with you," Zya says to Debra half-teasing. "Ashanti told me about you helping her when she was hurt at school."

Debra's face goes pale.

Stepping over to her, Zya puts her arm around her.

"Don't worry, I'm not mad. I was at the time, but it was more about the whole ordeal. I didn't want to bring this up while you were on bed rest, you were stressed enough. And that gave me time to think. As much as I would prefer my daughter come to me when she needs help, if she can't, for whatever the reason, I'm glad she's comfortable enough to ask you,"—motioning to all three of them— "to be there for her."

Zya turns towards Debra and says, "You made a promise to her you wouldn't tell me, and you didn't break it. You've proven to her you're a safe haven, and for that, I'm grateful—mostly grateful."

"I'm sorry, she put me in a very tough spot. She did make a valid point though about you moving back home," Debra says.

"I know. It would have been easy for me to just up and move. But then again, what if it happened again back home? We can't run away; we have to stay and fight. It breaks my heart to think about what she went through...I'm glad we didn't run, and I'm glad you helped her."

Zya hugs Debra smiling at her. "Now answer the damn question about Brian, we're all dying to hear the answer."

Debra says after laughing, "He's amazing and so patient and great with Little George. He's doesn't want to intrude, so he's giving me all the space I need—and then some. When I think back on the love triangle between him and Roberto, I shudder. I can only imagine what people must think of me."

"The only people that matter are the ones in this room, and in your home. The world can go to hell for all I care. Girl, no one has walked in your shoes—no one, but you can imagine what life was like for you when George passed. What's truly important is your happiness...are you happy?" Zya asks.

"I'm trying...I see George in his son, especially when he smiles. It makes me sad he's not here with us, but in some way, I feel like he is. He has George's eyes too. And before you say anything, yes, I know they could change color, but for now, he has George's eyes."

They chuckle.

Amber looks over at Zya. "Anything new on the home front?"

"Nothing really…just fighting with Doug for full custody of Ashanti because he thinks I'm an unfit mother—I'm a bad influence."

In unison, they say, "WHAT?"

"It's been resolved. And, I think we've distracted *Officer Home Wrecker* in the process."

"Do tell," Dominque asks.

Zya rehashes their meeting the night before with Cassandra. As she finishes filling them in, she looks at Debra, "Deb, Roberto had an assassination attempt on his life in Italy —he got away."

Debra spits out the wine she was drinking, spilling it all over the front of her onto the cocktail table. "Someone tried to kill him? And he got away?"

"Seems he's been running from the Italian mob. He must owe them money or something."

Amber looks over at Debra. "That's horrible, but it's starting to make some sense."

"I'm glad it is to you," says Debra.

"Think about it. He was in such a hurry to get married—even forceful. You said he was never that way before. It would make sense if he were desperate. You didn't miss anything; you were his way out. If you married him, he wouldn't have to go back home."

Zya interjects, "But wouldn't they have come here to find him?"

"Probably."

"Amber, thank God you were there that day, and you had your gun. What if I would have married him? We would have been in danger, and he would have put all of our lives in the crosshairs." Debra shudders.

"Thank God is right. Wow, I did not see that coming," Amber says, stunned.

"I don't think any of us could!" Zya says.

Zya catches Dominque stifle a yawn just as she begins to refill the glasses.

"You know, girls, I do have to get up early and get back into the studio. Dom, I'm sure you're exhausted too. It's been an eventful night. A fly on the wall would think we're actresses in a soap opera."

Focusing now on Dominque, she's not sure how she missed her tired, hollowed eyes. Amber jumps up to grab the glasses and help clean up the kitchen.

"I'll get it, don't worry about it. I'll take care of them," Dominque says.

"No can do—see I already got the soap out," Amber says as she washes the glasses.

Everybody takes part in wiping the counters, the wine from the cocktail table, and re-corks the bottle. Within ten minutes, the place is spotless.

"Since we didn't get a chance to discuss wedding plans, can we do this again in the next few days? You up for it?"

"Yeah, that would be great."

Debra says, "This time, my place."

"Right, like we'll get anything done with that handsome young man over there," Zya says.

Chapter Twenty-Six

"You ready for this?"

"As ready as I'll ever be," responds Amber.

"I want you there by my side, but remember, don't answer any questions, okay?"

She nods.

"Ladies and Gentlemen of the press, thank you so much for coming today. We are currently following up on several leads to help exonerate Miss Fiore in the murder of Mr. Paul Brettinger. I've asked you here today concerning the assault the late Mr. Brettinger inflicted upon my client on the day of his murder and the criminal case we are bringing against his estate. It has come to our attention, Mr. Brettinger had the reputation of demanding sexual favors and quite possibly assaulting other women. All the facts must come to light before we go to trial so that we can prepare properly. We ask you to put this request out if any women have had this experience with the accused to please call 1-800-555-2954. They may remain anonymous if they wish."

"Is Miss Fiore pleading insanity?" shouts a reporter.

"Isn't it true, you have security footage proving Miss Fiore is guilty?" yells another.

"Mr. Simpson, what's your relationship with Miss Fiore?" a reporter in the front row asks.

"Did Miss Fiore know he was interviewing her before she would be able to interview him?" the first reporter shouts.

"Miss Fiore, are you trying to tarnish Mr. Brettinger's reputation to save your own skin?" shouted from yet a different journalist.

"Miss Fiore is not answering questions today." Patrick clears his throat and grips the podium.

"Then why bring her here? To put out a sympathetic face for potential jurors? You don't have anything, do you?"

"Thank you all for coming, that's all for today," Patrick says as calmly as he can. He's so angry at the accusations; mad he didn't think the press would have her convicted already. Mr. Brettinger was a society icon, a generous philanthropist, and well-liked in the community. The monster inside was well hidden.

Patrick gets Amber settled in the car. "I'm so sorry, I should have prepared you better for that."

Amber is visibly shaking. "How could you have known? I knew this wasn't going to be easy."

"I'm going to get you through this, I promise. You're not going to jail. We're going to figure this out."

☯

"Mr. Simpson, you have a few messages on your desk. They're about the press conference you had earlier," Patrick's legal assistant notifies him as he walks in.

He's expecting the messages to be complaints from Brettinger's fan club, and the first two don't disappoint. It's the third one that catches his attention.

After several rings, she answers. "Hello."

"Hi, can I please speak to Rachael Moorings?"

"This is she. Are you the attorney I saw on TV today?"

"I am. I'm so sorry for not being here to take your call earlier."

After a long pause, she takes a deep breath then dives right in. "When it happened to me, I thought it was just a one-time thing, or maybe I just convinced myself of that. I needed the job, so I didn't report it, but then he kept after me like I was some quest. I tried to stay away from him, but he made sure we interacted daily. I had to accompany him to a meeting one day. I was so nervous but agreed, knowing a few other people would be with us. Once we got in the car and started to pull away, I asked about the others. He told me they had to stay behind. With mischievous eyes, he said, 'Don't worry, I'm not going to bite you.'

"Well, he did keep his word, he didn't bite me, but he sure did everything else. We went to the meeting as planned and stupid me, I let my guard down on the way back to the office. He said he had to make a pit stop at his house.

"He pulled into the garage and closed the door behind us. He wanted to show me something inside. I knew what he would he do if I went in, so I said I'd wait in the car. He opened my door, grabbed my hand, trying to get me out, but I stood my ground. Next thing I know, he pushed me down on the front seat so hard, I hit my head on the steering wheel. I saw stars for a few minutes or exactly as much time as he needed to pull my skirt up, rip my panties off, and get inside me. He had my hands up over my head...he was so strong. I was no match for him. I screamed, but he wouldn't stop. It seemed like an eternity; I kept praying for him to finish.

"When he was done, he said, 'See, that wasn't so bad now, was it? You've been playing hard to get. You won't do that anymore now, will you?' He was so proud of himself.

"I went to HR the next morning and asked for a transfer immediately to the Boca location. I said I was moving and couldn't drive the forty-five minutes each way. I was good at my job—an asset, so they exchanged me with another analyst in that office. I had to get away from him. I never wanted to see his disgusting face again!

"I had the TV on while getting dinner ready when I heard his name. Every time I hear it or see his beady eyes in the newspaper, I turn the channel or walk away. I couldn't do either today...Miss Fiore...Amber..."—she says sniffling— "I'm so sorry I didn't report it. Maybe if I had, he would have been stopped, and she wouldn't have gone through that. I was so scared."

"Rachael? Can I call you Rachael?"

"Yes."

"I'm so sorry that Paul Brettinger hurt you, and it's okay to be scared. I understand why you didn't say anything before...are you ready to say something now?"

"I am. I know he's dead, and he can't hurt anyone anymore, but I have to do what I can for Amber. I don't want to see her go to prison. He deserved to die, you know. That bastard got what was coming to him."

Patrick couldn't agree more.

☙

"Miss Dunham, thanks for coming in today."

"I didn't have a choice now, did I?"

"Can you please state your name for the record, your employer, and position."

"Maryann Dunham, I work for Brettinger Holdings. I've been—was Mr. Brettinger's personal secretary for the past eight years."

"Miss Dunham, do you know why you're here today?"

"Yes, I do, and frankly, I'm disgusted at the accusations. Mr. Brettinger has always taken great care of me and his other employees. He's been like a father figure to us—and now he's gone. I don't know what I'm going to do."

"Surely, Miss Dunham, with your record, you'll find another position within the company."

"That's not it—that's not what I mean…oh, never mind."

"Did you have a special arrangement with Mr. Brettinger?"

"No, no, no! He's my boss. He's just been, my boss."

Patrick realizes there's more to the story, but needs a different tactic. "Miss Dunham, do you remember seeing Miss Fiore on the day in question?"

Maryann slumps a bit in the chair. "I do, I remember her."

"Why was she there that day?"

"Mr. Brettinger wanted to meet her before he would grant her an interview."

"Mr. Brettinger was used to getting his way, wasn't he?"

"He was a very busy man. He had to be firm and direct."

"Miss Dunham, did Mr. Brettinger ever get short or mad at you?"

"Of course he did, I worked for him. I always tried to do better, but I wasn't perfect."

"And you worked for him for eight years. You must have been a great employee for him to keep you around for so long."

She begins squirming in her seat, nervous about where this line of questioning could end up. "I knew his schedule and what he wanted—or needed better than anyone."

"Back to Miss Fiore if I may, how did she seem when she arrived that day?"

"A bit nervous. I've read some of her articles—she's really good. She's pretty too."

"Was that important to Mr. Brettinger, her looks?"

"Not really. He admired her work."

"Was he pleased when he saw her?"

"I guess so. I didn't see."

"About how long was Miss Fiore in his office?"

"Fifteen, no sixteen minutes...."

"Exactly?"

"Yes, no more than sixteen minutes."

"How do you know that? Did you time her?"

"No, I went on break. Mr. Brettinger told me to go when she got there."

"Was that your normal break time?"

"I took my breaks whenever he asked me to."

"Miss Dunham, this is very important, did Mr. Brettinger ask you to go on breaks when he had female guests in his office?"

"I don't know—maybe."

Feeling the need to ease some of the tension, Patrick says, "Miss Dunham, you're not in trouble here, I understand you were close to your boss—this is hard for you. Do you have family here? Miss Fiore remembers seeing a picture of a young boy on your desk…your son?"

Her eyes get huge. "He has nothing to do with this. Keep him out of this—he's innocent."

"Of course, I apologize. Are your parents around, do they help you?"

"What does this have to do with Amber Fiore killing my boss?"

"It doesn't. I was just asking if you had any support to help you during this difficult time."

"Is that all then? Am I done? Can I go?"

"Yes, Miss Dunham, you can go. Thank you for coming in."

As he watches her leave, he knows there's much more to that story.

Chapter Twenty-Seven

"How are you feeling?"

"Scared shitless!"

"I bet. You have nothing to worry about. You're going to sail right through surgery and be back to your old self before you know it."

"I hope you're right. I'd be much better if they just tell me what to expect—no surprises. Everyone keeps saying, 'It's going to be fine, you'll be just fine.' I'm expecting the worst, hoping for the best. Wait, did you call me old?"

Tad chuckles as pulls her into his arms. "Glad to know you're paying attention."—he kisses her—"I get it. You're having major surgery tomorrow, I don't think it's going to be a walk in the park, but you'll be just fine."

"Thanks, I love you. I promise I'm going to listen to the doctors. I won't try to do too much too soon. They told me I'm probably coming home with drains, that should be fun."

"I've been doing some research on those. I'll take care of charting and emptying for you…your bandages too. You can call me Mr. Drano."

Dominque laughs. He's such a goofball, one of the many reasons she said yes.

"Hey, I know we don't want to think about it, but if something happens tomorrow and I don't make it out of surgery…"

"Bite your tongue! You're going to be just fine."

"I know, but something could happen. I just want you to be happy, please. Find someone to share your life with. Love someone the way you love me."

"I'll never love anyone like I do you." His eyes mist at the very thought. "I'm not losing you; you're going to be fine. When you open your eyes, Mine will be the first face you see."

They kiss each other fiercely—the idea that tonight could be their last, ignites an instant fire in need of extinguishing.

While their recent encounters have been gentle and slow, tonight is ferocious and urgent.

☯

Amber arrives at the hospital before Tad and Dominque. Focusing on Dom has given her some relief from her upcoming trial and reliving that day in January.

The wedding has been a minor distraction; however, now, as it's less than two months away, she'll need to pay more attention to the details. Dominque has planned it all perfectly. The doctors asked her to give herself six to eight weeks to recover fully, including radiation, so the wedding date is exactly seven weeks and five days away.

Tad and Dominque enter the hospital lobby, pulling Amber out of her thoughts with dark circles under their eyes and silly grins, requiring no explanation.

"Hey guys, great night last night?"

They gaze at each other and then hug as they chuckle.

Tad goes to the information desk and signs her in while the girls find seats.

"So, how are you doing this morning?"

"Nervous…I just want this behind me. I need to be on the other side. Then, I just have radiation."

"And then your wedding…"

A wide smile appears on her face. "I know, I can't wait to spend the rest of my life with him. By the way, I ordered the invitations yesterday; they'll be here in a few days. I figured it's something I can do while I'm recuperating. Anything else new about the wedding?"

"Really, I was just trying to get your mind into a happy place, you want to talk details now? Just before surgery?"

"I do, it takes my mind off the fact I'm about to be sliced open."

"Okay, well, Zya finished the sketches for our dresses last night…you are going to love them. They'll be ready for alterations two weeks before your big day. Do you want to have a bachelorette party?"

"No, not in the traditional sense. I'd love to get the girls together and party in my honeymoon suite the night before, kinda like a slumber party. I want to spend that night with my family."

Amber hugs her shoulders. "You got it. You've amazed me at how well you've handled all this. I don't know if I could be as together as you are—and you're planning your wedding!"

"Who are you kidding? Compared to what you're going through, I've got nothing on you, girl. You're the amazing one."

Tad comes back. "Dom, we need to get you checked in, window three is waiting for us. Amber, you can come if you want."

"I have an overseas call I need to make. I'm going to step outside, come get me before you go up?"

"Sure."

Amber steps outside just as her phone dings. *Who texts at six o'clock in the morning?*

"I knew you'd be by your friend's side this morning...It would have been so easy to take you, but I'm dying to see Dominque in her wedding dress and you on trial. I have no doubt your loverboy will get you off. Then...you'll be the one dying."

Amber throws her phone down, smashing it on the ground. She breaks down sobbing, falling to her knees.

Tad comes out to get her and finds her staring at the ground, hands clutched between her thighs, rocking back and forth on the ground.

"Amber, what's going on? What's wrong?"

Hearing her name, she turns her head toward him.

He sees her pained expression and asks again, "What happened?"

Tad helps her up from the ground.

She grabs a tissue from her purse, wiping her eyes and blowing her nose. "Another text, this fucking early in the morning. And on the day I need to keep my shit together for Dominque." Her eyes are threatening to drain again.

She puts her hands out in front of her firmly. "That's enough—I'll be damned if I'm going to let this person have this control over me. Enough! I'm here for Dom…and you."

Grabbing her hand, Tad says, "Are you sure? I can make up an excuse for you. We're heading up to the fourth floor. They still need to get her settled, so we'll be there for a little while. Her surgery is at eight."

"Thanks, tell her I'm on a call." Amber looks down at her phone, now in pieces on the ground. "I'll come up with something about that too."

Tad squeezes her hand again then goes inside to Dominque, who's waiting by the elevators.

Amber wipes her eyes then picks up her phone. After removing the SIM card, she tosses it in the trash. *Maybe it's time to get a new phone number.*

☯

"Hi, beautiful."

Tad's handsome face is the first thing she sees when she wakes up. She's groggy and sleepy, so her eyes stay open for only a few seconds.

Tad kisses her on the cheek. "Told you I'd be here when you wake up."

Amber leans over her. "Everything went great. Your sentinel node test came back negative, no cancer in your lymph nodes."

Tad adds, "They got clear margins, they got it all."

Dominque smiles, music to her ears as she drifts back off to sleep.

She awakens several times, briefly in recovery, and sees Tad right beside her bed, with a spoon full of ice chips.

When she's mostly awake and able to get up, they get her dressed in her button-down pajama top and sweat pants. They are moved to a waiting area until most of the drugs wear off. As soon as she sits, she yells for a bedpan. It's barely in her hands when everything she ate before midnight last night comes up. Mostly dry heaves, each one sends a thunderbolt of pain throughout her body.

A nurse rushes over, giving her a shot in the IV still in her arm to stop her body's reaction to the anesthesia.

Once the new drug has taken effect, and Dominque is comfortable, the nurse comes over to empty her drain. It's the first glimpse of her temporary attachment and the reddish liquid inside. "That's a lot of fluid; Is that normal?"

"Actually, it is. Better in the drain than inside you. It helps keep the swelling and fluid retention down. Your husband has been tending them…he's a pro."

Tad mouths, "Mr. Drano."

"Would you like to use the restroom before you head home?"

She nods. Once she's up on her feet, she shuffles to the door just twenty feet away, not realizing she had to go until the nurse mentioned it. Now she can't get there fast enough.

The nurse assists Dominque to the toilet. "I'll step outside. Do not get up without my help. Let me know."

Once the door closes, her bladder empties what seems like gallons.

The nurse taps on the door. "You okay?"

"Yeah, the river won't stop flowing."

"That's normal, we've given you lots of fluids."

Tad comes over once she returns. "Time to empty your drains," he says, way too cheery.

She watches as he dutifully drains the liquid and notes how much he's removing in a small notebook. "We track it, so we'll know when it's time to remove them," he says.

"Any idea when that will be?"

The nurse answers, "You'll be back to see Dr. Harris in a few days, hopefully then."

"Oh, that would be great. Can I ask another question?"

The nurse nods.

"Did they put in another implant during surgery?"

"Yes, they did. They needed to remove the old one to get to the tissue but they were able to replace it with a new one. It may not be exactly like the other side, but remember, you can have it fixed so they are perfect, whenever you like. Your insurance will pay for it."

The nurse goes over her release papers and home care instructions. "The bandages will fall off on their own. No showers until they come off, okay? Sponge bath only."

Tad's eyes light up. "Oh, that will be fun."

The nurse adds, "And no sex...not yet."

Tad blushes. "I know that. I just thought it would be fun to..." He stops himself once a naked image of Dominque enters his mind. "The square root of one sixty-nine is thirteen...," he says as he leaves to get the car.

Chapter Twenty-Eight

"Are you coming with me to see Dominque tomorrow?"

"Do you think she wants me there? I know some people are funny about having company after surgery."

"She would love to see you. Amber just called me and told me the good news."

"Good news?"

Debra fills him in with the results of the surgery. She beams as she explains everything. She couldn't ask him to watch the kids while she went to the hospital today, although he probably would have said yes, she just couldn't put that pressure on him. Besides, Megan is available tomorrow so they can go together.

Debra leaves Brian playing with Little George in the living room and heads to the laundry room to tackle the mountains that reside there. She looks at the washing machine and smirks, remembering their encounters to help her relieve some sexual tension last year, her pregnancy putting her desire in overdrive. "I'll see you later." She points to the relic with a spit-up stained onesie lying across the top of it. She grimaces as she gets a whiff. "That will definitely kill the mood."

Her mind wanders as she begins sorting through the baskets, trying to make sure she has the necessities done first. Brian's voice in the background brings her back to the present. She tiptoes to the doorway to eavesdrop.

"Hey, big fella, I want you to know, your Uncle Brian is here for you, for your mom and sister too. I'm sorry you never got to meet your dad. He was an incredible man, and he loved your mommy very, very much. He was funny—oh, how he made us laugh sometimes. You see, we used to play racquetball together, and I swear he'd tell us the lamest jokes just so we would miss the ball. We didn't mind because he had us in stitches. I hope you have his humor.

"He was kind...your dad was so very kind. He went out of his way to help people. He would give the shirt off his back to anyone who needed it, friends, co-workers, complete strangers. He was very generous, willing to give his time, money—whatever was needed...he was always the first in line to help.

"Most of all, he was loving. Your mom and dad had the romance of a lifetime...the kind novels are written about. Too good to be true, yet so true to be anything but genuine.

"Your mom may just be the love of my life as well. It's not hard—she's amazing. I may never get the chance to love your mom as your dad did, but I will love her with all my heart. I will never replace your dad, no one ever can, but I'll be that role model for you if you want. I promise you, I will always be here for you."

She begins to weep as she listens in on their private conversation. Part of her wants to run into his arms and tell him she wants him too. The other part—the sensible one she was missing before—keeps her feet planted. She still needs time to heal…to grieve. She wipes her eyes and smiles. *Brian, I love you. We will be together one day—not today, but one day.*

She turns to go about her monstrous chore and then remembers…"Brian, I forgot to tell you, someone tried to kill Roberto."

"Here, in the States?"

"No, as soon as he got back to Italy. Zya told me he got away. He never made it to the police station."

"That's weird and scary, both at the same time. I guess he had a reason to stay here. Maybe he was using you as an excuse."

"That's what the girls think, you think so too?"

"I know he cared about you, but I guess that's why he was so forceful? He was so desperate knowing he would be a dead man if he went back."

"You don't think he'll come back here to the States, do you?"

"How can he? If he tries, they'll arrest him."

"So getting a fake passport…that only happens in the movies?"

"Hmmm, I don't know. I guess it's possible, but don't you think there are other places he could go that are a lot closer?"

"Yeah, I guess. I'm just glad he's out of our lives."

Playfully she sashays over to him. "You're not in any trouble with anyone now, are you?"

Brian gulps as his temperature instantly jumps. He crosses his legs, pulling the baby blanket down and across his lap.

Debra's cheeks flush red as she realizes the effect she has on him—totally not planned. For lack of coming up with anything witty to say. "I'm just toying with you." *Maybe that wasn't the best choice of words.*

Chapter Twenty-Nine

"Great! I'm so excited. If I do say so myself, this year's line has some of the hottest swimwear I've ever seen. This show is going to be epic."

Tina walks over and hugs Zya. "I'm so very proud of you, you know that? I still don't know how you got all the designs done back in March. Your ads are plastered in every fashion magazine. That's some serious planning right there."

Zya chuckles. "I'm questioning myself how it all came together…it has been one hell of a year, and we're not even halfway through it yet. It can't get any worse."

"That means only good things from here on out. Your show next week is going to be as you said, epic! Dominque is getting married next month, and Amber's trial is a few months after that. She's not going to jail, Patrick is going to make sure there is plenty of reasonable doubt."

"From your lips to God's ears. I hope and pray, you are right."

"By the way, Cassie called today."

"Oh, do tell."

"Seems I'm an excellent matchmaker. She and Micki are alike in so many ways...they're getting pretty serious."

"Did she say anything about Doug's petition? It's been a few months now."

"He's moving forward with it. She's working on him, but he's a tough cookie."

"Really?"

"Yeah, you need to go ahead with your plan. She may have to go there."

"Okay, I'll handle that tomorrow. I was hoping I wouldn't have to. I'm sure he's going to make an appearance sometime to challenge me on it."

"Can I ask what you have on him?"

"It would be best if you didn't. Ignorance can be your saving grace. You know, I changed my mind, I would like to see the production if you're ready to show me."

"Absolutely! Prepare to have your mind blown," Tina says as she makes an explosion with her hands.

Zya pulls a chair over to the setup Tina prepared.

A voice booms through a single test speaker. "And now, Ladies and Gentlemen, the exotic designs of Label Zya, bring you the resort wear line of the century."

Tina set up a mock wall to simulate where the models will come out to strut their stuff. The lights splash the wall and the runway in every shade of blue. It's the Caribbean Sea of color.

Zya can't help but crack up laughing when she sees Tina come out, mocking the models with the front of her top pulled up through her cleavage, creating a faux swimsuit bra and her shorts rolled up, really high mimicking bathing suit bottoms. She loves the colors, the music—and particularly… her test model.

As Tina comes in front of her, still sashaying, Zya gets up and pulls her close, kissing her passionately.

After a long, sensual embrace, Tina pulls back. "Wow, whatever I did to deserve that, I'll do it again."

"I love you so much. I never in a million years would have thought the love of my life would be a woman—a drop-dead gorgeous, sensual one at that. I want to spend the rest of my life with you."

Tina is stunned. "I love you too. You are everything I've ever wanted. When I was a little girl, I would dream of riding off into the sunset with my queen, never a prince or a king…you've been my vision after all these years."

They kiss again, gentler this time.

It's that moment—that exact second, Zya realizes she's bisexual, and damn proud of it. No one has ever made her this happy before.

Zya has had a difficult time coming to terms with being in love with a woman. Tina has been very patient; she knew she'd come around eventually. In many cultures and religions, even Zya's, it's taboo. Becoming Muslim was Doug's doing, not hers. She was raised Christian; however, she changed to try and please him.

As she's grown away from him, she's found her way back to Christianity. She's always enjoyed the loving part of being Muslim, but getting back to her roots, the ones instilled by her parents have felt more natural.

Ashanti, knowing nothing except the Koran, has decided to broaden her horizons, studying all the different religions.

She's not changing, thinking there are no right or wrong ways to worship, it's what you choose to believe that matters.

Accepting her new sexuality has been a rocky road, but now all she can think about is how happy she is, and grateful Tina never gave up.

Zya grabs Tina's hand and pulls her over to the couch. Making love to a woman has come entirely natural to her. Tina can be delicate but tough as nails when necessary. She'll fight till her last breath for what she believes in, and she believes in them.

"I'm so happy right now. I can't wipe this grin off my face," Zya says as they sit down.

"Here, let me help." Tina straddles Zya and kisses her, making her lustful intentions known.

Zya's arms go around her, pulling her close, their breathing instantly becoming hot and heavy. Zya grabs Tina, positioning her on her hips.

Tina responds immediately, undulating and grinding her hips into her while their tongues dance.

With a pure animalistic impulse, Zya pulls Tina's top up over her head, admiring her breasts as the bounce to match the tempo of her hips.

Seeing Zya eyeing them, she grabs her head, pulling her to her chest to devour her breasts.

Zya complies as her hands each grab one. She pushes them up against her cheeks, making sure to capture her nipples between her fingers.

Tina's head rolls back as she increases the pace, grinding faster and harder.

As Zya's passion flares out of control, she grabs Tina under her arms and moves her to the couch, laying her down with lust burning bright in her eyes. She unbuttons and unzips her shorts, pulling at them anxiously, wanting them out of her way.

She leaves her wearing just her panties. Tina wears the sexiest French lingerie—worth every damn penny. While some women collect shoes, Tina hoards lacy undergarments, filling drawers and drawers with the sexiest—sometimes naughtiest—pieces.

Today her curves fill out a set made of French Chantilly leavers lace. Panties cut so low, they make Zya anxious and yearn for what lies just below. The easy-access, barely there, demi-bralette matches perfectly. Zya prefers to make love to her with her lingerie on. It's so sexy; it heightens the pleasure.

Zya admires the incredibly sexy woman lying in front of her, drinking her in. Her heart swells, knowing she's all hers. No, they are theirs. They belong to each other.

Rubbing her hands up Tina's legs, she pushes them to open wide when she gets to her knees. The wet spot on her panties gives away the effect Zya is having on her.

With pouty lips and sultry eyes, Tina begs, "Don't tease me, not today…please don't tease me."

Zya puts her hand over her pubic bone, grinding the palm into her.

Tina spreads her legs as far as possible, opening her lips wide, giving Zya's hand direct contact on her now swollen clit.

The feel of her engorged bud in her hand makes her desperate to touch it directly. She pulls her panties to one side, immediately taking her index finger and rubbing where her palm just was.

Watching Tina's head toss from side to side, Zya flips the lid off the box next to the couch. Inside is a small slippery pink toy.

Zya slips her finger inside Tina to test the moisture level; all systems go—green light. Zya flips the switch causing the toy to hum, placing the tip against Tina's swollen clit.

Tina jumps at the sudden sensation then rewards Zya with a huge smile.

Zya gently rubs it up and down. The vibration is gentle and titillating.

As Tina moans and pleas, Zya knows better than to listen to her; she loves being teased.

Just as Tina begs one more time, Zya penetrates her with it, letting the two ears protruding from the base now stimulate her while it hums deep inside. The overwhelming stimulation sends her immediately into orgasm.

Zya loves to watch her climax. The pure joy on her face makes her heart skip a beat. Watching her ride each crest, Zya unconsciously begins to rub herself. Unsure if it's pure love or pure lust, this woman turns her upside down.

Tina looks up, with her hair wild around her face. "Your turn."

"Oh, no, it's not. Right now, it's all about you, babe."

Before Tina can protest, Zya's mouth takes the pink toy's place. The height of the couch is perfect. Her tongue licks and flicks between her lips while her finger buries deep inside. The tip is pressing down around the edge as it pulses, in and out, hitting her G-spot. She knows if she applies just the right amount of pressure, she can send her crashing again. In sync with her tongue, she does just that. It took several sessions of exploration before Zya finally found it. Her only complaint—it didn't take long enough. Knowing how much she pleases her makes her want to do it more.

Tina screams as her body again convulses under Zya's expert touch. The double sensation causes her toes to curl. She grabs the pillow next to her to cover her screams.

While Tina tries to catch her breath, Zya's tongue swirls and explores around, careful not to be too firm; she doesn't want her to explode again—just yet.

Zya's other fingers have found their way back under her dress, slowly building her excitement. She thrusts her finger inside with the same tempo her tongue flicks against Tina's clit. Just as she's about to peak, she sucks hard, burying her other finger deep into Tina, causing them both to erupt together. No pillow can cover up the piercing screams from Tina. Once they both come down, Zya lays her head on Tina's leg to catch her breath.

Tina's head lies back as she looks up at the ceiling. "Wow, that was amazing, but you have to let me reciprocate, please," she pleads.

"No can do, gorgeous; I have a show to prepare for." She kisses her, feeling quite satisfied. Not only from her orgasm but also knowing the pleasure she gives Tina. She gives Tina a peck on her nose. "Feel free to stay here, just the way you are...for as long as you like."

As Zya stands, Tina grabs her hand, pulling her down for a deep passionate kiss. "I love you, woman."

261

Zya smiles and replies, "And I love you. Now rest, you look exhausted. What the heck have you been up to?"

Tina chuckles then rolls over. She is exhausted—maybe just a little nap.

Zya gets up, fixing her dress and heads over to her desk to go over a last-minute layout of the show. She sees all the sketches that have come to life already showing some of the most sophisticated, yet sexy swimsuit attire she's ever designed. She tries to keep her mind on her work, but her eyes wander over to her sleeping beauty.

I can't believe how much I love you.

She flips to the last sketch, the wedding gown. *That would be perfect.* She thinks as she imagines the final segment of her show.

Chapter Thirty

"You are so nervous, aren't you?"

"Come on, you mean you're not? It's Helen!"

"You're so funny." Mitch hugs Ashanti's shoulders as they walk into the studio together.

A stagehand on break is scrolling through his phone as they walk by. He can't resist the opportunity to snap a picture of the notorious bully and his victim.

As they're ushered into their room, Mitch grabs Ashanti's hand and pulls her along. Her palms are sweaty, and her eyes are huge like a deer in headlights.

Once inside, Mitch puts his hands on her shoulders and says, "You need to relax. Close your eyes, and let's just focus on breathing. Deep breath in, hold it, now let it out slowly—all the way out. Again, deep breath in, hold it, slowly release it."

It is impressive how they've come full circle from enemies to now friends, giving new meaning to the word frenemy.

Ashanti giggles as she thinks about how ridiculous she's being.

Mitch, looking at her adorable face, leans forward and kisses her on the lips.

Ashanti's eyes fly open as she steps away from him. "What was that? Why did you do that?"

Feeling foolish, he quickly replies, "I'm sorry, I wasn't thinking—it didn't mean anything." He turns away, reaching for a bottle of water.

"Seriously, why did you kiss me?" Ashanti asks as she turns him around to face her.

"I don't know—it was a spur of the moment. You've always been so strong, and in such control, it was cute to see you all nervous. When you giggled, I just couldn't help myself; it just happened."

"So what, now you're going to assault me too?"

Putting distance between them, he replies, "Whoa, whoa, let's not get carried away. I'm sorry, really I am—it won't happen again, I promise."

Ashanti turns around, mad at herself for lashing out like that. *That was a stupid thing to say, comparing a kiss to being assaulted.* Or maybe she's angry that her lips are still tingling—she can still feel his. "I was out of line; I shouldn't have done that. You just caught me off guard. Please, let's not do that again," she says.

"No worries—I won't."

☯

As they are being led to the stage to see Helen, Mitch's phone buzzes with a notification from one of his social media sites. 'TRENDING: Mitch and Ashanti,' with a picture of the two of them, Mitch's arm playfully over her shoulders. They are laughing, and she's leaning into him. It does appear very cozy.

He decides to keep quiet about it until after the show. He guesses at least the kiss gave Ashanti something to be more nervous about than meeting Helen.

Helen is excellent at putting Ashanti at ease once they are on stage. She has a way of taking a very serious subject—some taboo—and can ease the tension. "Ashanti, you and Mitch are friends now, right?" she asks.

"We are. It's funny how that all turned around, but yeah, now we're friends," Ashanti responds.

"I'm amazed at how you can be such good friends after the terrorizing, injuries, and final assault that brings you here today. It's a great example of how we can forgive if we truly want to. Now you two are only friends?"

Mitch and Ashanti turn toward each other, wondering if someone saw the kiss.

Mitch responds, "We're really good friends. I didn't see her for who she was before. I only saw what her religion—her skin color was. Now that I've gotten to know her, she's pretty cool. I'm sorry I ever caused her any pain, she didn't deserve it."

Ashanti, at that moment, takes Mitch's hand and squeezes it. Kiss crisis averted.

Helen flashes a picture on the screen behind them. "This photo is trending now with #HurtTheOneULove...what are your thoughts?"

Seeing Ashanti's eyes bulge and her hand flies off of Mitch's, Helen takes control, never wanting to make her guests feel uncomfortable, ...especially the young ones.

"From the look on your face, I see you probably didn't know one of the studio employees took this picture just a few minutes ago. You were nervous today, weren't you?"

Ashanti nods, wishing her chair would swallow her up.

"I'm not that scary, though—I promise. See, nothing to be nervous about, just three people discussing the bullying that went on in their lives. We just happen to be lucky enough to have your bully change his ways and take responsibility for his actions. I, on the other hand, have never confronted my bully. I envy the friendship you two have, and especially, letting him comfort you in your time of need—or nerves in this case. That truly is an amazing accomplishment—for both of you...you should be very proud."

"You were bullied?" Ashanti asks, astonished.

"I was back in middle school. Her name was Louise, and she picked on me every chance she got. I guess thinking back now, I did have a few angels help me. Whenever she was around, Victor and Cedric always seemed to have my back. Funny, I don't know what happened to them."

Helen turns toward the camera and says, "I'd like to say to you Louise if you're watching my show, shame on you for picking on someone so much smaller than you. And, thank you, Victor and Cedric, for always knowing when I needed you."

Helen gets up from her chair and hugs Ashanti. "You truly are an amazing young lady. You're going to go places, I know."

She then goes over to Mitch, hugging him as well. "You, young man, are a shining example of how, if we take control of our actions—own up to them, how much better we are for it. You will also go far. You're going to help put a stop to bullying, once and for all. Thank you for having the courage to come and talk to me—talk to us about this."

Chapter Thirty-One

The Ice Palace, just forty minutes south in Miami, is buzzing the morning of the big show. The location is close enough to the ocean to smell the salty sea; the air is thick with humidity. The seagulls cry overhead looking for handouts as the models, production assistants, and stylists file in for the big show. Stan is lining up the clothing, every piece precisely in its place. Changing is so crazy and hurried—everything has to be perfect to keep on schedule.

Hairdressers are working on updos, fully teased French twists, high, high hair. Makeup artists are at work, creating masterpieces on their flesh canvasses—all blues and turquoises. Airbrush artists create streaks of blue on one arm and opposite leg of the models wearing the swimsuits. Everything is perfect... precisely as planned until Tina sees Zya's face.

"What's wrong?"

"I'll figure it out, don't worry about it."

"H-E-L-L-O...it's me you're talking to—what's up?"

"Sylvia, the model who was supposed to wear the wedding dress, has pneumonia. I've got some calls in to the agency. I'm trying to find a replacement, but it's going to be tough; the dress was fitted for her."

"How about Dominque? Didn't she wear the wedding dress last year in Milan?"

"She did, but she'll never fit into this one. She's not busty enough. Plus, she's finishing up radiation, I'm not even sure she'll have enough energy to make it to the show this afternoon."

"Can any of your other friends wear it?"

"No, Amber and Deborah won't fit in it, and Ashanti's way too young to wear it. Damn!"

"How can I help? What do you need me to do?"

"Will you wear it?"

"ME? Are you crazy? I'm the last person you want to walk your runway."

"Actually, you'd be perfect. Your long blonde hair and bronzed skin—with that gown, ...you will be stunning."

"Did I just set myself up? You were hoping I'd ask what you needed, didn't you?"

"Well, it did cross my mind. You and Sylvia have very similar builds. She's maybe an inch and a half taller than you, but the dress already hangs past the ground in the back. I'd have to get the seamstresses to bring up the front a bit, so you don't trip over it."

"That would be perfect. Tripping over the dress, or my own two feet, and flying into the audience. You'd definitely be the talk of the town."

"Does this mean you'll do it?"

"If it will help, I guess. But I still have to run the production."

"I know. I'll get you into hair and makeup before the show starts. Once you've got it going, Stan will help you get dressed. I'll ask one of the assistants to oversee the rest of the production. You have it all set up on automatic, right?"

"I do unless something goes wrong."

"Then let's pray everything goes according to plan," Zya says as she crosses her fingers. She hugs Tina. "Thank you so much. This means the world to me."

"Yeah, yeah, yeah…you owe me. Stunning, huh?"

Zya turns away with a guilty grin on her face.

Amber comes backstage to wish Zya luck just before the show starts. "Zya, this place is packed. There are even people standing along the back. Wow, girl, standing room only. I think it's safe to say…you've arrived." Amber hugs her.

"By the way, why is Tina all made up like the models? You want your production director to match your show?"

"You'll see. Oh, by the way, could you please videotape the show for me? All the way, until the very end?"

"Sure, my phone okay? I had to get a new one, so I got the latest and greatest…the camera is awesome!"

"I was wondering when you'd break down and get a new phone. Not sure how you lasted this long. I have a videographer here for the media and marketing clips. I want one for my personal records."

"You got it. Now go break a leg."

"They only say that on Broadway, you know?"

"Okay, go break a catwalk then. That didn't sound right…good luck."

The place is full, as even more people try to pack in. Security is called to keep the numbers at the maximum before the Fire Marshall has issues.

Amber finds her seat between Dominque and Debra. She loves how Zya reserved three of the best seats in the house for her sisters. She even had their names put on them.

Just as Amber sits, the lights go completely out. Everyone starts catcalling and whistling in the pitch blackness. A faint, deep base beat can be felt vibrating their feet through the floor. Gradually getting louder, they feel the beat move up their legs. They're so distracted, they don't hear the faint noises coming from in front of them.

Suddenly, a blue spotlight comes on at the very end of the stage, illuminating a model wearing a tropical print swimsuit cover-up with a big white floppy hat and sunglasses. A loud drumbeat thunders as the light changes.

A different shade of blue spotlight comes on to show off the next model, dressed similarly yet in different colors right next to her, also in unison with another loud beat.

The drum beats continue at a faster pace, each one quicker than the one before. The runway is exploding with all different shades of blue as the models appear, one after the other, wearing similar cover-ups, hats, and glasses. Each posed uniquely and as beautiful as the one on either side of them.

"Ladies and Gentlemen, welcome to the House that Zya built. Introducing the whimsical yet elegant, spring 2019 resort collection of Label Zya."

The models turn to different sides, three times before following the one in front of them, to the end of the runway, then back behind the wall. They throw off the sunglasses and cover-ups to turn right back around and head out, revealing the swimsuits hidden beneath.

The fabric is exactly the same pattern yet different colors, with each one uniquely designed differently from any of the others. Full racerbacks to string thongs, one-piece suits with cutouts, making them more revealing than most two-piece suits. Everyone is stunned.

The show continues to wow the spectators as the collection showcases every style of resort wear imaginable; Casual shorts ensembles, flirty sundresses, and sophisticated evening wear. If Amber was going to a resort or on a cruise, her entire wardrobe could be planned tonight.

Three-quarters of the way through the show, Amber notices Tina is not at the sound setup. A young male has taken her place. Amber continues to videotape everything, pointing out the pieces she likes and will have to purchase.

Dominque picks a few pieces for her honeymoon.

As the show nears the end, the runway clears, and the lights dim. The music changes to a crisp tinkling of bells; the lights are now pale shades of blue.

Zya watches from offstage as Tina walks out. Zya, nervous and flustered, fights back the tears. This dress was made for her.

Tina walks out onto the stage and stops as directed. Oohs and aahs can be heard from every direction. The V-cut neckline shows off Tina's ample cleavage, stopping just below the bra line. The bodice, tight-fitting with boning, shapes the perfect hourglass down to her hips. No seam attaches the skirt, it just flows. From the sleeveless top to the long train, the dress is an engineering impossibility.

Each step Tina takes reveals the bright turquoise heels underneath. The gown is as stunning as the beauty wearing it.

As Tina makes her way down the runway, not walking too fast, she sees Amber, Debra, and Dominque in the front row with huge smiles plastered on their faces. Amber mouths, "You are gorgeous," as she passes them.

By the time she turns to walk back, she's more comfortable and decides to have some fun strutting her way back.

As soon as she's offstage, Zya is there to hug her. "You were amazing. Thank you so much."

"You owe me, now please take this off me before I damage it," Tina pleads.

"No, no, honey, you have to leave it on. You're going back out; it's the end of the show," Zya replies as she moves down the line of models repositioning the outfits and accessories as needed.

"You never mentioned that before," she replies, on the defensive.

The models begin their final walk. "Must have slipped her mind," Stan says, now fussing over Tina's gown.

Tina gets in line, behind all the models.

Stan holds her back, leaving more distance between her and the last model. "You're going to walk out and stop at the end. Zya will then be announced and join you at the end of the runway."

Tina looks at him, confused. She doesn't remember this happening in previous shows.

Watching her forehead crinkle in doubt, Stan quickly adds, "You've always been so busy, you just never noticed."

Still unsure, Tina does as instructed.

"Ladies and Gentlemen, please welcome the creator of Label Zya."

Zya walks out, grabbing a microphone as she passes the sound booth.

The room is loud, with everyone clapping and whistling —a standing ovation.

As Zya makes her way to Tina, she motions everyone to take their seat. "Thank you. Thank you, everyone, for coming tonight and sharing my latest masterpiece with me. They say, do what you love, and it will never feel like work. It never has, and designing this collection has been the most fun I've ever had. And, if I do say so myself, I think it's one of my finest."

The room explodes in whistles and applause again.

She continues once everyone has quieted down. "My success has a lot to do with being happy and fulfilled. That can mean so many different things; family, friends, but for me," — she reaches over taking Tina's hand—"happiness is this gorgeous woman, Tina, standing next to me." Zya turns and surprises Tina with a deep, passionate kiss.

The room erupts as everyone gasps at the unexpected display of love and affection on the runway.

Tina is stunned. Zya hadn't shown any desire to tell the world about her sexual preference. She certainly didn't think tonight would be the time she would share her secret.

"I didn't know I could love someone this deeply, this completely, until I met Tina. I wasn't prepared to meet my soulmate, and I certainly didn't expect that person to be a woman. She has helped me find myself—be all I can be. She completes me. They say behind every success story is a man or woman who helped make it real." She turns to Tina—. "My reality is, I can't do any of this without you. I don't want to do this without you. I want to wake up next to you every morning and go to sleep with you every night."

Zya pulls a diamond ring from her pocket, a two-carat oval diamond with a ruby halo.

Tina gasps, her tears silently rolling down her cheeks.

"Tina, will you spend the rest of your life with me?"

Totally surprised and speechless, she nods...the words just won't come out.

As Amber jumps from her seat to capture the romantic moment on her phone, a guest, who wasn't given access earlier, sneaks in unnoticed, making his way as close as possible to her. Very close now...so close...*Amber wears Coco Chanel...good to know.*

Chapter Thirty-Two

"Why don't we call it a night, okay? We still have all day tomorrow to prep. I'm beat, and I see the bags under your eyes. You're more than welcome to stay here tonight if you like. I'll make up the guest room for you."

Amber considers Patrick's offer for a moment before relenting. "Are you sure it's not too much trouble? It would be easier for us to get back at it in the morning. I have an appointment with my tech guy, Andy, in the morning too."

"Your tech guy? Having phone problems again?"

"Yeah, locking up like the old one did. I was hoping by upgrading to a newer version, I wouldn't have to deal with any of this."

"That's crazy—I thought you weren't supposed to have any of these issues with these phones."

"Me too! Andy is great. I bribe him with a dozen bear claws, and then suddenly, I have an appointment. I know that's not nice, especially with the long line I usually cut, but I just can't wait hours, and I don't get a heads up when this shit is going to happen…it's never convenient."

"I wouldn't worry about it." He gives her a peck on the cheek, "Give me a few minutes," he says as he leaves to ready her room.

After ten minutes, Patrick returns to the living room. "I took the liberty of starting you a bath. I hope that's okay. I know how much you love taking one and I'd bet about now, you can probably use it."

Amber looks at him in disbelief. *Who is this man? Why did I not see how amazing he was before?*

The pause causes Patrick to second guess his offer. "Unless you're too tired...it's no problem."

Amber, appreciating the thoughtfulness, gives him a big hug. He has tried to be careful and not overstep. After the attack, he decided they would be together on her terms. She would decide if, and when, they became a couple again.

She feels comfort as he wraps his arms around her, burying his nose in her hair. The trial is in just four months, and he's worked so hard looking for the evidence to prove her innocence. They've been through the case file so many times coming to the same conclusion...there's nothing.

As they pull away from each other, Amber touches his cheek. "I'm sorry for our torrid past and the part I played in it. I was so afraid of being hurt; I never allowed myself to love. You are everything I've always wanted but been afraid to ask for—or even admit."

Patrick takes her hand and kisses her palm. He doesn't dare say anything.

She lifts his chin and kisses him gently on the lips.

Sensing his hesitation—his fear, "It's okay...I love you, Patrick."

She shudders at the gentleness of his kisses as he places them delicately along her nose, her eyes, her neck.

He stops and looks into her eyes. She can sense his hesitation on continuing, as it's only been five months. "I want you—I need you." She gently takes his hand and leads him to the fragrantly filled bathroom. Candles flicker all around the tub, and a glass of wine waits for her. He even has a clip for her hair. It's so heavenly…and he did it for her.

Seeing this only heightens her feelings for him, so she takes the lead. Slowly she unbuttons his shirt, never taking her eyes off his. Her body starts to quiver when he takes her hands away from their task, kissing the tips of her fingers.

"Amber, I don't want to hurt you. Are you sure about this? I can wait. I'm not going anywhere. I love you so much—my heart hurts when I imagine the agony and pain you've been through."

"Let's try, okay? If I can't, we'll stop. I hate to do that to you, but I want to be with you. I want to feel our love…I need to make love with you."

She flinches when he puts his hand on the side of her neck, causing him to pull away. She immediately is taken back to when her attacker's arm was across it, pinning her down.

She takes his hand and puts it back on her neck, "Sorry, reflex, it's okay."

He lowers his hand to her shoulder instead and pulls her gently to him, kissing her. Using his lips, he retraces her face with light, featherweight caresses. Starting at her neck, he traces kisses down to her shoulder, causing a familiar tingle down to her toes.

She wills her mind to feel him and only him. For a split second, fear ventures in, trying to push this beautiful moment out. She pushes back, filling her mind with Patrick's face—his love—his gentleness.

Patrick's hand ventures down to her hip—with his lips, not far behind.

She wants to reassure him, so she places her hands in his hair and gently guides him. Her hips begin a subtle undulation nudging his lips closer.

He continues his butterfly kisses inside her thighs.

Her legs begin to tremble and go weak. The vanity bench is next to her, so he guides her over to it.

Wearing a wicked smile, he reaches for the bathroom rug and places it directly in front of her lowering himself to his knees, his lips returning to their task at hand.

After covering the inside of her knee, he begins to plot his course due north, still watching her face—her expression—for anything other than desire.

Part of her wishes, he would just get there and get it over with already. The other part wants to enjoy every single second of pleasure this man has to offer.

His trail eventually finds its destination, inhaling her sweet fragrance, eager to taste her. He exhales at the perfect moment, adding a small burst of hot air.

Her legs immediately squeeze together tightly against his head.

He jumps back.

"I'm sorry, I'm sorry, I didn't mean to do that, really… are you okay? I'm so sorry."

"Maybe it's just too soon. I'm okay. Not sure about my neck though," he says with a smile, trying to break the tension.

"Please don't give up on me, this is important. I'll be better prepared this time. Please try again."

Hesitantly, he goes back to kissing the inside of her thighs, positioning himself, so at the first flinch, he can get out of the way this time.

She doesn't flinch. It's tough when he goes back to the task at hand, but she keeps pushing the past out of her mind, focusing only on pleasure.

He continues his exploration, letting her hips dictate the speed and pressure.

As much as she would love nothing more than to climax, she can't let go, that might take a little longer. She gently puts her hands on his shoulders and pushes him away. She goes with him as he sits back on his heels positioning herself across his hips.

"Thank you for not giving up on me—on us."

Speechless, no words are adequate for how he feels.

His kiss—full of love, is so tender, yet passionate and full of fire. She doesn't need to hear anything; she can feel his love as well as his desire between her legs. He's made no move to enter her—she decides when she's ready.

She slowly starts to rub back and forth against him. Although she could not orgasm, the pressure of his hardness against her helps fuel the flame—ultimately pushing Brettinger out of her mind. As she rubs faster and faster, she starts to feel the familiar tingle in her toes. She reaches down and gently guides him just inside. It hurts—a lot, but she's determined to get past it.

"You sure? Really?"

"Yep, but can you do me a favor?"

"Really? Anything, you just name it."

"Can you put your thumb right there." She positions his digit right against her now super sensitive clit.

Needing no further instructions, he presses and flicks against it until she feels all tingly again.

She gently moves her hips, only slightly, so just the tip of him is going in and out.

He's doing everything he can to keep from taking over and just thrusting inside her. He wants it so badly; his body wants to take over—his brain struggles for control.

As he continues caressing her, she begins to take a little more of him—little by little, inching him further and further inside. The areas where she was torn, the scar tissue, is painful, but she's determined.

"Keep rubbing me baby."

He's trying every trick in the book to keep from exploding; unattractive important women, his most recent case, anything to distract himself.

With half of his length inside her, and without warning, she explodes.

His body takes over as he too climaxes.

She lays her head on his shoulder, trying to calm her breathing and stop herself from shaking. She did it. She got past it.

He was so nervous when they started, afraid of doing the wrong thing. The last thing he wanted was to hurt her, but he could see how much she wanted to get past the attack and find love again. His heart swells—it was one of the purest love experiences he's ever had.

"A penny for your thoughts?"

Her voice brings him back to reality. He looks into her eyes, seeing how vulnerable she is.

"You are everything to me. I can't believe I almost let you slip through my fingers. I love you, Amber Fiore, with all my heart, and I don't want to waste another day proving to you just how much, will you spend the rest of your life with me?"

Before she can respond, he holds his finger up in the air. "Wait, hold that thought." He gently places her on the vanity bench in front of him, then jumps up, stark naked, and runs into his bedroom.

With a big grin on his face, he opens the wooden box by his bed. He reaches in and grabs the ring box.

He rushes back into the bathroom, sliding along the floor, almost slipping, then drops down to one knee in front of her. He opens the box, "Will you do me the honor of marrying me?"

Chapter Thirty-Three

"I'm sorry, I'm staring, I don't mean to. It's just so eerie to be sitting here; you look so much like her. Duh, you're her identical twin, of course, you look like her."

"Would you prefer we go back to our Phone Fun?" Brandy asks.

"No, no, definitely not, I'm happy to see you, touch you…" Stewart feels the instant rise in his jeans.

Seeing the lust flash in his eyes, she removes her shoe and places her toes on his bursting seam.

He flinches. "Oh!" Then he puts his hand over her toes, pushing them down.

"You are one bad girl—you know that. The things you do to me."

"You mean, the things I'm going to do to you."

That's all the encouragement he needs. "Check, please."

As they leave the cafe, he puts his hand on the small of her back.

She takes his hand and places it under her short, short skirt. She doesn't care who sees.

Stewart moves his hand, so his fingers are between her legs—no panties. She stops to let a customer pass just as his finger slips inside.

Looking at him, she knows full well they'll never make it to a bedroom.

Once outside, she looks side to side for the closest place possible. If memory serves her, there's a park along the river, one block over. "Come on." She takes his hand and trots in that direction.

Not sure where they're going, he also feels the urgency and follows willingly behind.

Once she sees the park, she pulls him across the grass to the stage area. There are people all around walking their dogs or just taking a stroll. Behind the stage, the concrete rows of seats curve, so they are entirely hidden. That is, of course, unless someone walks back there. She sits on the first step and turns him to face her. Quickly, she unfastens his jeans, releasing his full, engorged length. Looking up at him, impressed, she puts both hands, one on top of the other, around him. The uncovered portion, she encloses with her mouth, sucking as she pulls back.

His knees go weak, so he places his hands on her shoulders to steady himself. She doesn't play around or start slow; she goes full throttle. Her mouth sucks so hard it's like she's fighting herself to keep him deep inside, down her throat. Her hands are busy as well, twisting and riding up and down in unison with her luscious lips.

He can't believe how quickly she's got him to full erection, and almost complete explosion. One more stroke and he's a goner, so he regretfully pulls away. He picks her up and pulls her to his hips. Needing no instructions, she wraps her legs around him. Just as he's about to enter her, his brain kicks in. He reaches inside his pocket and pulls out a shiny blue wrapper.

Her eyes light up as the sun reflects off the protective packaging. "I love a man who *cums* prepared." She grabs the condom from his hand, opens it, and slides it over the tip.

"Careful, you've got me very close. I'm not ready yet."

Taking his cue, she gently rolls it along his length. Must be extra, extra-long...it does the job covering him completely. She can't wait to get all of it inside her; she's giddy just thinking about it.

Once she's painstakingly completed her task, she places the tip just inside. "You drive," she says.

He pushes gently at first. She's so wet...hot and tight. The heat is almost painful—almost.

After two slow strokes, all the way in—all the way out, her head begins to thrash around. Not many men can fill her to capacity; the sensation of him filling her, sets every nerve ending on fire. She can never understand why some women complain about gifted men. Give her the biggest one, and she'll still want more. It might not be accurate, but she's always sized up a man by his hands and shoe size—no pencil pushers for her.

He can't hold back any longer. He takes a few steps forward to lean her against the back of the stage. It too is concrete, so it can't be comfortable, but she's oblivious to everything and everyone around her, every inch of him making her quiver and quake.

Pressing her against the stage, he thrusts faster and faster—deeper and deeper. His mind goes blank as he feels his orgasm start at his toes, exploding through his groin. They both scream out, not caring who hears.

They don't notice the two elderly ladies walking beside the stage. They can see and hear what's happening, so they hurry by not to disturb.

One of the ladies stops and goes back, peeking around the corner. Her friend joins her.

"Isn't that the girl that's on trial for killing that rich guy? I thought she was raped? I could be wrong, but I don't think any girl that was just attacked would be out here in public, screwing some guy."

"Hey babe, did you have a good day?" Zya asks.

"Yeah, it was okay," she responds, shrugging her shoulders.

"Just okay? Girl, you were on Helen—your show is airing tomorrow. Aren't you excited?"

"I am, it was a fun experience. Sorry, you couldn't come with us. Mitch's dad was great, but it wasn't the same."

Tina asks, "Any negative comments about the new trending hashtag?"

"Thankfully, it only trended for a few hours. Helen's replaced ours, #HelensBullyLouise, that's the big one now."

"Come over here and talk to me, there's more, I can feel it. What's on your mind?"

She thinks about not telling her mom, but then again, she tells her everything, why stop now. "Mitch kissed me before we went on set."

"He what?" Zya asks, astounded.

"It was out of the blue—spur of the moment, he said. I was nervous, and he was helping me by making me take deep breaths. I giggled because it was silly, and then he kissed me."

"Is this going to affect your friendship?" Tina asks.

"How can it not? What if he kisses me again? What if I want him to kiss me again?"

Zya smiles. "If you want that boy to kiss you again, I swear, you must be the holiest person I know. After everything he did to you—you've given him friendship, and now you think you might want more?"

"I know, screwed up, right?"

"Watch your language young lady—you're classier than that."

"Sorry, Mom, I'm just so confused. You're right, how can I want him to kiss me again after he had his thugs hurt me? It is scr—I mean messed up."

"You know, this might be something to discuss with your therapist. You get to see her one-on-one, right?"

"We do. I am a bit ashamed to talk to her about it, though. I mean, It's just a kiss, but it was so sweet and gentle. It was like it was from a totally different person."

"Maybe you're seeing the real him now. His mom really did a number on him, as did her family to her. Mitch almost lost his life...maybe he sees the light. A near-death experience can do that to you," Tina says.

Ashanti nods and thinks about it, "Mom, honestly—is this as crazy as it seems?"

"It is, but honey, I have to tell you, when you have feelings for someone, it can be crazy—crazy good, or crazy bad. I think you have to go with your instinct on this one, you've always had good intuition. Just follow your heart—don't worry about what others think. Protect yourself, of course, but be honest about your feelings."

"And talk to your therapist!" Tina exclaims.

Ashanti hugs both women, "Thanks—it's still messed up, but I do feel better. I love you."

Chapter Thirty-Four

"Patrick asked me to marry him tonight."

Zya starts to scream with excitement.

"I told him no."

"What do you mean, you told him no? Are you crazy? You love that man!"

"I do, that's exactly why I asked for a rain check."

"How do you ask for a rain check when a man proposes to you?"

"I told him to ask me again when I get that not guilty verdict, and we are out of the courthouse…that's when I'll say yes."

"Oh, I get it. You don't want to say yes in case it doesn't go in your favor."

"Exactly. If I go to prison, he'll work tirelessly to get me an appeal and a new trial. Everything is pointing to me being a murderer. I can't let him do that to himself. Who knows how long I could be in prison? What if I'm sentenced to life, or worse? Florida has the death penalty."

"What's going to happen is your soon-to-be fiancé is going to keep you from being put behind bars, he's going to get you that not guilty verdict."

"I hope you're right. Trust me, I pray every day. I just need to be a realist too and prepare myself for the alternative."

"Okay, but for me, I'm not going to think about anything other than, we'll be planning your wedding soon—too."

"Make excuses for me, okay. I don't want to have to explain this to everyone. Patrick is in the other room, and I'd like to stay with him tonight. As you can expect, his feelings are hurt. Not only that, I didn't say yes, but that I doubt he'll be able to keep me out of prison."

"Don't worry about it, I'll explain everything. You know, since you're not here, and the wedding is in a month... you're going to have to go with the dress design we pick for you. I have this bright chartreuse ball gown, with big puffy sleeves, that would be perfect on you."

Amber laughs. "Right, you would never design a puffy-sleeved, chartreuse ball gown, let alone, ever let me be caught dead in one."

"Go, be with your man tonight, I get it—no worries. I brought some sketches for you to look at, you and Dominque can pick out your dress tomorrow. I'll leave them with her. Now, we may send you a text from time to time. Just respond when you can."

"Oh, and please hug Debra for me. I know tomorrow is the first anniversary since George died. I'm sure it's going to be a tough day for her."

They didn't get much sleep that night for several reasons. They talked more about the case, and Amber tried to reassure him. Later, she got him to make love to her again. He knows she loves him, he can feel it, …he just can't shake this overwhelming sense of dread. But if it's the trial, or something else, he's not sure.

Amber can hear her phone buzz from time to time. She smiles, knowing it's the girls sending her photos—teasing her. And they are, all except one:

"So he popped the question? Isn't that sweet…and you turned him down? You broke his heart. I'll make sure I have him first before I get you. I bet he'd love to witness firsthand what I'm going to do to you. How I'm gonna make you scream. Your knight in shining armor won't be able to rescue you this time. I'm praying he gets you off—I don't want to wait years to get my revenge."

☯

The next morning over coffee, they pick up where they left off with the trial preparation.

"I can't wait until this is all over. I am going to marry you." Patrick looks up at her, awaiting her reply, and sees her face drained of all color.

She turns her phone around so he can read the text.

"Shit! I was hoping it was Roberto. And, it's from a different phone number again, but definitely the same person. Maybe we need to change your number."

"I was going to, but what's that going to accomplish? If this person wants to do me bodily harm, they're going to do it

293

regardless of what my phone number is," she replies, sharper than intended.

Amber pulls her legs up under her arms and rocks back and forth on the couch, tears streaming in a constant flow.

Patrick sits down, putting his arms around her. "I won't let anyone hurt you, I promise. He or she will never do anything to you."

"You can't guarantee that. I know you want to make sure no one ever hurts me again. But unless you are with me twenty-four seven, there's always the chance. I know we should be focusing on my trial, but where did we leave off on the list?"

"All the numbers were from burner phones purchased all over the place. I think one was even from Georgia. They only used the phone once and then tossed it."

"What about security cameras? Can't they search their feed and see who's buying the phones?"

"We were able to get a few. One person bought six phones all at the same time, but only one number was used. The other two were just random people."

"Can we talk to any of them?"

"These burner phones don't work that way. They usually pay with cash, and the names are aliases. I didn't pursue it any further when they picked up Roberto—we all thought he was your stalker."

"How do we start back up? I need to find this person, please."

"And we will. I know they're scaring you, and that's exactly what they're trying to do. It's of little comfort, but most of these people never do anything, they just want to frighten you. I'll see what I can find out, but understand, I need to focus on your case. Can we get the girls to help you?"

"I can ask Zya. She's good at finding the needle in the haystack."

"Maybe we should have her look at your case then too. I need to go to my office to pick up some files, come with me?"

"I think I'd like to stay here if that's okay. This person doesn't know where you live—I think. I want to take that bath I didn't get to take last night. I'll be okay."

"Okay, but don't answer the door. I'm not expecting anyone."

Shivers run up and down her spine as she imagines her stalker waiting on the other side of the door for her. "I won't, I promise. Hurry back."

In a stupor or just numb, she walks into the bathroom and starts the water. She finds the Epson salt container and mindlessly adds way too much. She's not really thinking of anything—trying to get her mind to go blank.

She slips into the hot water, it lightly scorches her, but she doesn't feel a thing. Her skin turns instantly, rosy from the heat, the steam rising from the surface.

She sinks lower and lower into the water until she's entirely submerged. Her eyes open, looking up to the ceiling, burning from the bath salts.

Chapter Thirty-Five

"To Dominque and Tad, may you find all the love you deserve, and more," Amber says as she toasts.

"And all the babies you can handle…," Debra adds.

"And all the sex you want!" Zya says.

They laugh and sip.

"I can't believe I'm getting married tomorrow."

Zya sits next to her. "Dom, with the year you've had, you deserve to be the happiest woman in the world."

"Yeah, from here on out, you should have smooth sailing. You've gone through more than most ever have to endure in a lifetime…it's your time now," Amber says.

"This is such a dream come true. I never really thought I could be this happy—that I deserved it. Tad is everything to me. I love you all, you know that, but he's just…it's hard to explain."

"You don't need to explain anything to us. He's a good man, and you deserve him, and he's proven himself to us. He deserves you too; you're perfect for each other—the stars are aligned," Debra adds.

They toast again.

Amber's phone dings notifying her of a text.

"Are you going to get that? It could be Patrick."

The hair stands up on the back of her neck, and her insides turn icy cold. "It can wait, it's Dom's time right now, no interruptions."

Debra jumps up and grabs her overnight bag. "Okay, girls, I have something for you."

She pulls out four teal blue, luxurious bathrobes.

Amber pulls hers up and reads the back. "Future Mrs. Simpson." She smiles, hoping this is indeed her future.

Dominque looks at hers, in addition to a fancy gold stitched border around the collar and her name, hers says, Mrs. Johnson. She still giggles when she sees that name.

Zya picks hers up. "Future Mrs. Tina? That's a good question? I have no idea if either of us is going to take the other's name or keep our own."

Amber grabs Debra's to see what hers says. "Mrs. Harris...no Future Mrs. Phelps for you?"

"I hope someday—I don't want to jinx anything. We're still great friends, and he's so wonderful with Little George. It's okay the way it is right now."

"How about some hot and heavy, get down and dirty, sex?" Zya asks.

Debra's cheeks instantly turn a rosy red. "You guys, you know I'm not that kind of girl. George—and Roberto—have been my only lovers. When the time's right, Brian and I will...get together."

Dominque asks, "Have you learned how to masturbate yet?"

Debra spits champagne out. Wiping the remnants from her face. "I think that came out of my nose."

Laughter fills the room.

"Didn't we have this conversation last year?" Amber asks.

"If you want to know if I have had the big O…," Debra forms an O with her mouth reminding Amber when Dom did it last year. "I have—I've found my pleasure tool."

"Pleasure tool? You went and bought a dildo? Or a vibrator?"

Debra's cheeks burn bright again. "No, I don't have one of those…I have an old washing machine with a very bouncy spin cycle."

Zya falls back on the bed in hysterics.

Amber and Dominque look at each, the crack up.

Debra shyly smiles.

"We're not laughing at you, honey, we're laughing with you. You have to explain to us how that works?" Zya asks.

"I can't—I can't tell you that…it's too embarrassing."

"That's okay, we'll use our imagination," Dominque says as she takes a sip from her glass.

Amber, feeling happy and in a kidding mood, something she hasn't felt in a long time. "I think I have some laundry I need to do. Debra, can I come to your house and use *your* washing machine? Wait a minute…I've done laundry for you in your machine." Amber thinks, imagining Debra's washing machine. "Oh, I get it! If you press up against the corner when it starts to spin, it does buck and jump!"

Debra jumps up off the bed. "Okay, who needs a refill?" she asks, ignoring the girls rolling around in hysterics.

☯

Tad's parents are already seated when he arrives at the church. He sends his best man, Patrick, in search of his dad for pre-wedding photos. His parents are still angry at him for living in sin. They understood why he stayed with her when she was recovering from surgery, but that was almost two months ago. They still don't buy the excuse they were getting married anyway. But it didn't seem right for him to move for just a few weeks.

His dad comes into the room where Tad, Patrick, Stewart, and Brian are waiting. The photographer poses them for a few shots. He says while frowning, "Okay, let's try something a little different. Mr. Johnson, when you got married, what did it mean to have your father there that day?"

His dad's face softens.

Tad remembers what happened that day. His dad told him about it when he graduated from college while giving him the 'You're a grown man now' speech. It was the best day of his life. He was marrying his best friend. Tad's grandfather was tough and never really liked his mom. He made sure to point it out the day they were getting married. He was miserable that day.

He turns to Tad, takes him in his arms, and hugs him tightly. "I'm sorry, son. Today isn't about me, or your mom, it's about you and Dominque. I see how much she means to you and how much you love each other. It hasn't been ideal, but you two fit. I love you, and we couldn't be happier for you. Forgive an old man for being so set in his ways?"

"Oh, Dad, I love you too. I know you don't approve, but I do love her with all my heart. Today I get to marry my best friend. Today is the first day of the rest of our lives."

Tad awaits at the altar for his bride to be. He watches as Debra and Brian take the aisle. *They are perfect together. One day Brian, you'll have her in your arms.*

Zya, the African beauty, leads the surfer dude, Stewart, next. It's obvious she's pulling him along.

He notices her lock eyes with Tina as she passes her row…another fairy-tale ending.

He watches as Amber takes Patrick's elbow as they start down the aisle. He prays for their own happy ending.

The music changes as everybody stands. This is it, the moment he's been waiting for.

He watches as Dominque comes out from the right, stopping at the end of the aisle. They lock eyes, never looking away. *She looks so beautiful. Today she becomes my wife.*

As she makes her way toward him, he sees how beautiful and happy she is. She opted to go with her own hair, tossing the wig aside. Her short, European chic hair looks as if she spent a fortune on the cut and color. She glides down the aisle with Tracey in front of her, dropping rose petals, each step bringing their fate closer together.

Dominque always dreamed of getting married at the famous Pier 66 resort along the Intracoastal Waterway, until she saw the prices. Her tribe insisted she would have her fairy tale, pitching in one-fourth each. When Patrick and Brian found out, they helped as well, unbeknownst to the future Mr. and Mrs. They even surprised them with the cocktail hour in the revolving top.

All seventy-five guests enjoy cocktails and multiple serving stations. Each table towers with mini-appetizers, gazpacho shooters, jumbo prawns, oysters on the half-shell, and other delectable delights. The slowly-turning outside ring of the room can cause quite the problem for some guests when they retreat to the restroom, as their table is never where they left it. The entire outer walls are made of glass, floor to ceiling windows. These become virtual photographs as the city lights begin to dot the horizon, changing the scenery by the minute.

To the east, the ocean turns a dark blue as the stars start to spot the sky. You can see the lights from boats and ships miles out from the shore.

To the west, the sunset casts a warm glow in shades of orange, peach, and rust behind the downtown high-rises.

Due north, multimillion-dollar homes with their yachts line the finger channels of the Rio Vista neighborhood and the Las Olas Isles—the Venice of America.

Just south, over the bridge, is the port. Ships carrying thousands of passengers back and forth to their tropical destinations pass through every day.

Looking southwest, you're likely to see many planes in the air from the airport just minutes from the port. The Port Everglades pulled Fort Lauderdale into World War II before the United States entered in 1941. In 1939, A British cruiser chased the German freighter, *Arauca*, in where she remained until the U.S. seized her in 1941. By December, that same year, the

Army Corps of Engineers, began transforming an abandoned 9-hole golf course and the Merle Fogg Field into a naval base, now referred to as the Fort Lauderdale International Airport.

"Thanks for inviting me. I wasn't sure if you'd ever want to see me again. I'm really sorry. I don't want to jeopardize our friendship."

"Are you really sorry for kissing me?"

"Don't ask me that," Mitch says.

"Why not?"

"Because then I'll have to lie to you."

Ashanti reaches out and kisses him on the lips. "There, now we're even."

She turns and walks away, proud of herself for having the guts to kiss him. Forgiveness is something that's always come easy for her. Maybe it's her Muslim upbringing or her mother's influence. She's always been able to see the good in people—even those who don't deserve it.

Once they move to the ballroom, everyone anxiously awaits the announcement of the bride and groom. They float in, holding hands—so happy. The gown has clips to bustle the skirt at the top of each gusset, eight in all, showing the vivid colors and making the dress more fun.

Tad twirls Dominque onto the dance floor as they hold each other close, floating to their song.

After a few minutes, the disc jockey invites the bridal party to join in.

Brian takes Debra's hand and walks her to the floor. They've both been cautious, trying to keep their distance. They have refrained from cuddling in each other's arms since their wet dreams before Little George was born. Now, it's a reminder of that day—just how perfectly they fit together.

She rests her head on his shoulder and closes her eyes.

It's been a year since George's death. Maybe it's too soon.

"I love you," he whispers in her ear.

She looks up into his crystal blue eyes. "I love you too."

He gently tilts her chin up and kisses her—a loving peck at first, which quickly turns more passionate, causing their pulse to race.

Without having to say a word, Brian takes Debra's hand and leads her off the dance floor.

Patrick is holding Amber, but she's rigid, on guard. "Everything okay, you seem tense?"

She pretends to relax in his arms, failing miserably. She can't tell him—not now. He's been so focused on her case, determined to find something, anything to clear her name. The last thing she wants to do is show him the last text she received. The one from last night…maybe the final one.

"Don't worry, you're safe tonight. I wouldn't dream of hurting Dom; she deserves happiness. You on the other hand... I don't think your man is going to get you off. I don't think he found any more evidence. Tell you what, I'll make sure you never go to trial—or prison. I'll even promise I won't hurt Patrick. I'll leave this number active for the next forty-eight hours. Just say the word, and you'll be mine before September."

❧

Amber, unable to sleep, gets up and retrieves her phone. She dials the number. It's answered on the third ring. "I hoped you'd be calling..."

Chapter Thirty-Six

"Okay, I know we've gone over this at least a hundred times, but jury selection starts in two days. Let's go through it all once more, okay?"

"Alright."

"We have five minutes of lost time on the security footage—exactly five minutes—right down to the millisecond. Glitch on the times...possible."

Amber nods.

"When we overlap the first and last image, they are identical. You haven't moved, not a hair out of place, that we can see."

Amber nods again. "That's not good, is it?"

"They may cancel each other out. The possibility of Brandy setting this up so perfectly may be just as insane as losing exactly five minutes."

"Okay, let's view the lab reports again," Patrick continues.

"The assault took place around 3:40 p.m., and your blood was drawn around midnight that night, that's a window of about eight and a half hours. There's no trace of any drugs in your labs; however, GHB can only be detected up to eight hours, so it's possible. It would have shown up in your urine sample, but that test came back inconclusive."

"So, what would cause my urine test to come back like that?"

"Your urine might have been contaminated, or the actual test itself. There's any number of reasons."

"So, GHB could have been detected in that test?"

"Yeah, for up to twelve hours. Your hair sample though should have detected it…that's where I'm lost."

"My hair sample? She didn't take a hair sample."

"That's strange; it says here your hair sample came back clean."

"She picked up some pubic hair on the paper she had me standing on. It wasn't mine; it must have been his."

"That's odd, and she didn't ask you about it? She didn't take any hair from you?"

"No, and I didn't question her, she's the expert."

"During her exam, she would have to notice you don't have any pubic hair. She would know it was his. You did say they treated you as if you were guilty. Brettinger was well-liked in the community. I would hate to entertain the idea that she would have rushed through the test because of her personal feelings. Can you think back for me and tell me exactly how the rape kit testing went?"

"When they arrested me, the cops were very short and cold. I was in shock—they could see I was abused, but they were still rough with me. They pushed me into the back of the car. When I got to the station, they went through the procedure of fingerprinting me, taking my picture, etc. I didn't say much —in fact, I don't think I said anything at all until you came in to find me. They didn't believe he raped me. You put the wheels in motion to get the nurse out to test me."

"She came in about twenty minutes after I saw you. She kept saying I could stop this at any time. I think she has to say that, but I felt as if she didn't mean it that way. She could see I was abused. She wasn't rude—she wasn't nice either. She was rather cold about the whole thing—robot-like, unfeeling."

"Okay, I need to see if I can add her to our witness list."

"You think she'll be on our side?"

"I don't know what to think except this hair sample test is wrong. I'll see if I can talk to her tonight. If I can prove she didn't follow procedure, that may give us some time."

"Okay, go back to this GHB and tell me more about it. Why do you think this is the drug they would have used?"

"Let's say Brandy drugs you when you run into her coming out of his office. When injected, GHB's effects are felt pretty quickly, within fifteen to twenty minutes, and can last up to three to four hours. This fits our timeline. It clears the body quickly, which is why we didn't see it in your blood test. Like I said earlier, it would have been detected up to twelve-hours in your urine if that test had come back with any results. A hair sample can show it up to four weeks."

"How about testing the hair in my brush? I know it's been seven months, but we might find hair there that's within that period of time. Wait a minute,"—she runs to get her purse — "I forgot I have this travel brush. I'm sure I've used it at least once since then. I forgot about it, so I haven't cleaned it."

"It takes seventy-two hours to get hair sample test results back. I don't think we have enough time."

Chapter Thirty-Seven

When she left that morning, John, the building security-doorman, hugged her and said, "There's no way they will find you guilty. It will all be okay, you'll see." His attempt of trying to comfort her was sweet and served its purpose—until now.

Her heart is racing, and she knows all eyes are still on her. She takes her seat beside him and drinks from the water glass in front of her. Somehow her hands on either side of the cold vessel calm her, give relief to her sweating palms.

After the jury files in, the judge comes into the room, and everyone rises. Amber's chair gets stuck as she pushes it back, causing her to lunge forward. The judge notices and nods to her as if to ask, *You okay?*

Amber nods in return, pulling the chair free from the lifted tile.

Jury selection only took one day, although Patrick was hoping he could push it to two, especially with the news coverage this got. The prosecutor and the judge would not have it; they got down to business and went through the potential jurors like clockwork. He was confident several of the jurors were lying when asked if they knew about the crime Amber was on trial for, but he couldn't just call them out, that would be unprofessional. He was warned several times by the judge; he couldn't push his luck any longer. It's been forty-six hours since he dropped off the hair samples to the lab…he has twenty-six hours before he can hope to get any positive results, negative ones sooner. No way this trial can be over in one day.

He's had the sheriff's office out searching to serve Brandy, to no avail—she's nowhere to be found. Stewart claims he hasn't seen her, so it's assumed she's left the area.

The prosecution's opening statements are brief and right to the point. They will prove, beyond a reasonable doubt, that Amber Fiore murdered Paul Brettinger. They did not mention she had motive, that would mean they would have to allow her attack as part of the trial—they don't want to go there, this will be a swift and uncomplicated trial.

"The defense will prove Miss Fiore was drugged and set up for the murder of Mr. Brettinger. We will prove Mr. Brettinger's reputation was not as perfect as the prosecution and the community would have you believe."

"Careful, Counselor," the judge warns.

Patrick changes his tactics, telling the jury about Amber's stellar reputation, her community activities, and her special reports she does to help when all else has failed. When he's sold them on her reputation, he closes his opening remark. "The prosecution's case is not as airtight as they would like you to believe. You will have reasonable doubt, and you will have no choice but to return with a not guilty verdict for Miss Amber Fiore."

"Is the prosecution ready to call upon your first witness?"

"Yes, Your Honor, the prosecution calls Miss Maryann Dunham to the stand, please."

After raising her right hand and repeating to solely swear, she sits nervously in the chair.

"Miss Dunham, you've been working for Mr. Paul Brettinger for eight years now, is that correct?"

"Worked—yes, I worked for him for just over eight years."

"I apologize, and I'm sorry for your loss. I understand Mr. Brettinger was very good to you?"

"He was, he took me under his wing when I first came to Brettinger Holdings."

"That must have been exciting for you, the CEO of a big company trusting you with such responsibility."

"It was. I was fresh out of college, but my grades were exemplary. He took notice of all my hard work and said he would make sure I didn't get lost in the shuffle."

"Miss Dunham, have you ever seen the accused, Amber Fiore, before?"

"Yes."

"When did you see her?"

"On January 16, 2018, she had an appointment that day."

"An appointment at Brettinger Holdings with Mr. Brettinger personally?"

"Yes, with him, personally."

"Can you tell us the nature of that appointment?"

"Mr. Brettinger had recently been railroaded by a reporter in the Sunshine Herald. She and Mr. Brettinger didn't see eye-to-eye, so her article was not very flattering. Mr. Brettinger sued the Herald and swore off any more interviews."

"Did Mr. Brettinger request Miss Fiore himself?"

"No, his CFO talked him into doing one with a respected journalist to help shine a better light on him and help take the other article out of circulation. He thought Miss Fiore would be the perfect professional for the job. He met her at an event and asked if she was interested."

"Did Miss Fiore show up on time for her interview?"

"Yes, in fact, she was fifteen minutes early."

"And how did Miss Fiore appear to you?"

"She was fine…maybe a little nervous."

"And how did Mr. Brettinger seem to you before the appointment? Did you see him before she arrived?"

"Yes, he met her at his door. He even picked up her portfolio from one of the waiting area chairs."

"How long was Miss Fiore in Mr. Brettinger's office?"

"She was there for sixteen minutes."

"And did Miss Fiore remain in his office during that entire time?"

"I think so—I don't know for sure."

The prosecutor's forehead wrinkles; it's not the answer he was expecting. "Were you not at your desk during this time?"

"No, I went on break. That's how I know it was exactly sixteen minutes. I left as soon as she went in, and when I came back, she was coming out of his office."

"And how did Miss Fiore appear to you when she left?"

Looking down at her hands, she's careful about her words. "She seemed okay."

"Did you say anything to each other?"

"I asked her if she wanted to make that appointment, and she said she'd call me back, then she went to the elevator and left."

"And then she came back, right?"

"Yes, about fifteen, maybe twenty minutes later she came back and said she left her portfolio in his office. She didn't wait for me to check; she just let herself in. As she left, she informed me he was in the shower. I could hear the water running when she opened the door."

"You think he was still showering?"

"Well, if she killed him before she left the first time, the shower would still be running, right?"

"Objection, Your Honor."

"You're objecting to the witness's answer, Counselor?"

The courtroom laughs.

"I'm sorry, Your Honor."

"So you heard the shower running when Miss Fiore left the first and second time?" the prosecutor asks, looking around at the jury to make sure they got every word.

"Yes," she answers, unsure if she heard both times.

Patrick makes a note.

"How long was Miss Fiore in for the second time?"

"Not long at all. Um, maybe ten minutes."

"Doesn't ten minutes seem like a long time to go in and grab a portfolio?"

Definitely confused, she replies, "Yeah, maybe. It didn't seem like it to me at the time. I took a call, and she left while I was still on the phone. Maybe it was more like five minutes."

"Miss Dunham, I know this is very painful for you, Mr. Brettinger was like a father to you, but can you please tell us what happened next?"

Tears threaten the corners of her eyes, and she fidgets with her hands. "He liked to take long showers but never thirty minutes. It seemed too long, so I went in to check on him to make sure he was okay."

"And what did you find, Miss Dunham?"

Tears are now streaming continuously. "He was dead. The water in the shower was red. I couldn't see his face, but I saw the ice pick sticking out of his neck. She stabbed him. She killed him!" she says as she stands up, pointing at Amber.

"Nothing further, Your Honor."

"Your witness, Counselor."

Patrick brings Miss Dunham a tissue from his pocket. "Would you like a glass of water?"

"Yes, please."

Patrick pours her a glass, allowing her to compose herself.

"I know this is very hard for you, you and Mr. Brettinger certainly had an extraordinary relationship."

She looks up at him, nodding.

"You mentioned earlier, you asked the accused, if she wanted to make that appointment before she left, is that correct?"

"Yes."

"How did you know he would want the interview? He was meeting her to decide if he wanted it, right?"

"Mr. Brettinger did that all the time. If I didn't hear from him by the time they got to my desk, I was to ask for the appointment."

"Had Mr. Brettinger, at any time in the past, asked you not to make the appointment?"

"He did, it was rare, but he had."

"And on these occasions, were they women or men he had in his office?"

"Objection, Your Honor. Not relevant."

"Sustained."

"Miss Dunham, did Mr. Brettinger ask you to take your break when Miss Fiore went into his office?"

"Yes."

"Was it your normal time to take a break?"

"Objection, relevance?"

"I'm just trying to establish the timeline here and any abnormal behavior," Patrick says.

"I'll allow it, continue."

"So, was it your normal time to take your break?"

"There was no set time for my breaks. I took them when he asked me to."

"When he wanted you to, did you always get breaks, every day, the same amount?"

"No, some days I never took breaks, other days I would take three or four."

"Did he ask you to run errands for him during these times as well?"

"Sometimes, I'd pick up his dry cleaning or get a bottle of wine or a trinket for a date."

"And did these breaks and errands coincide with when he had appointments?"

The prosecutor looks at Patrick, warning him.

"He always had appointments. He was always seeing someone. It probably did but purely by coincidence."

"Miss Dunham, if you weren't there the entire time while my client was in his office, is it possible, someone else joined them? Could someone else have gone into the room?"

"I guess it's possible, but why would someone else go in there?"

"I'm just clarifying it's possible since you were not at your desk. You did not see who entered or exited his office for sixteen minutes, correct?"

"Yes, it's possible but highly unlikely," she answers, confused.

"You said you heard the shower running both times? When Ms. Fiore left the first time, and when she came back and left again, right?"

She's been caught. "I definitely heard it when she left the second time."

"But maybe not before?"

"I don't know, maybe…I can't quite remember."

"So isn't it possible, Mr. Brettinger was very much alive when she left the second time, going into the shower as she mentioned when she left?"

"It's possible but no one else was in there. It couldn't be anyone else but her."

"But you weren't there the whole time, so it is possible someone could have joined them?"

"I guess."

"Miss Dunham, was there anything different about Miss Fiore's appearance when she came back the second time?"

"She didn't have her coat with her."

"Did you notice anything about her appearance that was different…maybe a tattoo on her shoulder?"

"A tattoo? No, I didn't see a tattoo." Trying to remember, she thinks back.

"Anything else? Did she seem hurried? Scared?"

"No, in fact, she seemed quite happy. She had a pencil in her hand. She placed it on my desk."

"Are you sure? Wasn't her hair up in a bun, held with the pencil?" He's trying desperately to trip her up.

"I saw a pencil. It was definitely like the one she had in her hair…the one she put on my desk…they were the same."

"Anything different about the way she walked to the elevator?"

"Objection, Your Honor. What is the counselor trying to prove here?"

"May we approach, Your Honor?"

She motions them forward.

"Your Honor, Miss Fiore, has an identical twin sister, Brandy. They have been estranged. Brandy was just released from jail last year and has made threats against Miss Fiore's life."

"Your Honor, the defense has been unable to locate and serve this, Brandy. She is not a witness in the trial; she probably doesn't even exist. This line of questioning cannot be allowed."

"Doesn't exist? Do you want a copy of her birth certificate? Of course she exists," Patrick says aggressively to the prosecutor.

"Mr. Simpson, please calm down, this is your last warning. One more outburst and I will have you in contempt of my courtroom. I'm sorry, but I agree, I cannot allow this questioning, do you understand?"

Patrick nods.

He takes a few deep breaths before continuing. "I apologize, Miss Dunham. Can you remember anything else that might be helpful?"

"She had this scary look on her face when she put the pencil down?"

"Scary? What do you mean by that?"

"Like she was possessed or something."

The prosecutor jumps to his feet, but Patrick waves him down. He turns to walk away but then turns back. Throwing all caution to the wind, Patrick says, "I'm sorry, just one more question, were you and Mr. Brettinger having an affair?"

The courtroom erupts.

The judge yells, "My chambers now, both of you! This court will take a ten-minute recess."

Patrick sulks into the judge's chambers with a red-faced prosecutor. "Your Honor, what was that? How can you allow that?"

"I'll ask the questions if you don't mind. Mr. Simpson—Patrick, what are you doing? Do you want to lose your license?"

"Your Honor, Mr. Brettinger has a reputation of being a womanizer, and at times, it's not reciprocated."

"Your Honor, that's not been proven, he has never been convicted or charged with assault, rape, or sexual harassment. This is all hearsay."

"I agree. Patrick, where are you going with this?"

"I have a witness, someone who used to work with Mr. Brettinger, an analyst who was assaulted by him."

"Rachael Moorings?" the prosecutor asks.

"Yes."

"She never filed a suit against him, and I believe she was fired from her job. She has an ax to grind. You can't call her, I'm sorry, I won't allow it."

"Mr. Simpson, your client did not plead insanity, or even self-defense—she pleaded not guilty. I don't quite understand why tarnishing Mr. Brettinger's name would be helpful in this case."

"Your Honor, my client and I both feel very strongly— she has been framed. This murder could have been premeditated, and we'd like the opportunity to present it."

"And your person of interest is her identical twin sister, right?" the prosecutor asks.

Patrick addressing the judge says, "I know it's strange. Miss Fiore—Amber, has been receiving these threatening texts, possibly from her sister. These texts are scary; they know everything that's happening in her life. It's someone that has a connection close to her. Let's assume Brandy knew Amber had that meeting. And given Mr. Brettinger's lust for the opposite sex, had she gone back in Amber's place and killed him setting Amber up. Brandy is cruel, downright mean—she would do this."

"Really! That's absurd! You have no proof of this!" the prosecutor exclaims.

"You're right, not yet, at least. I'm waiting for a hair test to come back from the labs. If she was dosed with GHB, Liquid Ecstasy, her test will come back positive—it fits!"

"Your Honor, you can't let him do this, it's a wild goose chase."

"Maybe, Counselor. I tell you what, Patrick, I will only allow that line of questioning, if—and that's a big if—your hair test comes back positive. I'll allow you to introduce it into evidence and recall any witnesses you need. You cannot introduce that line of questioning until then, understood?"

"Seeing how it's nearly impossible for this test to be back in time, I'll allow it, Your Honor."

Patrick sneers at his opponent. He'd be doing the same if he too was madly in love with his client.

"All rise," the bailiff says as the judge and attorneys come back into the courtroom.

"Ladies and Gentlemen of the jury, please disregard that last question from the defense and strike it from the record. Unless you have anything further, Counselor..."

"No further questions, Your Honor, however, I reserve the right to recall the witness at a later time." Patrick is looking for anything at this point to stall the trial.

"Would the prosecution like to redirect?"

"Yes, Your Honor, may I approach the witness, please?" The judge nods.

"The prosecution would like to introduce Exhibit A, the coroner's report. Miss Dunham, can you please read to the courtroom the approximate time of death?"

"Between 4 and 4:30 p.m."

"No further questions, Your Honor."

"Miss Dunham, you may step down," the judge instructs.

Amber looks at Patrick, confused. "Patrick put me on the stand."

"I don't want to do that to you."

"We don't have a choice. If you ask me about what happened during our meeting, I can tell them about the attack, right?"

"Prosecution will object, but it's possible the judge will allow it. I'm sorry, but you may be right. I don't want to do this to you—have you rehash it all—but I don't think we have a choice."

"Your Honor, the prosecution rests."

Patrick is shocked his opponent has decided not to show the jury the security footage as planned. He's rushing the trial—hoping Patrick can't get the lab results back in time. But then again, by playing that video, does it open the door for their 'setup' theory? *I have to try and hope the judge doesn't stop me. I don't think he can object since it was part of his discovery.*

"Mr. Simpson, your show."

"Thank you, Your Honor. Ladies and Gentlemen of the jury, I'd like to introduce Exhibit B, the parking lot security footage for the day in question." Patrick sets up the video monitor, just waiting for the judge to say something—she doesn't.

He goes to press play but rewinds a little further back instead. He's decided to take everyone back to when Amber comes out of the building. The camera angle isn't the best, but they'll see the crowd at the door as she's exiting. It could help if the lab report gets back in time.

"At 3:54 p.m., the accused can be seen walking out of the building. She'll appear in just a second as she passes through that crowd." Patrick also knows it's crucial for the jury to see her behavior, how she was walking, comparing with the other direction. He can't say anything about it, but he can make sure they see it, just in case he's unable to show the video again.

He lets the video play to just past the lost five minutes. "In case you might have missed that, allow me to play that back again."

He rewinds to just before the time glitch and plays again, stopping only after. "Did you see it?"

Confusion is visible on the jurors' faces.

"One more time." He repeats playing that section; however, this time, he points to the time counter and makes sure everyone can see the lost five minutes.

"Objection!" the prosecutor yells out.

"And what are you objecting to, Counselor?" the judge asks.

"The defense did not announce this in their discovery."

Patrick retorts, "We only just discovered this recently."

"You had access to this footage, is that correct?"

"Yes, Your Honor."

"Objection overruled, continue, Mr. Simpson."

"I'd like to call Mr. Howard Fiennes, cybersecurity specialist, to the stand please."

After being sworn in, Mr. Fiennes takes his seat.

"Mr. Fiennes, thank you so much for taking time out of your busy schedule to be here with us today. Can you state your name and your profession for the jury please?"

"Mr. Howard Fiennes, I specialize in cybersecurity or otherwise known as computer security of hacking prevention. I own Eye-Spy, Florida's leading cybersecurity company."

"Mr. Fiennes, have you had an opportunity to review the security footage we've just seen?"

"I have. However, I was focused mostly on the five minutes in question. I did not review the previous section."

"Understood. To the best of your knowledge, what can you make of the loss of time?"

"It's strange, losing exactly five minutes, down to the exact millisecond, it's bizarre."

"A computer glitch, maybe?"

"Unlikely, it's too precise."

"So, what do you think happened?"

"It's possible someone tampered with the time stamp, but I can't understand why."

Patrick attempts to distract Mr. Fiennes, knowing what he's about to say. "So you think, in your professional opinion, the time stamp was tampered with? That this footage has indeed been hacked and changed?"

"Maybe, but for what purpose?" He continues, "The image doesn't change; it stays exactly the same. The chances of someone changing anything during those five minutes, and then going back to the same position…it's one in a million. But the odds of the time stamp glitching on its own, that's one in a billion. The odds are better, someone hacked into the footage."

Damn, I was hoping he wouldn't go there.

"Mr. Fiennes, what's the quality of the footage?"

"It's a little grainy, but it's not bad. I've seen worse."

"But you usually see better, right? Higher resolution?"

"I work with all types, but yeah, the resolution on this footage is lower than usual. With the money that company makes, I'm surprised they didn't invest in better quality."

"I don't know that much about security cameras, however, can you verify that the distance the camera can see is dependent upon the length of the focal lens, is that correct?"

"That's true."

"And what is the size of the focal lens of the camera that recorded this footage?"

"It's actually a *varifocal* lens, adjustable from two-point-eight to twelve millimeters; it was set at six."

"And about how far away from the accused is the camera?"

"Just over forty feet."

"As I said, I'm no expert, so can you tell us how far, at a six-millimeter setting, you can see clearly?"

"Somewhere between thirty and thirty-five feet."

"So is it possible, because the image isn't as crystal clear as it could be, the images might not be as exact as you say they are? Could you be missing some small details because of this?"

"It's possible—yes, maybe. I just kept putting one image over the other, and I didn't see anything out of place. It was like she was just sitting there in her car, not moving for five minutes."

"If the camera was hacked, could the focal point on the lens be changed as well?"

"For sure."

"So just to be clear, is it possible, because the accused was just over forty-feet away from the camera, you can't see every detail because of the focal setting, correct?"

"Yes, but…"

"Thank you, Mr. Fiennes, that's all I have."

"Counselor, would you like to question the witness?"

"Oh yes, I would, Your Honor, thank you."

"Mr. Fiennes, you said the image is exactly the same just before and just after the time glitch, is that correct?"

"Yes, exactly."

"And the odds of pulling that off are one in a million?"

"Maybe even higher, it's impossible."

"No further questions, Your Honor."

Patrick gets to redirect the witness. He can't ask about not moving for five minutes for fear it will hurt him if he can discuss the attack. It would be odd but not for someone who was just raped; they might do just that…sit in their car, in shock, for five or more minutes.

"Just to be clear, because of how far the camera was, and the lens setting, we may not be seeing every detail?"

"Yeah, I guess."

"No more questions, Your Honor."

"Counselor, do you have any other witnesses you'd like to call up?"

"Yes, the defense calls Mrs. Elizabeth Robbins."

"Objection, Your Honor, Mrs. Robbins, is not on the witness list."

"She was a late add-in just yesterday. I won't be held accountable if your office didn't inform you, Counselor," the judge says.

"Can you please state your name and occupation for the record please?"

"Elizabeth Robbins, I'm a forensic nurse for the Broward Hospital district."

"Mrs. Robbins, have you met the accused before?"

"I have," she says, looking stern.

"Can you tell us how you came to meet Miss Fiore?"

"I was called to the jail on the night in question to perform some tests on the accused."

"What kind of tests?"

"Objection, Your Honor. We both know where this questioning is going to lead, and it cannot be allowed. Mr. Brettinger's actions are not on trial here, Miss Fiore's are."

"I'll rephrase, Your Honor," looking at the judge. "Mrs. Robbins, when you do the type of testing that was required on the night in question, do you take hair samples?"

"I do."

"Did you test the accused's hair during your testing?"

"I did."

"Are you positive, the hair you tested belonged to the accused and not the victim?"

"Objection, Your Honor!"

"Counselor,"—looking at the prosecutor— "If you don't mind, I'd appreciate it if you'd let Mr. Simpson conduct his case please. He's already on thin ice, and he knows it."

The prosecutor nods.

"Please answer the question, Mrs. Robbins."

"I'm positive."

"Where did you get the hair sample? Did you get it from her scalp?"

"That wasn't necessary; there were hairs on the paper she was standing on, so I took a few of those."

Patrick knows if he asks the question he really wants to, the judge can throw him out of court.

"Is it possible, the hair was that of the victim and not the accused if you didn't pull it out of her scalp?"

Flustered, she's not used to anyone questioning how she does her job. "It's...I don't know, maybe it's possible. I don't make mistakes, though."

"Thank you. No further questions."

The prosecutor waves her off when the judge asks if he would like to cross-examine, probably not the best action toward the judge.

"Your Honor, the defense wishes to call Miss Amber Fiore to the stand, please."

"Objection, Your Honor! I know Miss Fiore is not on the witness list."

"Your Honor, you've asked me to remove part of my case, the least you can do is allow the accused herself to tell her side of the story."

"I'll allow it, however, let's break for lunch first."

Patrick smiles, knowing full well the judge just gave him a gift.

Zya hugs Amber as she passes her, leaving the courtroom. The whole tribe, including the guys, are there for moral support.

After watching Patrick and Amber walk down the hallway, Zya turns to talk to Tad, who's checking his phone for texts from his boss. Someone brushes between them in such a rush, they knock the phone from Tad's hand.

"How rude!" Zya exclaims.

They watch as the woman rushes in the opposite direction, toward the elevators. The scarf falls off her shoulder, revealing a two-tone, round tattoo.

Chapter Thirty-Eight

"All rise, the court is now back in session."

Most of the seats are full by the time they get back, forcing them to sit apart spread out around the courtroom.

"Counselor,"—the judge nods at Patrick— "your next witness, please."

"Thank you, Your Honor, the defense calls the accused, Miss Amber Fiore, to the stand."

The tribe all find each other and lock eyes.

At that exact moment, the same woman who rushed past earlier enters the courtroom. She's wearing large round sunglasses, and her scarf now across her shoulders. She sees an empty spot up front, right behind Amber's seat. She takes it as Amber takes hers by the judge.

They've agreed to take it nice and slow through the questioning. Amber needs to be careful about how she answers and reacts. Once the prosecutor gets his chance to cross-examine, that's when the show will really begin, hoping, of course, he takes the bait.

Amber is sworn in and says her name. "Miss Fiore, can you please explain to us the nature of your profession?"

"I'm a journalist. I've been one for the last sixteen years."

"And what type of articles do you write?"

"Most of my work is interviewing South Florida celebrities, CEOs, models, entrepreneurs, philanthropists, and other rising stars in the community."

"You were approached by the CFO of Brettinger Holdings earlier this year, is that correct?"

"I was at a charity function, and he approached me about interviewing with Mr. Brettinger."

"That was an honor, right?"

"Yes, I was aware of the last article that had been written about him."

"So here you are being given the opportunity of a lifetime."

"Absolutely. It would make my career for me. Being granted an interview with him would help open so many other doors."

"When you scheduled the meeting with Mr. Brettinger, were you under the impression you would be doing the actual interview at that time?"

"No, his secretary, Miss Dunham, told me on the phone, it would be him interviewing me, before he would decide whether or not I would get the job."

"During Miss Dunham's testimony, she mentioned she asked you if you would like to schedule that interview before you left, is that correct?"

Amber hesitates, thinking about how she felt when she left his office. "She asked, and I told her I would call her back."

"So, you wouldn't have anything to gain by killing him then, would you? You wouldn't get that interview?"

"No, I would not…I did not kill him."

"No further questions, Your Honor." Patrick holds his breath, hoping he's gauged his opponent's ego to be big enough not to be able to resist. "Your witness."

It takes a few moments, and then the prosecutor stands.

"Miss Fiore"—long pause, choosing his words carefully—"Did you like Mr. Brettinger?"

Amber feels the hairs on the back of her neck stand up. *Breathe girl, just breathe…* "I respected him in the community. I did not know him personally," she replies.

That a girl, Amber. Don't take the bait—not yet.

"Did you find him attractive?"

She's grabbing the sides of the chair so tight, her knuckles are white, and her nails are leaving marks in the wood.

"He was a handsome man, that was common knowledge. He wasn't my type though," she answers with daggers in her eyes.

"What exactly is your type? Your attorney, Patrick Simpson?"

"Objection, Your Honor, what does this have to do with anything?"

"Sustained. Please keep your line of questioning on the subject at hand. Her romantic life is not on trial here."

"So you meet the CFO at this charity event, and he just says, 'Hey, have I got an interview for you?'"

Amber chuckles slightly, probably not the reaction he had hoped. "The CFO sought me out at the event. I was at my table, enjoying my dessert when he came up and introduced himself. I knew who he was, but I had never met him personally. He complimented my work, including the article I wrote about Mr. Simpson, titled The Ethical Attorney," she says, emphasizing the last three words.

"You agreed right away to the interview? Did you have any questions?"

"I had plenty, but the request humbled me."

"You're already one of the top journalists in town, how much could this interview change your job?"

"Thank you...I think. Local interviews are great, and they've helped me make a solid career for myself. Interviewing Mr. Brettinger would help me break into the national market."

"But even without this interview, you have a great career. You make a very nice living, correct?"

"I do have a great career, and yes, I'm comfortable—I'm goal-driven, always reaching for the next level. It's how I've gotten to where I am."

"So it's possible this interview might not change it all, isn't that right?"

"Yes," she answers reluctantly.

Ask her about the appointment, go ahead you know you want to. Patrick is willing his opponent.

The prosecutor attempts to ask the next question without giving her an opening. "How long was your appointment with Mr. Brettinger that day?"

Amber knows she has to get him to be more specific. "About fifteen, twenty minutes, I don't remember exactly."

"But this was the opportunity of a lifetime. You don't remember?"

Bingo, Amber, can now let out her emotions. She begins to weep quietly at first for fear of letting it all out at once. Her shoulders and arms start to shake.

He realizes he's just made a big mistake. The prosecutor says, "Miss Fiore, I'm sorry for upsetting you. We could take a break if you like." *So I can get my shit under control.*

"I'm fine. I don't remember because Mr. Brettinger attacked me—he raped me that day. Excuse me for being a little confused about the exact time my abuse took place."

The jurors and courtroom guests gasp. They knew about this; however, the raw emotion that spews out as she says the words, make it all so real.

"Objection, Your Honor. I ask that be stricken from the record. Mr. Brettinger is not the one on trial here today."

"Counselor, I believe you've opened that door. I'll allow it. Overruled."

Red-faced and trying to think fast on his feet, he attempts to steer the conversation in another direction. "Have you interviewed other powerful men like Mr. Brettinger?"

"Plenty of Fortune 500 CEOs, I even interviewed the Saudi Prince when his boat was docked at Pier 66. They never attacked me—they never raped me. They respected me and my work."

He switches tactics. "If Mr. Brettinger raped you, that gives you motive, doesn't it, Miss. Fiore? You came back and got even with your attacker. You came back and killed Mr. Brettinger in cold blood."

Wild-eyed, Amber shouts, "NO! No...I didn't kill him. I'm glad he's dead, any man who assaults a woman—hurts her and makes a game of it, doesn't deserve to live."

"No further questions, Your Honor," the prosecutor says with a wide grin.

"Mr. Simpson, would you like to redirect?"

"Yes, Your Honor. Miss Fiore, your appointment didn't go as expected, did it?"

"Objection."

"Overruled, continue, Counselor."

"No, it didn't. I was there exactly sixteen minutes—"

"Sure, now she has a grasp on time!" the prosecutor interrupts.

"Careful, Counselor, you may be the one on thin ice now. You opened this line of questioning."

Patrick nods for Amber to continue.

Amber repeats, moment by moment, what happened that day. Patrick told her it was going to be hard. She would have to relive each painful second. She pauses a few times to drink some water and calm herself.

It was so painful to watch the torture. He couldn't touch her—he couldn't comfort her.

"Miss Fiore, I'm so sorry you had to rehash all that. Can you tell us what happened when you left?"

"I wanted out as fast as possible. I just grabbed my purse and ran. As I got to the door, I saw my coat on the rack, so I grabbed it. I kept my head down; I didn't want Miss Dunham to see me—I couldn't look her in the eye.

"She asked if I wanted to make the appointment. I thought I would throw up at the thought of seeing him again. I just said I'd call and got to the elevator. When I got downstairs, I turned the wrong way at first. Once I got my bearings, I ran for the door. I know I literally ran…I was going to throw up.

"As I got to the door, there was a group of people coming in. I couldn't wait, I just pushed my way through them. I know it was rude, but I had to get away."

"Can I stop you right there? Anything odd happen when you bumped into that group?"

"Objection, Your Honor. This definitely is leading in the direction we agreed would not be allowed."

"Sustained. Next question, Counselor."

"Do you remember getting to your car?"

"I do. I had to get right back out and vomit next to the car in the grass, and then I hurried back in. I sat behind the wheel for a moment, just trying to catch my breath."

"What do you remember next?"

"I forgot my portfolio upstairs. I remembered when I was waiting for the elevator. I was trying to decide if I should go back up and get it or not. The next thing I remember, I woke up in my car. It was parked in my condo's parking garage in my space."

"Miss Fiore, was Mr. Brettinger alive when you left his office?"

"Very much so."

"Did you go back up to his office to retrieve your portfolio?"

"No, I did not."

"No further questions."

"I'd like to ask the witness another question, please," the prosecution asks.

The judge nods, allowing it.

"You didn't leave with your portfolio the first time, did you?"

"No, I left it behind."

"Was it in your car when you woke up?"

"Yes."

"Thank you."

Patrick looks down at his phone, willing the text he needs from the lab on the hair results to be there...nothing.

"Do you have any further witness or evidence to present at this time, Counselor?" the judge asks Patrick.

"Yes, Your Honor, the defense recalls Miss Dunham to the stand."

Amber gives him a questioning look.

"He cracked the door, so I'm about to open it the rest of the way."

"Miss Dunham you mentioned earlier in your testimony you worked for Mr. Brettinger for about eight years now, is that correct?"

"Yes, a little over eight years."

"In that time, how often would he ask you to take your breaks when he had visitors of the opposite sex?"

"Objection, Your Honor, where is the defense going with this? How many times do I have to state, Mr. Brettinger is not the one on trial?"

"Overruled, I'll allow it."

"Miss Dunham, do you need me to repeat the question?"

"No, most of the time, I was asked to take my break."

"Would you say ninety percent of the time? Ninety-five percent..."

Becoming defensive, she says, "Ninety-five percent of the time."

"And do you have any idea why that would be?"

"No, I don't!"

"Miss Dunham, isn't it true, your boss, Mr. Brettinger, was known as a ladies' man?"

"Objection, Your Honor."

Patrick takes two big steps toward the prosecutor, causing him to take two steps back. "If you'll stop interrupting me, I'll get there."

The judge, not sure if she should be amused or mad, chooses the first. "Gentlemen, this isn't a playground; this is my courtroom." Motioning to the prosecutor, she says, "You, sir, take a seat, and let's allow the defense the opportunity, un-interrupted to get on with his questioning."

"Yes, ma'am, I'd still like the record to show I objected."

"Duly noted and overruled." Looking at Patrick, she says, "I suggest you get to your point and soon, Counselor."

"Miss Dunham, have you had sexual relations with your boss, Mr. Brettinger?"

The courtroom gets noisy as the prosecutor stands.

The judge motions with her finger for him to sit back down.

With tears threatening, she asks, "Why would you ask me that question?"

"May I remind you, Miss Dunham, you are under oath."

"Yes, we had an affair," she spits out.

The courtroom again is all abuzz.

The judge hits her gavel. "Quiet, please. I ask you all to be quiet, or I'll clear this courtroom."

"Miss Dunham, isn't it true Mr. Brettinger asked you to take your breaks when he had a female guest because he planned to have sex with them and due to your past relationship, you had become jealous, angry at him?"

Whispers murmur around the courtroom—no one wants to be removed.

"Yes, he knew it hurt me when he had women in his office, so I asked to take breaks."

"When my client, Amber Fiore, went into his office, you were mad, weren't you? Another one of his quests—and not you?"

She tries hard to keep her composure. "I had gotten used to it. It didn't bother me anymore."

"Are you sure, Miss Dunham? Weren't you so angry at him for taking yet another beautiful woman into his office that you murdered him?"

The courtroom erupts, the judge slams her gavel down hard several times until she can gain control.

"Objection, Your Honor, Miss Dunham is not on trial here today."

"No, she is not, but if you don't mind, I'd like to know the answer to that question too, overruled," the judge says.

She fidgets with her hands, tears threatening to drop. "I didn't kill him...I wouldn't kill him."

"And why is that Miss Dunham, because you loved him?"

"No, because he's the father of my son."

Chapter Thirty-Nine

The judge is the last to enter after the recess. "Ladies and Gentlemen of the jury, I apologize for the outbursts from the gallery. I assure you, the next time there is any disruption, I will clear the courtroom. Miss Dunham, will you please retake the stand."

Patrick continues his questioning. "Miss Dunham, I'm so sorry for upsetting you earlier."

"No, you aren't."

"I assure you, I had no idea Mr. Brettinger was the father of your child. Is that why you remained his secretary even after your affair ended?"

"Yes, he wanted to be a part of Daniel's life, he promised me I would always have a job with him if I allowed it and didn't tell anyone who his father was."

"And did you tell anyone?"

"No, not until today."

"Not even your parents or best friend?"

"I told no one. He said if I did, he'd deny it and turn his back on us. No more support, and he'd fire me."

"Thank you, Miss Dunham, no further questions."

"Counselor, would you like to cross-examine?"

The prosecutor steps up. "Miss Dunham, did Mr. Brettinger have you in a will, or was there any documents of any kind drawn up for support for Daniel. Any kind of trust or special account for his future?" he asks.

"No, there wasn't."

"And you're positive about this?"

"Yes, he refused. He told me it was his insurance to make sure I'd keep my mouth shut."

"So you needed him alive right? To help pay for Daniel's school, clothes, medical bills, etc.?"

"Yes, there's no support anymore now that he's dead. I have to do it all on my own."

"Thank you, no more questions, Your Honor."

"Mr. Simpson, do you have any other witnesses to call at this time?"

Patrick's shoulders drop, and he answers, "I do not, Your Honor...the defense rests."

It's a fifty-fifty shot now. He hopes he's been able to create enough doubt. It's late in the afternoon, and he was hoping to extend the trial until tomorrow at least in time to get the lab report. He goes through his files one last time as the prosecution gives his closing statements.

"Ladies and Gentlemen of the jury, you've just heard testimony from Mr. Brettinger's secretary, a cybersecurity expert, a forensics nurse, and the accused herself. Miss Dunham has stated, the accused, Miss Fiore, was the last person to see Mr. Brettinger alive. There is the case of the missing five minutes which sounds like a good book plot to me."—the jurors laugh— "That's just as unbelievable as someone setting Miss

Fiore up and positioning everything so perfectly. Finally, Miss Fiore herself admits she left her portfolio in his office, and then magically, it appears in her car later that evening. Did she blackout somehow from the so-called attack she received? Did she go back up with so much hatred and anger that she just doesn't remember? Or maybe she conveniently chooses to forget. There is no other logical explanation here. You must find Amber Fiore guilty of murder in the second degree."

Their time is running out, still not text regarding the hair sample.

And all too soon it's Patrick's turn. "The prosecution is telling you to find Miss Fiore guilty, but they haven't proven anything. The burden of proof is on them. Five minutes missing on the tape is plenty of time for someone to set Miss Fiore up. Our cyber specialist confirmed the resolution on the footage was not that great. He couldn't see all the details. Was it possible for someone to set it up, almost perfectly—yes, it was."

"Miss Dunham also admits someone else could have entered Mr. Brettinger's office while she was on break. Could someone have entered while Miss Fiore was being abused... unnoticed and killed Mr. Brettinger after she left? It's possible. The office is hectic. Someone could have slipped out of his office before Miss Dunham found him in his shower.

"There are just too many other possibilities here. The prosecution did not provide proof my client killed Mr. Brettinger. No fingerprints, no evidence of any kind, it's all theory. Therefore, you have no choice but to find Miss Amber Fiore not guilty of second-degree murder."

The prosecutor gets back up. "Jurors, it's highly improbable someone would enter his office while he was there with a client. Your proof is this wild theory that someone, who looks exactly like Miss Fiore, goes back upstairs, looks directly into Miss Dunham's eyes, grabs her portfolio, and leaves. Regardless of whether she remembers or not, Miss Amber Fiore went back upstairs and killed Mr. Brettinger."

The judge gives the jury their instructions and releases them to private chambers. It's too late for the lab results. They cannot introduce new evidence once the jury is in deliberation. It's after 6 p.m. also, they would be closed for the day.

Patrick was hoping the judge would release them and have the jury deliberate tomorrow. Who conducts a murder trial in just one day after jury selection? He knows she can't play favorites, but he had a feeling she was on his side—on Amber's. Either she thinks they will come back with a verdict of not guilty, or she just wants to clear her docket for tomorrow. Patrick chooses to believe the former.

Amber grabs Patrick's hand under the table. "You did everything you could. It's not in your hands anymore. No matter what, I love you so much. I can't thank you enough for everything."

"Don't give up yet. We've given them plenty to think about."

Amber smiles at him, trying to conceal her concern, but fails miserably. She's scared, and it shows.

He squeezes her hand to reassure her. There's no way they can send her to prison. She didn't do it—she's innocent.

"You think it would be okay if I went to the ladies' room?" she asks.

"Yeah, sure, there will probably be a female sheriff that will accompany you—sorry."

"I understand." Amber gets up and exits the courtroom with the sheriff within her shadow.

Once inside the restroom, Amber walks to the sink to splash water on her face while sheriff waits just inside the door.

Zya, Debra, and Dominque enter and go straight to her, wrapping her in their arms. The sheriff, unsure if Amber wants the attention, asks, "Miss Fiore, are you okay?"

"Yes, I'm fine, these are my friends, it's okay."

"All right ma'am, I'll be right outside if you need me."

All four are crying, worried, she can't go to jail.

Zya asks, "That was rough there during your testimony. How are you holding up?"

Debra adds before Amber can answer. "We know you didn't do it. You couldn't kill anybody—it's not in your DNA. When he was attacking you maybe, but to go back up and kill him, there's no way. They have to find you not guilty."

"Thank you, and of course, I didn't kill him. If they find me guilty, we can ask for an appeal based on the lab test find-ings."

"Lab test?" Zya asks.

"We didn't realize until just three days ago, the hair sample they tested wasn't mine. We grabbed some hair out of my brush, hoping there were some old enough to show that I was drugged."

"So the test came back, you were drugged?" Debra asks.

"We don't have the results yet, and even if they come in now, it's too late. It's the only thing that could've happened. We've been over it so many times; there's just no other way."

"And Brandy is the murderer?"

"Yes."

The sheriff enters the bathroom. "Miss Fiore, your attorney is looking for you."

"Already?" Debra asks.

Patrick meets Amber as she exits the restroom. "The jury hasn't come back yet, but they are asking to see the security footage, up close. This is good—this is real good," he kisses her, the sheriff looks away.

Amber looks at her tribe. "I love you all. Whatever happens, we'll deal with it—together. No matter what, knowing I have all of you beside me will get me through."

The sheriff walks up. "They're ready for you now."

"That was too fast!" Debra explains and throws her arms around Amber. Zya and Dominque do the same. "Okay, let's do this," Amber says as she bravely pulls away.

Patrick grabs her and hugs her tight before they leave. "I love you, future Mrs. Simpson."

Amber smiles. "And I love you, Mr. Simpson hyphen Fiore."

Patrick returns the smile, holding her elbow as they slowly walk to the courtroom. Patrick puts his hand on the door handle while looking at her. She's very strong—stronger than any woman he's ever met.

Once they are seated, the jury files back into their assigned seats. The clerk of the court walks over to the jury captain to retrieve the verdict.

The judge motions to the jury foreman she'd like to read it first before it's read aloud. She scans the page with a poker face, revealing nothing. "Miss Fiore, will you please rise."

Amber and Patrick both stand.

Patrick's phone dings announcing a text.

The clerk of the court announces, "In the matter of the State of Florida vs. Miss Amber Fiore, we the jury find the defendant guilty of murder in the second degree."

- Is Amber found guilty? What is the result of the hair sample?
- Who is Amber's stalker? Who gets who first?
- Does Doug gain sole custody of Ashanti or will Zya and Tina break up to keep her at home?
- Do Brian and Debra find true love or will Roberto make an unexpected appearance and take it all away?
- Does Dominque make a full recovery? Does she and Tad have that Happily Ever After, or will their strength and courage continue to be tested?

The answers to these questions, and many more will be in the final book, "Cést la Vie," to be released in December 2020.

Thank you for coming along this ride with me and the Unbroken Series' characters. I'm sure by now, you've become quite fond of most of them. Would you please take the time to write a review of Déjà Vu from your retailer? If you purchased your book from a book signing, you can still write a review at Amazon, Goodreads and other retailers. Be kind. Be honest, but please be kind. Constructive criticism is always welcome when it's done in a positive, helpful way. I know I can't please everyone, however, I try. Thank you.

Be sure to "Stay Tuned" on my website to get sneak peeks into future releases, not available to the public, along with special offers and giveaways available only to my Unbroken Series readers. Your information will never be shared or sold. I appreciate my privacy as much as you do yours.

https://www.MelodiousEnterprises.com/unbroken-readers.html

Melody Saleh - Author/Storyteller/Escape Artist

The inspiration for the Unbroken Series originally came from *Sex in the City*. The hit series and blockbuster movies *Fifty Shades* added additional creativity. The opening chapter in *Facade* was written many years ago, she had no idea where her characters were going to take her. "The story basically wrote itself. It was like a movie projector playing in my mind," is how she describes her experience. It soon became apparent, their voices were not to be silenced, hence the "Unbroken Series" was born. *Facade* was published on December 31, 2019 followed by *Deja Vu*, released June 23, 2020. *Cest la Vie*, the final book in the trilogy is to be released in December 2020.

Melody lives with her husband in her native home state of Florida. She's blessed to be alive today after two cancer diagnoses and enjoys watching her grandchildren grow up. Something she never takes for granted.